44076231

MAY 2 2 2001

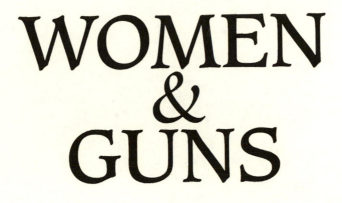

# WOMEN
# &
# GUNS

# WOMEN
# &
# GUNS

## Politics
## and the
## Culture of Firearms
## in America

## DEBORAH HOMSHER

*M.E. Sharpe*
Armonk, New York
London, England

**Library of Congress Cataloging-in-Publication Data**

Homsher, Deborah, 1952-
  Women and guns : politics and the culture of firearms in America / Deborah Homsher.
    p. cm.
  Includes bibliographical references and index.
  ISBN 0-7656-0678-X
1. Gun control—United States—Public opinion. 2. Women—United States—Attitudes.
3. Firearms and crime—United States—Public opinion. 4. Violent crimes—United
States—Public opinion. 5. Public opinion—United States. I. Title.

HV7436.H65 2001
363.3´3´0973—dc21                                                        00-041018

Printed in the United States of America

The paper used in this publication meets the minimum requirements of
American National Standard for Information Sciences
Permanence of Paper for Printed Library Materials,
ANSI Z 39.48-1984.

⊗

BM (c)    10    9    8    7    6    5    4    3    2    1

*It is a surprising and memorable, as well as valuable experience, to be lost in the woods any time. Often in a snow storm, even by day, one will come out upon a well-known road and yet find it impossible to tell which way leads to the village. Though he knows that he has traveled it a thousand times, he cannot recognize a feature in it, but it is as strange to him as if it were a road in Siberia. By night, of course, the perplexity is infinitely greater. In our most trivial walks, we are constantly, though unconsciously, steering like pilots by certain well-known beacons and headlands, and if we go beyond our usual course we still carry in our minds the bearing of some neighboring cape; and not till we are completely lost, or turned round,—for a man needs only to be turned round once with his eyes shut in this world to be lost,—do we appreciate the vastness and strangeness of Nature. Every man has to learn the points of the compass again as often as he awakes, whether from sleep or any abstraction. Not till we are lost, in other words, not till we have lost the world, do we begin to find ourselves, and realize where we are and the infinite extent of our relations.*

*Henry David Thoreau*

# Contents

About the Author                                                                        *viii*

Acknowledgments                                                                          *ix*

Chapter 1.  Meeting                                                                      3

Chapter 2.  American Stories                                                             31

Chapter 3.  Fields Near Home                                                             47

Chapter 4.  Self-Defense, Part I: Combat by Story and Statistics                         79

Chapter 5.  Self-Defense, Part II: Looking for the Bad Guys                              99

Chapter 6.  Gun Games and Homegrown Rebellion                                            131

Chapter 7.  In the Cities, on the Edge                                                   161

Chapter 8.  Conclusion                                                                   197

Index                                                                                    239

# *About the Author*

---

**Deborah Homsher** graduated from Brown University and received an M.F.A. in fiction writing from the Writer's Workshop at the University of Iowa. She was a Wallace Stegner Fellow in fiction writing at Stanford University and in 1990 received a Fellowship in Nonfiction Literature from the New York Foundation for the Arts. Her first book, *From Blood to Verdict: Three Women on Trial,* examined local criminal trials involving female defendants in order to study how combative courtroom rituals function as machines for processing tragedies. She lives with her husband and sons in Ithaca, New York.

# *Acknowledgments*

---

I wish to thank the many people who contributed to this study. Most important were the women and men who agreed to speak with me about their experiences and their opinions. A few of these individuals are not named in the text, most notable among them David Corina, a storyteller and hunter, and Marie Corina, Donna Freedline and Ray Freedline, Dr. Arthur Smith, who took me hiking to look for rattlesnakes when I thought this book would be about something else, Bebe Smith, and the guides at Turkey Trot Acres. I would also like to thank Lisa Erbach Vance, who coaxed me to expand this study at an early stage and who provided incisive editorial advice; Stuart Basefsky, whose great enthusiasm for and knowledge about online search engines guided me to a rich field of new material; Rose Batt, who suggested I contact Stuart Basefsky; Peter Coveney, my editor, who read and approved the manuscript and offered insightful suggestions; my sons, Kevin and Michael Egan, who figure significantly in this discussion, though they remain behind the curtain; and my mother and father.

Special thanks to Mark Selden—if it were not for his editing and generous intervention, this book would still be a loose manuscript in a basket—and to my husband, Hugh Egan, for his abiding good sense and love.

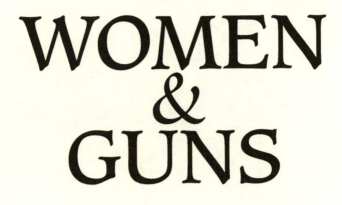

# WOMEN
# &
# GUNS

# 1

## Meeting

### Making Histories

This book is about American women in the 1990s, their experiences with guns, and their responses to the national public debates about guns and violence. It aspires to give voice to citizens who hold divergent political opinions and, in this way, to find out something about life in the country as it is perceived and interpreted by people who call themselves Americans.

The efforts of these women to define their own histories and the history of the nation based on personal experiences, political analyses, and news reports reveal politics in action at the most basic level. The women whom I interviewed commonly explained what they thought about guns in the United States by telling anecdotes. Frequently, they used popular political messages to shape or conclude these narratives. Yet now and again their own experiences proved to be too complex or contradictory to match the gauge prescribed by agendas that had been forged for political combat. When this happened, when women began telling personal stories that didn't teach a simple "pro-gun" or "anti-gun" lesson, stories that defied the established categories, I felt that I came closest to watching a citizen at work.

We live in a vast, combative democracy that encourages people to take sides. Many women I interviewed had committed themselves to one side or the other in the gun-control debates, and they had adopted the positions, the "talking points," of partisan advocacy groups organized to mediate between the government and the people. These advocacy groups clearly sought to influence public policy by cultivating, and educating, a constituency, be it a constituency of hunters or "concealed-carry" supporters or gun-control advocates. These citizen groups were held together by friendships and get-togethers at the local level, but guided by pronouncements from various national headquarters that sought to represent their interests. I was always curious to see what happened at this intersection between the national and the local—what messages got transmitted straight through and which were lost or altered in transmission—and also to see what happened at the intersection between traditionally masculine organizations and their female constituents. As one might expect, local women very often adapted programs to fit their needs, borrowing some sections of a platform while discarding others. Occasionally they were able to join special women's programs designed to accommodate and attract them. But individual women also adapted themselves; they shaped their identities and their visions to accord with national agendas. I believe democratic nations are created in this way. Any working definition of "we the people" can never fully accommodate an actual, various, changeable, motley citizenry. Somebody is always spilling (or being pushed) outside the frame. But we can't manage without a frame. To feel ourselves citizens, we must have some concept of what it means to be American . . . or alternately, un-American. Right here, in this territory where citizens gather to hammer together the framework of the nation and of themselves, the United States is perpetually recreated.

I found it heartening to listen to women talk about their memories and their opinions, but this did not happen because they were uniformly optimistic. They were not. A number of the people I interviewed felt that the nation was declining and becoming an unrecognizable entity. The most partisan blamed their political enemies for the citizenry's loss of essential, decent qualities that, in their opinion, defined what it meant to be genuinely American, and they were intent on asserting their identities in the face of the opposition and on claiming recognition and respect.

When making such judgments about the state of the country, women were influenced variously by their own experiences, their local cultures, by newsworthy events of the last few years, and by heated public discourse, including the gun debates that repeatedly flared and dimmed through the 1990s. Often these public debates featured women as *women*, for instance, as bereaved mothers or wives who could advocate effectively for stricter gun-control laws, or as potential victims who could advocate effectively for "right-to-carry" legislation that would allow them to carry concealed handguns in public for personal self-defense. Thus the discourse explicitly invoked assumptions about gender. But since certain women presented themselves as avidly pro-gun, while others were just as passionately anti-gun, anyone could see that gender wasn't the only factor determining female constituents' inclinations. Their opinions about the proper role of the federal government, or, more broadly, about American independence and self-reliance, American character, and American history—both distant and recent—were significant factors as well, and these opinions bound them as allies not only to other women, but very obviously to a range of individuals, male and female, whose political attitudes matched theirs on the conservative/liberal spectrum in evidence through the 1990s.

This was the decade of William Jefferson Clinton and his impeachment, the Brady Bill and the federal anticrime bill of 1994, welfare reform, Bill Gates, a World Wide Web, the European Market, mutual funds, the rise and fall of Newt Gingrich, genetic engineering, the bombing of Iraq and Yugoslavia, Nintendo and Doom, the bombing of a federal building in Oklahoma City, and, a series of "school shootings" in the United States, including an attack inside Columbine High School, Littleton, Colorado. The years 1995 through 1999 were distinguished in the United States by a booming economy, falling unemployment, and a surprising decline in the nation's crime rate (including a notable decline in the rate of violent, urban crime). Yet not all news was good. The American prison population expanded enormously as a result of stricter sentencing laws, and outbreaks of rogue violence punctuated the decade. The most unsettling and widely publicized acts of violence were perpetrated by white men who seemed to have ingested half-baked ideas about American outlaw "resistance" and, in response, outfitted themselves to attack institutions (and the people inside them) that represented the oppressor. In 1995, two self-styled "patriots" bombed the Alfred P. Murrah Federal Building in Oklahoma City. Then between 1997 and 1999, various lonesome, vengeful pre-adolescent and adolescent boys carried out a spate of copycat school shootings.

These violent events, perpetrated by these few isolated, but well-equipped, men and boys, came to be accepted as meaningful signs about the state of the whole nation, and they generated intense public discussions about what ought to be done to heal our sick nation. Women with whom I spoke responded to news of violence and even memories of violence in different ways, and since we were talking about guns, they focused on questions having to do with weapons. Some proposed to strengthen gun control legislation as part of an effort to limit the availability of weapons in the United States and cure the nation's "epidemic" of violence, while others favored right-to-carry laws that would insure women retained their constitutional right to purchase and carry their own weapons for self-defense, a move intended to grant more power generally to law-abiding citizens. A few straddled the political divides and offered hybrid proposals. And in the course of speaking about guns, these women also spoke about neighborhoods, families, partnerships, attacks, tradition, the good old days, good government, the modern world, and the future of the country.

It makes sense that shocking national events would be followed by exercises in national self-criticism. Many people sensed that these explosive dramas were recognizably American, engendered by a popular culture we know and movies we've seen, and that the men and boys reenacting familiar dramas had badly missed the point. They knew how to plan and stage their attacks, but they had confused good guys with bad guys. They seemed ethically, morally blind . . . very badly educated. It was reasonable to ask, then, whether certain aspects of American life contributed to this sort of terrible blindness, just as it was reasonable to ask what security measures could be implemented to prevent disturbed people from acquiring weapons and gaining easy access to federal buildings and schools in the future.

On the other hand, any instant analysis of the United States based on the most recent front-page news will be skewed, especially if it focuses on the actions of a few isolated individuals, and the loudest public responses to the news will often be politically motivated. There are many quieter, neglected stories that must be considered by anyone who hopes to study the state of the nation. For instance, as certain journalists (notably Jonathan Alter of *Newsweek*) have noted, African-American and Hispanic students in the United States have been getting shot and killed at a far higher rate than white students for years, yet these victims and their attackers attract relatively little media attention. I believe this happens in part because these students constitute only a marginal segment of the "country" that many people imagine as their own, so that their deaths register as the deaths of foreigners.

I am interested in these neglected stories and curious about the state of the nation as it exists below and behind sensational news reports and strident public debates. For this reason, I have chosen to focus on citizens whose engagement with guns is variously recreational, peripheral, or terribly accidental, and whose engagement with contemporary debates about guns is therefore usually nonprofessional. I will not describe the careers of public women who have established reputations as spokespersons for or against gun control, nor do I interview American women engaged in careers and directly involved in institutions (e.g., law enforcement agencies and military institutions) that require weapons training.[1] Some of the individuals interviewed in this book have studied and written position papers or essays, but most have not. The majority gather information on political issues in their off hours. They subscribe to magazines, read newspapers, and watch television. They talk with friends. A few surf the Internet or attend conferences. And from this hodgepodge of sources, they decide how to vote, to act, and to define themselves as citizens of the United States of America.

### Shirley Lyon's House

Most of the women with whom I spoke were unaccustomed to conversing across a tape recorder. But they did not mind being questioned. They were ready to be questioned. One particular interview took place at night in the living room of Shirley Lyon, a woman who had owned a gun store in New York State for a few years and had only recently quit the business because the paperwork had become too cumbersome. At my request, Lyon had invited to her house a group of her acquaintances who used and kept handguns and had attended classes in firearms self-defense. It was clear from the beginning that these women would speak in accord with standard pro-gun doctrines that I recognized but did not accept as my own. I was not raised in a hunting family (though my father hunted for squirrel and rabbit as a boy growing up in Kendalville, Indiana), I favor most gun-control legislation, and my husband and I do not own or keep guns in our house. Still, I had explained my position to Lyon earlier and felt that we each, warily, understood one another.

Perched alone on the sofa in Shirley Lyon's living room, I set my tape recorder on the coffee table as far out as it would go, hoping it would pick up the voices of the guests who had pulled up chairs in a broad circle. Stefani Woodhams sat near the window. A lean, attractive woman with a thick braid down her back, Woodhams told me that she carries a knife in her pocket because she needs it in her maintenance work at a local nursing home. She once scared away an intruder (who had followed her in his car one night across an open field to the isolated cabin where she lived at that time) by dragging her big poodle outdoors and bellowing: "GET OUT OF MY FLOWERBED!" Next to Stefani sat Joan Rupe, a customer service supervisor at Hills Department Store, who has wrestled shoplifters to the ground, but who presented an overall impression of quietness, even paleness, and who wore a loaded .38 revolver hidden under her clothes as we spoke. Rupe and her husband had bought guns for their grandchildren: "We have four grandchildren, and part of our inheritance for them is, we have bought specialized guns. For one granddaughter, we bought her a LadySmith. It's in a safe, and it's got their name on it. When they get old enough, it's theirs." Near Joan sat Carol Stauffeneker, a home daycare provider who had purchased her first handgun in response to a gruesome local murder. Lyon's fifteen-year-old daughter, Jolene, stood against a wall near Carol.

All of these women professed deep distrust of the U.S. government. When I asked if this distrust started with the inauguration of President Clinton, there was a flowering of women's startled laughter: "No! Oh no!" When I asked how they pictured the National Rifle Association (NRA), two of them said: "We're the NRA!" and laughed again. At one point, we tried to count up the handguns they owned. Lyon's family had seventeen in the house. Her daughter Jolene was soon getting a type of handgun called a Glock. Rupe also had about seventeen, since both she and her husband were involved in "practical handgun shooting," a sport based on police pistol training where participants engage moving targets. Stauffeneker had three guns. Woodhams said most of the guns in her house arrived with her second husband: "I got involved with Bill. He came with all the guns."

And what would they do, how would they feel, if someone came in and tried to take away their guns? "You're in trouble," said Rupe. Then: "I'd feel naked."

"I'd have to depend on the men in the house, and if they aren't there, well . . ." said Stauffeneker.

"I would have to live back in that fear, being afraid to walk, being afraid to go out. If you take it away from me, now I've got to walk a little faster, look over my shoulder a little bit more," said Lyon, who retained a New York State dealer's license and told me she would sell firearms to people she trusted, even though she had closed her shop.

Woodhams said: "I would manage just fine. I don't carry a gun with me. But I'd make sure my knife is in my right pocket."

Like the other women in the room, Lyon supported the "constitutional right" of private citizens to own and use guns and generally opposed efforts to pass gun-control legislation: "As if criminals obey laws, they really do, right?" She herself owned and practiced with guns alongside her second husband and had taken a self-defense course offered by the Lethal Force Institute of Concord, New Hampshire. She said that if she had a shotgun in the cabin instead of a big poodle that one night: "I'd take it out, man, and I'd grab the shotgun and I'd go KA-KLICK—WHAT'S YOUR NAME? . . . And if he called my bluff, well, that's the last thing he'd do." At the same time, she agreed that people ought to try and keep guns out of a household where there are "unbalanced" family members; her judgment in this case was based on experience, for she had been threatened with a shotgun by her first husband once. She described the night:

> My first husband years ago was kind of, well definitely, an alcoholic, and then he got into cocaine. Bad combination. Well, this guy had guns, and in fact, he's the one who taught me to shoot, and it was fun.
>
> But, unfortunately, when you have an unbalanced person in your family, the last thing you need is a gun around, and in this case Sarah Brady's right. If there's someone in your home that has access to those guns who you do not trust, get rid of the guns, or better yet, jump ship. It's scary when you have someone threatening you with a firearm. It's horrible.

He had been drinking and doing cocaine and came in late, and I asked him if he'd fed his beagles. And he just went completely off the wall. I didn't realize he was that bad because I'd been working around the house. Then I looked at him and I realized that there was nothing in his brain; there weren't two brain cells that were functioning together, and I had a madman on my hands. So he proceeded to attack me physically, and I kind of held him back a little bit and yelled at the kids to go upstairs, so they did. And then he grabbed a hold of me and held me against the wall and said: "I'm going to get the gun and blow your head off." I'm thinking: "Ohhhh, crap." So he let go of me and went up and got his shotgun and came back down, and he's holding the shotgun there, and I grabbed hold of the barrel and held it up, and he shot through the ceiling.

Asked why the experience didn't make her hate guns—after all, when this shotgun fired up through the ceiling, her children were standing somewhere on the second floor—she replied:

The *gun* didn't do it. *He* did. I think I'm fairly smart and that gun was sitting right there, by itself, upright in the closet there, and it didn't do a thing. He grabbed it and used it. It meant nothing more to me than if he'd gotten a hammer. It's a thing. It doesn't have a life of its own. It doesn't attack people. And having been in that situation, I know what Sarah Brady and her crowd and all the people who have lost people in their family, I know what that's like. I do. But it's not the gun. It's people.

Woodhams chose to conclude with a stock pro-gun message: "It's not the gun; it's the people." This surprised me a little because I found her to be such a vibrant, original storyteller. I was surprised again, in a different way, when the interview was over and Lyon and her husband led me out across the gravel driveway to their dark, side yard near a forest gully where they had built a shed for a pair of very small goats. I would never have predicted that this family kept miniature goats. These animals were part of a familial context that I could analyze but not fully comprehend. In short, the women with whom I had just spoken could be categorized as "pro-gun" advocates but they also resisted categorization.

The few minutes when Shirley Lyon and her husband introduced me to the goats penned on the edge of the gully educated me, alerted me, warned me to take care. Behind every speechmaker's phrase, every short-cut political analysis, unidentified households wait in the dark. Trying to imagine or characterize *real life* in America, we have to acknowledge the likely proximity of unnoticed rooms and unnamed companions. At the same time, of course, public discourse enters each one of these households, so that almost any meeting with a new person will expose a set of adopted, even hackneyed, arguments, phrases, and perceptions. The impulse to prove oneself an individual is counterbalanced by the impulse to fit oneself into an identifiable category and show allegiance to a group by repeating its creed. And all of these are mussed and muddled by realities.

## Hammer or Hazard?

Partisan political groups in the United States have identified two essential, but contradictory, aspects of a gun: pro-gunners insist that guns are inert tools, as Woodhams argued, while anti-gunners maintain that they are active, alluring agents. This disagreement raises questions not only about the *real* identity of a gun, but about the composition or character of the American people. Relatively conservative men and women who advocate for the Second Amendment right to "keep and bear arms" insist that noncriminal American citizens can and must be trusted to make decisions about owning and carrying guns for themselves. Relatively more liberal men and women who advocate for gun-control legislation insist that a "free market" in guns endangers the citizenry and should thus be approached and confronted as a public health problem, akin to the problem posed by cigarette smoking. These two proposed agendas obviously rely on different assumptions about how guns function in the United States—as useful tools or viruses—and about how individuals function as members of a civil body. This last consideration leads directly to questions about proper government: how should individual citizens be governed in a democracy so that their constitutionally prescribed rights are protected but their actions are at the same time restrained so that they don't hurt their fellow citizens?

Female gun owners whom I interviewed insisted that firearms could not shoot themselves. Every gun tragedy or victory required human agency, and responsibility for each tragedy ought to be accepted by the shooter, not transferred to the machine. On the other side, anti-gun advocates speak of "gun violence" repeatedly as a kind of disease spawned by the presence of active, viral agents—firearms—in the United States: "Gun violence in America has reached *epidemic* proportions" (Sarah Brady, Handgun Control Inc., fundraising letter, undated, c. 1995). And they never hesitate to introduce guns as active subjects in their declarations: ". . . a handgun in the home endangers its owner's life rather than providing for protection and safety" and "it is the concealable handgun that threatens and intimidates the citizens of the United States" (conference publications, Coalition to Stop Gun Violence).

In the late 1990s, this political definition of a gun's—particularly a handgun's—"identity" as a public health hazard sparked a new anti-gun initiative, as cities throughout the United States began to file suits against gun dealers and manufacturers for the damage sustained as a result of these "unsafe" products and the gun industry's allegedly irresponsible sales and distribution policies. The City of Chicago and Cook County filed a multimillion dollar lawsuit against the gun industry in late 1998. Mayor Daley announced that a police undercover operation had determined suburban gun dealers were selling arms without conducting background checks and, as a result, flooding his city with illegal firearms. The suit named twenty-two manufacturers, twelve stores, and four gun distributors, and it was based on "a new legal theory, that the gun industry causes a 'public nuisance' by creating excess costs for Chicago's police, fire department, and public hospitals." A lawyer for the city of Chicago compared the spread of guns from the suburbs into the city to "a suburban industry polluting the city with poison gas."[2] A number of these suits were guided by lawyers who had earned their spurs in recent civil actions against cigarette manufacturers. Dennis Henigan, an active anti-gun litigator,[3] teamed up with the Castano Group, a syndicate of lawyers who directed many of the successful suits against "Big Tobacco." Describing Henigan's approach to the issue, a journalist wrote: "Henigan told the Castano lawyers about the many studies that have considered guns in an epidemiological context; in other words, guns should be thought of as pathogens, and gun ownership, perhaps, as a disease."[4]

Persons who insist that guns are passive, not active, agents are offended by suggestions that their own households might be infested by violent gun pathogens, that they themselves might be "sick" because they own guns, and that they can't be trusted to establish responsible control over their tools, selves, and family members and to judge and govern their own households without intervention. This response will be discussed in greater detail in chapters 4 and 5 but I note it here because it is an important element in a politically conservative response to perceived liberal elitism and condescension. Pro-gun authors rail against biased public health leaders who interpret "violence as a public health crisis and the firearm as something akin to an infectious disease."[5] One of the NRA's Internet postings (copyrighted in 1996 by the NRA lobbyist and spokeswoman Tanya Metaksa and still online in 1999 though it had disappeared by January 2000) complained that "the Clinton Administration has greatly energized efforts to frame violence as a public health, rather than a criminal justice, issue. To Clintonites, especially those at the taxpayer-funded Centers for Disease Control, guns are germs and gun owners the new 'Typhoid Marys.'"[6]

And according to Karen MacNutt, a columnist for the magazine, *Women & Guns*:

Let's get something straight: "Gun Control" is not about crime. It is about a snob elite that looks down its nose on the working men and women of this country. It is about an elite who believe the average American is too criminal, too irresponsible, or too irrational to be trusted to make his or her own decisions or handle dangerous machinery. [7]

More than three years later, commenting on an editorial that recommended "junk food" be taxed to protect the general health of Americans (encouraging the consumption of fat-free yogurt), MacNutt reiterated:

The glory of the American system is in its trust of the common people. . . . We as a society must stop trying to regulate everything. . . . If you want to live in a free society, you must allow people to make their own decisions about their own personal welfare, even if you think those decisions are wrong.[8]

Karen MacNutt for years authored a legal column, "Legally Speaking," for the national magazine *Women & Guns*, which in 1995 was published monthly but by 1999 had been reduced to six issues a year.[9] Here she expresses one of the most enduring resentments of pro-gun conservatives, who feel that they are misjudged and belittled by liberal elitists allegedly eager to invade their homes, trample their rights, and regulate their lives.

MacNutt clearly implies that these ivory tower elitists don't know much and don't care about the lives of the "common people," real down-to-earth Americans, and that their vision of these people, The People, is warped. It's fictional. In response to such assertions, liberals generally argue that the conservative's vision of a nation peopled by upright, responsible gun owners is itself a convenient fiction, for households that contain guns are in fact more likely to be visited by accidents, violence, and tragedy. In this debate about what constitutes real America and real Americans, the nation seems to have discovered its own perpetual motion machine; back and forth, the argument goes on, energized by a laudable desire to comprehend this mammoth country, as well as by a national propensity to conduct our political debates as team sports. Statistics and personal stories are all mustered to establish which of these images of the nation is more accurate and thereby determine what actions should be taken, what legislation passed, to improve things. Yet the picture never seems to get any clearer, in part because the most committed warriors in these public debates are outfitted for battle, not for exploration. Divisions between the partisans are strongly marked, and passionate enmities have emerged; one finds evidence of these divisions and enmities in the respective web postings, speeches, and publications broadcast by "pro–Second Amendment" and "pro-gun-control" organizations, notably the NRA and Handgun Control Inc./Center to Prevent Handgun Violence, the advocacy group headed by Sarah Brady.

Evidence brought to bear in these contemporary debates is not limited to statistics or stories about this year, or even this decade, because the partisans have very strong opinions about how the nation has evolved, how it has developed and changed over time. They graph trends. They concern themselves with traditions. Because they hope to influence the future, they become engaged in retelling and interpreting the past. They're concerned with history. In my opinion, the national gun debates become especially fascinating at this point, where they begin to "make" history by selecting facts to create politically useful stories.

The facts and stories most important to relatively conservative organizations that advocate for "gun rights" focus on the origin and meaning of the Second Amendment to the Constitution, and also on America's revolutionary and frontier traditions, which characterize our citizenry as distinctly, perhaps even uniquely, self-reliant and independent. I would argue that our influential canon of factual *and fictional* stories about the American frontier life are largely grounded in male—more specifically, white male—adventure tales. Unlike Europe, the United States has no history that predates firearms. The merry men who inhabit our mythic wildwoods, roaming free of taxes, wives, and religious services, carry not long bows, but long guns.

The collective image of self-reliant American heroism and American character advanced by these wonderful frontier adventure stories was forcefully challenged in the 1960s, and our politics continue to be strongly influenced by the sharp political rifts that developed in the 1960s. Debates about violence, guns, and gun control in the 1990s often make reference implicitly or explicitly to the 1960s, when America's forefathers were exposed to question, and the iconic American frontiersman was redefined, in some quarters, as a murderous thug. Questions about the essential gender of America arise here. If our nation and its citizens have been influenced by a powerfully masculine tradition, should we now seek to alter that condition and remake ourselves as a more feminine, "gentle," "compassionate" country?

## Politics Since the 1960s

Richard Slotkin, a scholar who has compiled an encyclopedic three-volume study of gun myths in America, argues that our nation is a "gunfighter nation," so steeped in tales about the independent, armed frontiersman that those narratives shape both our identity and our policies.[10] An abiding respect for this hero can be said to undergird American conservative ideology, and an abiding distrust of him typically energizes liberals. American liberals have challenged national narratives that honor white male frontiersmen, hunters, or soldiers, and these liberals have called attention to the victims. Our history comes heavily packed with "carcasses," many of them dark skinned—Iroquois, Sioux, Filipino, Vietnamese, African—and in the United States increased recognition of those who have died, and a reappraisal of the gunmen (generally white men) who took aim at them have irrevocably altered the American histories that many citizens accept as true. The rebellious political movements of the last forty years advocating the rights of minorities, women, and gays and opposing the Vietnam War have also demanded a reevaluation of our white male forefathers, a reevaluation commonly tagged as "liberal" and "politically correct." These movements threatened to strip the archetypal Anglo-American explorer of his glory and transform him into an imperialist killer. According to these reinterpretations of America's frontier fathers, the guy in the coonskin cap shoots whatever gets in his way—usually indigenous American wildlife and Native American human life. His firearm excites in him the most dire masculine impulses. He is dependent, *not* independent; short-sighted, *not* keen-eyed; alien, *not* native; and childishly brutal, *not* heroic. Good-bye Columbus.

Critiques generated in the 1960s reached strongly into the 1990s and continued to influence our politics. Reevaluations of the cultural roles and even the essential natures of women and men as they related to one another, to the country, and to Mother Earth were key to these debates. By the 1990s, of course, "feminist," "environmentalist," and "multicultural" critiques of this kind had roused a spirited and practiced conservative opposition. In the pivotal years of 1994 and 1995, especially, the power of the Angry White Male as a political force appeared to be on the rise in the United States. Post-election reports in 1994 often focused on the leverage of the male, pro-gun, pro-NRA vote in support of conservative Republican candidates who had unseated a number of Democratic incumbents and had given the Republican party majorities in both houses of Congress. Handgun Control Inc. reported with dismay that the balloting had stuffed the Congress with a majority of members (237 out of 435) who had earned either an A+ or A rating from the NRA for their voting records in favor of Second Amendment rights and against gun control. Just a few months after the election, President Bill Clinton was quoted in the *Cleveland Plain Dealer* as saying: "The NRA is the reason the Republicans control the House."

It is difficult to remember now how common it was at that time for news analysts to dismiss Bill Clinton—a reliable proponent of gun control who had supported passage of the 1993 "Brady Bill" mandating background checks of gun purchasers and the 1994 anticrime bill (the Violent Crime Control and Law Enforcement Act of 1994) banning certain high-capacity, automatic weapons—as a "lame duck" president and to speculate about which Democrat would replace him as the presidential candidate in 1996. It's also difficult to remember what power the Republican Speaker of the House, Newt Gingrich, wielded at the time and what terror and horror he roused in liberal Democrats.

But then Timothy McVeigh and his partner, rogue patriots allegedly inspired by militia rhetoric, bombed the federal building in Oklahoma City in April 1995. This action prompted journalists to turn the lights on the far-right militia "movement" in the United States. It soiled the public image of the Angry White Male and changed the political landscape, though probably not to the extent that people believed at the time. Over the next few years, the NRA would lose some influence and members—membership would fall 18 percent from its peak in 1994 and 1995—and the Republicans would suffer losses, many of them attributed to the party's poor showing with women.

Yet many of the conservatives' gains held, even as their momentum diminished. Republicans, led by Senate Majority Leader Trent Lott (rated A+ by the NRA), maintained their majorities in Congress from 1994 through 1999. What's more, their "revolution" altered legislation in a number of states. Between the years 1994 and 1997, fourteen states passed right-to-carry legislation guaranteeing law-abiding citizens (those with no criminal record) the right to purchase and carry guns concealed on their person in public, largely unhindered by local licensing requirements. In Texas George W. Bush, son of the former president, promised to pass a right-to-carry bill and won the election, unseating a liberal favorite, Ann Richards, and gaining a platform that would enable him to run for president in the year 2000. After passage of the Violent Crime Control and Law Enforcement Act in 1994, no substantial new national gun-control measures made it through Congress for the rest of the decade.

When high school students Dylan Klebold and Eric Harris used guns in a surprise attack that killed twelve of their fellow students and a teacher in Littleton, Colorado, in April 1999, gun control became a front-page issue again. Gun control advocates pressed with renewed hope for a number of measures, including the proposal to ban importation of "high-capacity magazines" (magazines holding more than ten bullets) and the requirement that unlicensed dealers conduct background checks of individuals buying firearms at gun shows. Public pressure drove the Senate to approve measures that required background checks of customers at gun shows, mandated the sale of safety locks with new guns, and banned the importation of high-capacity magazines. But similar legislation died in the House.

News analyses throughout the 1990s followed these shifting moods of the nation with interest. They generally identified a strong pro-Republican and pro-gun vote as masculine and a Democratic "gun control" vote as comparatively feminine, or, at least, less masculine. These broad categories were loosely grounded in actual voting patterns, but they obscured the many voters who crossed over, those who refused to vote "straight ticket" on candidates or issues.

This doesn't mean that "crossovers" were ignored, however, for they made good news/feature stories. As it happened, one of the figures who attracted the most attention in the mid-1990s was the armed American woman. Public interest in the subject sparked when a number of publications reported that American women were swarming to buy handguns. It appears now that this news was based in part on a deceptive study funded by Smith & Wesson. But for a time in the mid-1990s, it was widely reported that more women were purchasing firearms, and these reports roused political debate and activity. Pro-gun organizations applauded the reports and encouraged the "development" when they could. The NRA elected to foreground two women, Marion Hammer and Tanya Metaksa, as representative spokespersons, and it actively promoted its own "Refuse To Be a Victim" program, which recommended that women consider acquiring handguns for self-defense. In states where right-to-carry legislation was being proposed, women often came forward as pro-gun advocates and attracted media attention.

Understandably, liberal feminists interpreted promotion of the new image of this gunwoman as part of a general, cynical bid to fuel the firearms market and sweeten the image of essentially sexist, reactionary organizations. *Ms. Magazine* published a full issue on the question—the introductory article was titled "Is This Power Feminism?"—challenging the idea that guns could protect or somehow strengthen women, and other publications followed suit, many noting that statistics showed guns in a home actually endangered family members.[11]

Debates of this sort necessarily rely on broad assumptions and make broad assertions about women's lives and natures, the conditions they face collectively, and the identities of their general enemies or allies. Many of the speakers who contribute to the debates are interested not only in winning a constituency, but also in proving, or suggesting, that they in fact have a large constituency, because this is how one gains the political influence needed to advance a public agenda. Following these debates, I became interested in the many unknown women who were being collectively described, allegedly represented, and readily advised by the various spokespersons. I wondered how they fit into the picture. And I wondered too where I fit in.

## "Becoming an Outdoors-Woman" Conference

I had mentioned to Stefani, Joan, Carol, and Shirley that many people considered the gun organizations' interest in women to be part of an ugly marketing ploy, a trick to convince women that guns could actually protect them from harm, when actually studies showed that household guns increased chances for tragedy. Joan Rupe responded: "Women aren't getting pushed towards guns. Women are *asking*." Shirley Lyon, who had owned the C&S Gun Shop, said that most women who came in the door of her establishment to purchase their first handguns had never even heard of the NRA. "Most of them go, 'NRA what's that?'" In short, these female gun owners resisted two assumptions commonly made by anti-gun liberals: first, that women were being duped by the advertised attractions of firearms, and second, that it was men who were duping them.

Around the country, conferences and competitions were—and are—being scheduled to attract fledgling female shooters. These events are generally sponsored by organizations with vested interests in gun sales or gun sports—firearms manufacturers, shooting clubs, state wildlife agencies. It's clear that these traditionally masculine organizations hope to attract women, "nontraditional clientele," as new members, consumers, and allies. In fact, statistics show that the market for new guns has been declining through the 1990s: in 1993 Americans purchased 5.2 million new guns, but by 1997 that number had fallen to 3.7 million.

The Women's Shooting Sports Foundation (WSSF) was organized in 1993 by the National Shooting Sports Foundation (NSSF) and sponsored Ladies Charity Classic shooting competitions in a number of states throughout the 1990s. Also, the "Becoming an Outdoors-Woman" Program—sponsored by the NRA, Federal Cartridge Company, Whitetails Unlimited, Browning, National Shooting Sports Foundation, Ducks Unlimited, National Wild Turkey Federation, North American Hunting Club, and Thompson-Center Arms, among others—has scheduled "BOW" workshops throughout the 1990s. Their schedule of workshops for 1998 lists programs held in more than forty states and a number of Canadian provinces. Judging from the list, the program thrives most heartily in the Southeast and the cold, forested states of the North; it was founded by and, at this writing, is still under the direction of Christine Thomas, of the University of Wisconsin, Stevens Point College of Natural Resources. The first "Becoming an Outdoors-Woman" session took place in 1991 and was spearheaded by Christine Thomas and Tammy Peterson, U.S. Fish and Wildlife Service, Oregon. Thomas and Peterson published their reasons for initiating these clinics, which were meant to teach women basic, introductory hunting or fishing skills in a congenial environment. As state "resource management" professionals, these women were worried by the decline in the sale of hunting and fishing licenses nationally between 1985 and 1991 and concerned about predictions that the situation would worsen, given various cultural and demographic trends, including the growing influence of single mothers on the nation's youth:

> It has also been determined that mothers play a dominant role in shaping the recreational choices of children. . . . With predictions regarding children born in 1989 indicating that 60 percent will be reared at some point in their first eighteen years by a single parent (usually a woman), it is clear that if hunting and fishing are to survive the next century, women will play an important role.[12]

Other wildlife management researchers joined with Thomas and Peterson in recommending that outdoor sports enthusiasts start catering to women:

> That conservation agencies have neglected women is rather remarkable. Across the nation, wildlife agencies have recognized the decline in hunters, the growth in anti-hunting sympathy, and the great need to better sell wildlife programs to the public. The majority of the non-hunters, the majority of the "anti-hunters," and the majority of the public are women. Given no changes in the status of current trends, the rapid evolution to a non-hunting ethic will prevail.[13]

In a published introduction to one of their workshops, Thomas and Peterson list a number of "barriers" that generally discourage women from becoming hunters and recommend strategies to help them overcome these barriers. For instance, they suggest that hunting and fishing ought to be marketed as family activities and that advocates should "Promote the aspects of the sport that are not directly related to 'Killing.'"[14]

I attended a "Becoming an Outdoors-Woman" conference sponsored by the New York State Department of Environmental Conservation (DEC) and located at a YMCA camp in Huguenot, New York. Nearly eighty women participated; one man signed up, but had left by Saturday morning. Over the course of the weekend, classes were available in "Beginning Muzzleloading," "Beginning Shotgun," "Beginning Rifle," "Beginning Trapping," "Deer Hunting," "Turkey Hunting," "Fly Tying," "Edible Wild Plants," "Beginning Archery," "Beginning Kayaking," "Outdoor Photography," "Wilderness Camping" or "Taking Children Outdoors." Saturday afternoon, I switched my schedule, and replaced "Taking Children Outdoors" with "Beginning Rifle."

### Beginning Shotgun/Beginning Rifle

It was high season October. A long, reflective pond lay between our cabins, and behind the pond was a tall hill massed with yellow and copper trees. The camp food was plentiful, the female organizers, buoyant and low-key. We slept in bunks, on pillows hard as folded newspaper. A number of young participants arrived with coolers of beer. Over the course of the weekend, I met ponytailed hunters' wives; genteel trout fisherwomen outfitted in handsome sweaters; a shaggy, gracious muzzleloading enthusiast, mother of teenage sons, who kept her flintlock (long gun) wrapped in striped blankets; a female moose hunter from Maine who used draft horses to drag out her trophy; and one Everglades canoeist who told an unforgettable pissing-by-watermoccasin story (. . . standing with one foot propped in the canoe and one foot on a wet log, she happened to glance down near her heel and saw . . .). I also met Darlene Dillon, a private detective with a moon-goddess face, and Lt. Carol Drury, a DEC officer who regularly nabs guys attempting to truck dead deer across the bridges into Manhattan and who knows all the spots where thriving, contaminated, off-limits shellfish colonies bed in the waters around New York City.

Everybody wore blue jeans. No one carried a purse to the dining hall. Women wearing plaid flannel jackets and Patagonia fleece sat together around the breakfast tables, but the outfits were not reliable indicators of a person's background; the lady in red plaid might have been a contractor's wife, a stenographer, or a tax lawyer. Hairstyles varied from gray coifed to youthfully loose. Women willingly wore name tags, even on the second day. By Saturday morning, we each knew a few names.

The "Beginning Shotgun" class started on Saturday morning at a local trap shooting range. Our instructor arrived in a van with a pile of new Remington 1100 semi-automatic shotguns, and it took a long time to unload them, and then a longer time to go through safety information, questions and answers, and negotiations with the range members, two gray-haired men who knew how to run the trap machinery. Hours passed before the gun cases were unlatched. The researcher and freelance writer who had come along to photograph women holding guns looked weary. Then the cases were unlatched. The mood changed.

When an inexperienced female student first picks up a shotgun out of its case, her physical expressions are hesitant and apologetic. She's uncertain whether to use a thumb or two fingers to push the shells into the magazine and uncertain how much force to apply. She checks the red-ringed safety button many times, and if she's accompanied by a female instructor eager to encourage female shooters, she will ask a lot of questions and be reassured by her instructor that every question is a good question.

It doesn't take long for a woman's movements to change. Two turns at the firing line on the trap range, and she feeds the shells straight in with her thumb, pauses for breath and permission, then lifts the shotgun hard against her cheek and shouts: "Pull." The orange disk floats out of the box. There's a shot. Usually the disk continues its flight, undisturbed by the shot, until it spatters on the hillside. To score with trap, a person has to paint a line of shot across the sky and get the clay pigeon to fly into it.

Our "Beginning Rifle" class began that afternoon in the modest headquarters of a local Huguenot shooting club. The meeting room was utilitarian, skimpily decorated with antlers and one big NRA "Qualification Program Progress Chart," a large, sturdy but worn sheet of paper covered with names and adhesive silver stars. After the requisite review of firearms safety rules, Darlene Dillon led us through a door and back into the narrow shooting range—an enclosed, gloomy, private place outfitted in plywood, red warning lights, and nicked, gray concrete walls, something like a gutted bowling alley or a burial cave.

Each woman was assigned a partner, her own plywood stall with shelf, and a pad of worn red carpeting on which to prop her elbows. When it was time to shoot, she received an Anschutz bolt-action rifle and a tiny serving of three brass .22 bullets. In the distance, at the end of the firing alley, NRA official 50-foot slow fire pistol targets had been stapled to plywood sheets with most of their centers disintegrated by gunfire shots. Given permission to engage the target, the shooter loaded her gun, took her stance, and forgot about the others. Given permission to fire, the shooter sighted her gun. The sight at the end of the barrel wove and dipped. Distance did not appear to be a factor; only fitting the black target spot into the sight's wedge was important. Frequently, the sight marker at the end of the barrel cupped the small black spot on the target exactly, in passing, but by then it was too late to decide *and* pull the trigger. At last, the shooter compromises. BOOM. Stand up. Work the bolt.

When the "Beginning Rifle" session was over late Saturday afternoon and we exited into the wide open sunlight, I had a summer camp craving for food that wouldn't be served in the dining hall, and I also felt the need to calm down. So I drove off on a hunt for a bottle of red wine to slow down my pulse. Yet my experience tells me that this "Becoming an Outdoors-Woman" conference did little to convert the participants and that the motives of the original conference organizers, "resource management" professionals eager to sandbag against the gradual erosion of American sport hunting, had a minimal impact on the individuals who arrived in Huguenot. Participants who had been curious about hunting or sporting clays signed up for gun classes. Those who were not interested in firearms signed up for kayaking, wilderness camping, and outdoor photography. Certainly the conference was designed to place hunting and target shooting—gun sports—in a friendly context, but most of the women who arrived eager to fire already knew about guns in context, because their fathers or husbands owned firearms. Two young wives said that they were tired of dusting around their husbands' shotguns without knowing how to check whether the safety was on and the magazine stocked with live shells. They wanted to learn about guns partly in order to unload them.

## An Anti-Gun Conference in the Capital

One month after attending the Outdoors-Woman Conference in rural New York, I drove farther south and arrived at the Sheraton–Washington Hotel in DC to attend a conference sponsored by the Coalition to Stop Gun Violence (formerly the Coalition to Ban Handguns) and the Episcopal Diocese of Washington.

I expected the voices at this urban conference to be more strident than the voices at the BOW workshop. Many of them were. I also expected, without fully realizing it, that the people at this Washington, DC, conference would be less compelling than the ones I'd bunked with in Huguenot. I had enjoyed the summer camp atmosphere at the BOW workshop, where women modeled their camo green face nets like raucous brides and traded advice on how to ease the sting of a bowstring burn. In short, I expected that the more explicit political agenda of this meeting in the Capital would both magnify and dull the individual voices of the participants. I was not prepared for exact personal stories about death and loss told from the podium, in the corridors, over dinner, and during luncheon.

A woman named Patricia Murray met up with her sister at the conference. Murray's son had been shot twice and was serving time in jail; her husband had been shot and killed in 1968. Surgeons from Chicago, New York City, and Camden, New Jersey, participated in the conference. They had seen plenty of bullet holes. And there was Camille Gianaris, an emergency chaplain for St. Luke's Roosevelt, a hospital in Harlem, New York. She had seen plenty of dead men. She described what happens when gunshot victims arrive at the hospital: "They're either being rushed to the operating room, and I'm literally running with them and their family member, or I am standing over them, giving the ironic benediction."

When the victim dies on the table:

> I bring the staff back in, and I bring the EMS people back in, and I say: "We're all going to put our hands on this person. An hour ago they were alive, and when they were born, there was a whole cast of human beings around, but when they died, they're laying here all alone, so we're all going to put our hands on this person." This person is—I say if I know what

faith they are—and then I start in with the prayer that honors their faith. And if I don't know it, I make it general, and I thank all the people who tried to save their lives so they will be grounded in that person, and I thank God for the presence of that life.

Almost invariably, Gianaris said, the victim is male and the mourner in the waiting room female:

Always the survivors who arrive are women. I pick them up off the floor. Their mothers and their aunts and their grandmothers. That's the way it is. The women are African-American and Latino females who cannot understand what's happened. I hold them, and then I take them in there with their loved one, and we do the prayer again.

The conference continued, generating stories into the night. After a candlelight vigil organized in front of the White House, I ate with a middle-aged woman, a grandmother, named Carole Hockmeyer and a young woman whose brother had been shot in the back and killed in Washington State; his attacker was acquitted after pleading self-defense, even though the woman's brother had only been "armed" with a flashlight. Hockmeyer attended the conference because as the victim of a gun attack, she was eager to learn strategies from other people involved in grassroots efforts to reduce the availability of firearms in the United States.

I interviewed Hockmeyer in her hotel room Sunday morning, minutes before both of us were about to depart for home. Telling her story made her short of breath, but she finished it.

She had worked as administrative assistant in the town of Newbury, New Hampshire, for ten and a half years, up until November 1, 1993. The town was fighting a court battle with a man named John,* who had put money down on a number of "owners unknown" properties in the mid-1980s but then lost control of those properties when the Merrimack County Register of Deeds failed to document the tax sales. John had hired five different attorneys over six years to try and get his land. In November 1993, the case was finally scheduled to go to court. On November 1, Hockmeyer looked through a window and saw John pull up outside the town hall and park near the front door.

I thought to myself: "I wonder what John wants." And the next thing, I heard what I thought were firecrackers, two pop pop noises, and I thought

*Described by first name only.

Sue Webster, the secretary in the town, was playing a prank because it was the day after Halloween. So I got up from my desk and walked around into the office where Sue was. When I got to the doorway of the office, I saw John standing in the doorway with a gun in his hand. It was not a hand-gun—it was a long-barreled assault-type weapon. What I didn't know was that Maribeth . . . the two pop pop's I heard was John shooting Maribeth. He shot her in the head. Maribeth had just buzzed Sue to tell her she had a phone call, so Sue was in the process of getting up from her desk to walk across the floor, and she was very close to where John was. John opened fire and fired at Sue, once. Sue fell on the floor. I was quite a distance away from them. It was a long office—it was in the selectman's area, so it had a long conference table in there—and I screamed: "Oh my God he's going to kill us," and the only thing John ever said was: "I'm not taking any more bullshit from this town." That's what I think he said. He made one state-ment and fired at me. And I put my arm out, and I took the first bullet in my left arm.

Hockmeyer lifted her arm, where a long, tucked scar ran down from her wrist towards her elbow, and gave it a light slap.

Then I turned around and started screaming and running back through my office, I believe. I'm not positive because even in therapy I've tried to remember what happened after the first shot. I remember him shooting me again, but I don't remember if I went through my office. I think I went past Maribeth* because I'm sure I recall seeing Maribeth face down on the carpet. Our town office building used to be a school, so it was like two huge classrooms on either end of a long narrow building, and I started running down a hallway and feeling stings from other bullets because . . . for some reason . . . I was told this by the state police. His first weapon jammed and then he shot me with a .22. He shot me twice in the left but-tocks, once in the right thigh, and once in the back. I also think I fell down once. I have been told since that there was a pool of blood on the carpet in the hallway where I ran, and I was the only victim able to move, so we're pretty sure that did happen to me.

She ran toward a room where the state assessors were working, but they had recognized the sound of gunfire and already cleared out. She ran into a bathroom and locked the door. "And all the time this was going on I was saying: 'Is this real? Is this really happening to me?' Because it was in slow motion." She removed a screen from the bathroom window and screamed

---

*Described by first name only.

for help. One townsman started running toward the building from over near the fire station but then turned around again. Hockmeyer spotted a police cruiser coming up the street. She heard two more gunshots: John had shot himself in the head. She believes he must have seen the police cruiser, too. "Then I heard the police chief's voice, and I came out of the bathroom, and I came walking up the hall, and as I came around the corner, the police chief had a rifle pointed at me."

The police quickly took over; rescue workers arrived. Hockmeyer called to Maribeth and got no answer. She called to Webster and heard: "I need help. I need help. I'm hurt." Hockmeyer was bundled into the rescue vehicle. Once in the hospital, she was put under the care of a surgeon who had seen duty in Vietnam, but even he had trouble mapping her injuries:

> I had so many holes in my body that they had me in and out of X-ray for hours, trying to figure out where the bullets were. They couldn't understand why I had so many holes, but bullets weren't showing up on the X-rays. What they found out was, for every bullet, the four bullets I took from the .22, I had an entry and an exit wound, so I had two holes for every bullet. And finally around three o'clock I went into surgery.

Hockmeyer survived surgery. John did not. Sue Webster did not. She had been shot in the chest, the bullet ripped one of her large arteries, and her blood pressure was measured at zero in the ambulance. In the hospital, because the victims had been numbered 1, 2, 3, and 4, personnel kept calling Carole "Sue." Hockmeyer said that when she drives by Webster's house or sees a red Ford on the road, she thinks of her friend. And she thinks of Maribeth, who was left face down on the carpet until 6:00 that night, when the medical examiner arrived. "They told me her face was black."

She thinks of John with his two guns, one big, one small. She remembers the police chief with his rifle. She lives with constant physical pain and nightmares. Once a well-wisher delivered a big package to her door and she panicked, thinking it was a bomb: "I saw this black bag on my porch, and I was afraid to go out. I thought somebody was trying to kill me. Finally I talked myself into opening the door, and it turned out to be a shopping bag that had a zucchini lasagna in it or something." And in New Hampshire, a state with a granite Republican tradition and hunting tradition (and a markedly low gun-homicide rate), she has switched political parties—from Republican to Democrat—and has developed a sensitivity to the sight of dead deer.

> I don't want to see even a dead deer, and I don't want to hear about it, but I grew up with it. When I was younger, it didn't bother me; but it has bothered me even before I got shot. . . . Hunting is unnecessary. We don't

hunt because we need the meat, but because it's a manly thing: it's a macho thing. Men get together and go into the woods. They gang up on a poor innocent deer, and I just can't deal with it. I feel sorry for an animal that has to put up with it.

Carole Hockmeyer's grandson swore off toy guns immediately after she was shot. Six months later, he eased back into playing with water pistols. His father, her son-in-law, has hunted in the woods of New Hampshire for years. "It's a boy thing," she said.

Hockmeyer's report concluded with a message and a few important loose ends. Two new characters stepped into the landscape: her son-in-law, who hunts deer in season, and her grandson, who temporarily swore off guns for his grandmother's sake but then one day saw a bright squirt gun and asked for it. By mentioning her two beloved "gunmen" who are linked to John because "it's a boy thing," Carole Hockmeyer inadvertently joins the company of American women who have lived with, thought about, and reported on guns in real life as they know it.

## The Debate Continues . . . Paralyzed

America's public gun debate did not progress or evolve very much between 1993 and 1999. Though the web sites for the chief advocacy organizations grew more sophisticated and measured in tone, and new methods of combat—most notably the barrage of public interest lawsuits against gun manufacturers—showed results, the terms of the debate did not really change. Partisans returned again and again to the same trampled fields, prepared to resume their passionate fight over the meaning of the Second Amendment and the validity of studies, first published in the late 1980s and then again in the early 1990s, proving (1) that guns are used by American citizens to stop crime much more often than they are used to commit crimes, or (2) that guns pose a serious risk to anyone who keeps and carries them. A few different reasons help explain this fiery, yet frozen, situation.

First, the gun debates do offer citizens an excellent stage for debating the transformation of the United States since the 1960s, a transformation that began with challenges to traditional assumptions about what constitutes American heroism, individuality, citizenship, culture, history, manhood, and womanhood. In his book, *The Politics of Gun Control*, the political scientist Robert Spitzer notes that "whenever the government seeks to apply its coercive powers directly to shape individual conduct, the prospect of controversy is great." He remarks that such "social regulation greatly expanded at the national level in the 1960s," when the federal government addressed such issues as "abortion, crime control, women's rights, pornography, school prayer, gay rights, civil rights, affirmative action, and gun control" and passed laws to regulate both institutional and individual conduct in these matters. According to political scientists quoted by Spitzer, when the government introduces and then enforces "social regulatory policy," it exercises "legal authority to modify or replace community values, moral practices, and norms of interpersonal conduct with new standards of behavior."[15] It is just this sort of intervention, this sort of broad government intrusion, that individuals who advocate for the protection of the Second Amendment rights often decry, finding it condescending and insulting.

A second reason for the intractability of the gun debates may be that advocacy organizations that have evolved and grown to fight these battles now rely on the funds generated by them. And there are other reasons, more difficult to articulate, having to do with flesh, wounds, and death.

At the NRA's annual meeting in 1998, Tanya Metaksa began her keynote speech with quotes from Samuel Adams and Thomas Jefferson, and then she called on stage a small group of newly designated American heroes. The last to join her was Jake Ryker, the student who helped wrestle Kipland Kinkel, age fifteen, to the ground after Kinkel began shooting his classmates in Thurston High School on May 21, 1998. Jake himself had been shot in the chest. Jake's father, Robert Ryker, had worn his NRA cap to interviews the day after the shooting. In this way, Robert Ryker displayed his conviction that it was Kinkel who shot his son in the chest (and killed four people and wounded twenty-one others), not Kinkel's gun. The gun was not guilty. In his mind, guns and gun-owning men were not collectively guilty for this act of "gun violence." Kip Kinkel was the sole guilty party.

Based on my own conversations with men and women who share this perspective, I judge that Robert Ryker would not interpret the shooting of Carole Hockmeyer in the same way she did; he would not listen to her story and conclude that legislation should be passed to reduce the availability of guns in the United States. Following the school shootings at Littleton, Colorado, one NRA spokesman argued that the whole situation might have been turned around if the school guards had been armed; in his opinion, general disarmament of the citizenry posed a greater threat than an excess of armaments. What if Carole, Sue, and Maribeth had guns of their own hidden in their desks? Replay the scene. John bursts in . . . and Hockmeyer rises calmly to greet him with a pistol in her hand.

And I feel that Hockmeyer would be intimately offended by this pro-gun reinterpretation of her experience and its moral, just as I expect that the father of Jake Ryker would be mightily irritated by an anti-gun reinterpretation of his family's experience. At this point, we discover another factor that helps explain why the American gun debates are so heated, but frozen, so stubbornly, persistently irresolvable. Because bullet wounds are real, and the people who witness them, in the flesh, come away convinced that they know and comprehend what they have seen. Blood is deafening.

The following discussion relies on interviews, tales, news reports, Internet postings, polemics, and bits of history to illuminate the significance of contemporary political debates about guns in the United States. It also seeks to track down America in the 1990s . . . while trusting that this cumbersome beast will elude capture.

The examination begins with a review of our nation's frontier stories—including reports from nineteenth-century frontierswomen—and the heroes they offer as models. The next chapter focuses on women hunters. Liberal critics have tagged the American hunter as a piggish spoiler, an enemy of the natural world, and in the process they have aroused and offended people who consider the hunt to be an essential part of their heritage. *Female* hunters confuse the images and thus help expose some of the assumptions that generally underlie these polemics. Women who hunt easily with their fathers and brothers do not fit gender roles assigned them by traditional frontier adventure stories or by liberal activists. They challenge us to test our own assumptions about the nature of nature, and of men and women.

Women can be predators. More typically in our imaginations, however, they figure as prey. The central chapters of this book introduce women who imagine using guns, or who have used guns, to defend themselves against attack. In this arena, the tool of choice is usually a handgun and the enemy a man . . . sometimes real, often a phantom. Predictably, a woman's vision of this man determines how she fantasizes resisting him. In this process, in the fantasizing, a woman partially defines herself and defines the country surrounding her. I will argue that women I spoke with who advocated for right-to-carry laws were determined not only to defend themselves against physical threats, but also against lack of recognition, against perceived threats to their identities as law-abiding, trustworthy American citizens. They demanded that authorities acknowledge them as the good guys, not the criminals. By contrast, typically liberal women were not so focused on "criminals" nor so confident that these criminals could be easily distinguished from honest citizens. In the world as they perceived it, one of the most dangerous threats to women was not the feral stranger, but the outwardly respectable, familiar batterer, who was much more difficult to identify confidently and shoot. They were convinced that guns generally endangered women more than they protected them and that the false promises made by gun advocates misled women, blinding them to the kinds of action that would actually most benefit and protect them: concerted community action and large-scale liberal reforms.

The impulse to practice "self-defense" expands readily to meet the size of the proposed enemy, and as the enemy expands, it can become terrible, or it can turn clownish. Men and women who participate in a national gun sport, "Practical Pistol Shooting," gather on weekends to shoot down hosts of cardboard bad guys planted in rickety outdoor sets variously furnished with doors, toilets, aluminum foil spaceships, and bells. Is this gun game indicative, ominous, or is it a just a wacky, theatrical adult sport? If we say it is just a sport, then what about other local exercises or drills that involve guns and are fueled by more explicit political agendas? Female militia members in New York State gather with their friends to drill for, prepare against, and assert their right to resist very large aggressors. They perceive the U.S. federal government as an encroaching threat and America, as redefined by the reforms of the last forty years, to be an alien country.

The final chapter in the book records interviews with African-American, urban women who have observed what happens to kids living in neighborhoods plagued by crime and well-supplied with guns. These women speak matter-of-factly. Many of the arguments advanced by pro-gun and anti-gun advocacy organizations are not entirely relevant to their situation. Their neighborhoods are already "controlled" in many ways—many of the men they know are in prison or have been in prison—so they're not especially enthused by proposals for new gun-control legislation. But they also don't trust the promise that advocating for the "Right to Keep and Bear Arms" and ensuring the availability of firearms to law-abiding citizens will improve conditions for their families. They look for other measures, other kinds of resources and inventions, to reconstruct their sections of the city, and in doing so they prompt us to think about the wide range of efforts and different kinds of heroism needed to build a fair nation.

## Notes

1. See Mary Fainsod Katzenstein, *Faithful and Fearless: Moving Feminist Protest Inside the Church and Military* (Princeton: Princeton University Press, 1998) for a study of women in the military. Prof. Katzenstein explores the different routes military women and churchwomen have followed in accommodating themselves to, while at the same time seeking to alter, the (typically male-dominated) institutions they have decided to join.

2. Quotations from Fox Butterfield, "Chicago Is Suing Over Guns from Suburbia," *New York Times*, November 13, 1998, p. A-18. According to a Harvard law professor quoted in the same article, the "public nuisance" approach sidesteps Second Amendment challenges because Constitutional guarantees don't extend to corporations and manufacturers.

3. When Dennis Henigan spoke as a representative of Handgun Control Inc. before the Senate Judiciary Committee in September 1998, this note was entered into the record:

> General Counsel, Handgun Control Inc. and Director of the Legal Action Project at the Center to Prevent Handgun Violence, Mr. Henigan has written and lectured extensively on the Second Amendment. Among other articles, he is the co-author of "The Second Amendment in the Twentieth Century: Have You Seen Your Militia Lately?" *University of Dayton Law Review* 15, no. 1 (Fall 1989) and the author of "Arms, Anarchy and the Second Amendment" *Valparaiso University Law Review* 16, no. 1 (Fall 1991). He also is a contributing author to *Guns and the Constitution: The Myth of Second Amendment Protection for Firearms in America* (Aletheia Press, 1996).

4. See Peter J. Boyer, "Big Guns: The Lawyers Who Brought Down the Tobacco Industry Are Taking on the Gunmakers and the NRA," *New Yorker,* May 17, 1999, p. 60.

5. See Don B. Kates et al., "Bad Medicine: Doctors and Guns," in *Guns: Who Should Have Them?*" ed. David B. Kopel (New York: Prometheus Books, 1995), p. 236. Kates's notes include a list of public health articles that identify firearms as "disease 'vectors,' 'toxins,' and/or causes of an epidemic." Ibid., p. 286, n. 24.

6. When this posting was on the NRA web site, the address was http://www.nra.org/politics96/bewar.html, "Clinton, Guns, and the CDC."

7. Karen MacNutt, "The Big Lie," *Women & Guns* 6, no. 8 (September 1994): 50.

8. Karen MacNutt, "Junk," *Women & Guns* 9, no. 2 (March–April 1998): 59–60.

9. Throughout the second half of the 1990s, the publisher of *Women & Guns* was Julianne Versnel Gottlieb, wife of Alan M. Gottlieb (chairman of the Citizens Committee for the Right to Keep and Bear Arms), and the executive editor was Peggy Tartaro, daughter of Joseph P. Tartaro (editor of *Gun Week* and president of the Second Amendment Foundation). The magazine was published by the Second Amendment Foundation, and the address listed for the Foundation, for *Women & Guns*, and for the Citizens Committee for the Right to Keep and Bear Arms was: James Madison Building, 12500 NE Tenth Place, Bellevue, WA 98005.

10. For the first volume of the trilogy, most applicable here, see Richard Slotkin, *Regeneration Through Violence: The Mythology of the American Frontier, 1600–1860* (Middletown, CT: Wesleyan University Press, 1973).

11. *Ms. Magazine* (May/June 1994).

12. Christine Thomas and Tammy Peterson, "Becoming an Outdoorswoman: Concept and Marketing," p. 3. Paper presented at the Becoming an Outdoors-Woman Conference, September 24–26, 1993, Turner, Oregon.

13. Robert M. Jackson, Shari McCarty, and Doris Rusch, "Developing Wildlife Education Strategies for Women," in *Proceedings of North American Wildlife and Natural Resources Conference* 54 (1989): 452.

14. Thomas and Peterson, "Becoming an Outdoorswoman," p. 8 [see note 12].

15. Robert J. Spitzer, *The Politics of Gun Control* (Chatham, NJ: Chatham House Publishers, 1995), pp. 3, 5. Spitzer quotes Raymond Tatalovich and Byron Daynes, "Introduction: What Is Social Regulatory Policy?" in *Social Regulatory Policy*, ed. Tatalovich and Daynes (Boulder, CO: Westview Press, 1988). It is interesting to con-

sider the assertion that U.S. federal social regulation expanded in the 1960s. In many cases, the federal legislation of the 1960s was meant to challenge, and ultimately undo, a loose network of comparatively conservative state and local regulations that reformers perceived as racist or discriminatory, such as antimiscegenation and literacy laws throughout the South and antisodomy legislation in some states. Thus the reforms of the 1960s may have revoked old social regulations as often as they imposed new ones.

# 2

---

# American Stories

In the hands of a woman, the gun itself does not change. It remains a tool that can only accomplish two actions, to threaten or to discharge. It can't be used to cook an egg. But one's image of this new composite, the woman-with-firearm, does change because this hybrid challenges our assumptions about the "gender" of the firearm and the proper situation of the person. Many people associate guns with penises for obvious reasons; they point, they ejaculate, they penetrate, they can be shocking when exposed, and they usually can be found adorning men. A woman carrying a 12-gauge shotgun, therefore, illustrates some elementary lessons. This wooden and metal object is not a penis, which means a firearm should not be carelessly interpreted as a natural or metaphorical extension of someone's masculinity. We cannot assume that touching a gun or even firing it will transform any woman (or any person) into either a patriotic hero or a testosterone-maddened brute.

The woman-with-gun is a hybrid who provokes observers to reassess which qualities are inherent in the firearm and which are really associative or metaphorical. She also raises questions about which qualities in the shooter are inherent and which are culturally assigned.

Questions that ask one to discover and untangle the sources of any identity—be it national or individual—are notoriously difficult to answer. Yet a host of American stories and characters continues to influence our political dialogues and, in my opinion, to guide our imaginations and, therefore, our actions in ways that we seldom notice. They do this by portraying, and thus offering as models and imaginary companions, American heroes. Some of these national heroes were real people, others are fictive, but all have been reshaped by storytellers interested in discovering some essential elements of the nation and its ongoing life. Traditionally, these heroes have been male, and they've displayed some part of a constellation of traits—independence, self-reliance, curiosity, adaptability, mobility—that would supposedly enable them to survive, and even savor, life on a frontier. What's more, the most notable are portrayed apart from women, so that their independence involves *independence from women,* thus posing an obvious dilemma for women who hope to model themselves on their example. It is useful to remember this canon of stories—our classic, segregated, national literature—as we attend to American women telling their own stories about hunting, self-defense, target shooting, resistance, and tragedy.

## The Lonesome Frontiersman

The critic Leslie Fiedler argues that ever since Rip Van Winkle first climbed into the mountains with his dog and gun to escape the carping Dame Van Winkle, "the typical male protagonist of our fiction has been a man on the run, harried into the forest and out to sea, down the river or into combat—anywhere to avoid 'civilization,' which is to say, the confrontation of a man and a woman which leads to the fall to sex, marriage, and responsibility." [1]

Our classic stories teach that a true American is baptized and strengthened by his passage through some kind of frontier experience. Just after the American Revolution, when the Constitution was in the process of being written, a book entitled *The Adventures of Colonel Daniel Boone* appeared. This well-timed volume created a prototypical hero incarnate for the new nation, which required prototypes to engender its identity. John Filson, the author, had interviewed the real Daniel Boone at length, then recreated him as a grandiloquent first-person narrator. His literary Boone is initiated into natural mysteries during his experiences as a captive of the Shawnee, who are impressed by his abilities as a hunter and wish to keep him in the tribe. Boone eventually escapes his Indian brothers, however, and returns to Boonesborough, where he leads the settlers in their resistance against the Indians. Later, after Boone has visited Carolina to retrieve his wife and family who believed him to be dead, the clan returns to Kentucky and rejoins the settlement, which is about to be attacked by a confederacy of Ohio tribes. At Blue Licks, Boone's son is killed, along with sixty-seven other white Kentuckians. But these tragedies never dim the frontiersman's great hopes for Kentucke. He joins a successful expedition against the Shawnee, his former brothers, and recognizes that their land is fertile. This land will be a fitting home for a new generation of (white) men, trained by the wilderness to be independent, reverent, wise, and free.

Early in the narrative, Filson's poetic Boone overlooks this new land from an elevated seat:

> I had gained the summit of a commanding ridge, and looking round with astonishing delight, beheld the ample plains, the beauteous tracts below. On the other hand, I surveyed the famous river Ohio that rolled in silent dignity, marking the western boundary of Kentucke with inconceivable grandeur. At a vast distance I beheld the mountains lift their venerable brows, and penetrate the clouds. All things were still. I kindled a fire near a fountain of sweet water, and feasted on the loin of a buck, which a few hours before I had killed. The sullen shades of night soon overspread the whole hemisphere, and the earth seemed to gasp for the hovering moisture. . . . I laid me down to sleep, and I awoke not until the sun had chased away the night.[2]

The scholar Richard Slotkin has identified a significant irony in the Daniel Boone story. He argues that Americans who accepted Boone as a model were entangled by the "dilemma in their perception that the achievement of true title to the wilderness seemed to require both the adoption of Indian lifeways and perspectives (Boone's vision) and the pragmatic elimination of the real Indians from the scene (Boone's victory)."[3] In short, our wide, generous dreams camouflaged a rigid program of national expansion. Following Slotkin, one might also notice a significant absence in the Boone autobiography as shaped by Filson: that absence is Rebecca. Documents show that the actual Rebecca Bryan Boone was a tall, strong woman, an accomplished hunter herself. When her husband disappeared for years, she hoisted up her family and moved to the Carolinas. In Filson's tale, Rebecca plays virtually no part in the story, except to make a brief appearance as metamorphosed prey, whose eyes shine like a deer's in the night forest and nearly get her killed by her future husband.

Daniel Boone—adopted brother to the Shawnee, killer of the Shawnee—started up a long line of romanticized American male hunting heroes who continued to beget one another without the help or interference of any woman. Davie Crockett was one. In his 1834 biography, the noisy Crockett counts up all the bears he kills, but fails to report news of his three wives. A host of fictive wilderness hunters sprang up during America's literary renaissance—one thinks of Cooper's Deerslayer and Melville's Ahab—followed by their progeny, dime Western novel heroes and hard-bitten detectives, as well as Faulkner's and Hemingway's lonesome outdoor boys. America's lone, masculine explorer is armed with weapons, of course, but in classic American stories the strength of the weapon shrinks in comparison with the titanic, shifty powers of his wild opponents, who live at home in the element the hero has chosen to explore. In many of these tales, the passionate union of the American hunter with enemy, hunter with prey, hunter with male friend, or hunter with nature replaces the union of hunter with wife as a prime source of generative, creative power. Fiedler was one of the first to recognize how often red-skinned and black-skinned men befriend our romanticized explorers. Chingachgook loves Hawkeye, the Shawnee wish to adopt Boone, Queequeg sleeps with Ishmael, Jim mothers Huck, Sam Fathers baptizes Ike McCaslin, Tonto sticks by the Lone Ranger. In each case, the explorers win "native" loyalty because, according to the standard plot, their experiences out-of-doors have liberated them from genteel, "civilized" (female) prejudices. They have busted out of the parlor to discover and confront the real world.

Firepower reportedly has little to do with our Romantic heroes' victories; they manage in the wilderness thanks to quick reflexes and a profound, respectful, even *humble* comprehension of their prey. So William Faulkner in *Go Down Moses* could sing praises to religious, communal male hunting rituals more than a century after John Filson:

> It was of the men, not white nor black nor red but men, hunters, with the will and hardihood to endure and the *humility* and skill to survive, and the dogs and the bear and deer juxtaposed and reliefed against it, ordered and compelled by and within the wilderness in the ancient and unremitting contest according to the ancient and immitigable rules which voided all regrets and brooked no quarter; . . . There was always a bottle present, so that it would seem to him that those fine fierce instants of heart and brain and courage and wiliness and speed were concentrated and distilled into that brown liquor which *not women, not boys and children, but only hunters drank*, drinking not of the blood they spilled but some condensation of the wild immortal spirit, drinking it *moderately*, *humbly* even, not with the pagan's base and baseless hope of acquiring thereby the virtues of cunning and strength and speed but in salute to them.[4] (author's emphasis)

Again and again in our stories women are asked to take their positions as the pious, hypocritical lawmakers while true-hearted, even tormented, men and boys rebel against the status quo. In *Go Down Moses*, Ike McCaslin's wife performs a nasty striptease to tempt her husband into accepting his propertied inheritance and renouncing the wilderness. In *The Adventures of Huckleberry Finn*, Miss Watson tells Huck he's doomed to hell for swearing, then makes plans to sell her slave, Jim, downriver. In Hemingway's collection, *In Our Time*, Nick's mother is a dazed Christian Scientist who lies in bed with the shades drawn and murmurs silly things to her husband, who subsequently picks up his gun and heads off into the woods to escape her. Harold Krebs's mother in the same collection is worse—this dim woman asks her grown son, who has returned shell-shocked from the carnage of World War I, to kneel and pray with her. She reminds Harold: "I held you next to my heart when you were a tiny baby." In response "Krebs felt sick and vaguely nauseated."

This common equation of women with genteel "civilization" makes them responsible for a wide network of injustices. Such an assignment of responsibility to women as the "civilizers" also conveniently beclouds the plain fact that American men have been much more responsible for shaping national policies of aggression than women have been; it invites the reader to forget that in the eighteenth and nineteenth centuries, women enjoyed virtually no civil authority and lacked means to help govern the country in which they lived.

Nonetheless, the story lives, and the frontier hero survives in our imaginations and actively invites young men to costume themselves, pick up a gun, and follow him. As a fictional construct, the frontiersman is a Romantic figure meant to distract us from remembering the influence of certain potent forces in American history: domesticity, on the one hand, and also technology, particularly weapons technology, on the other. An extraordinary number of our stories are nostalgic, written by men hoping to reclaim an element in life they feel has been endangered as they, or the country, have grown more "civilized" and modern, entrapped by domesticity and enmeshed in a technological net that frustrates anyone who wishes to prove himself simultaneously heroic and humble. Revolutionary American political writers frequently contrasted decadent, effeminate Europe with the hardy, manly New World. Twentieth-century American nostalgia owes much to the earlier varieties; all identify the wilderness as the place citizens must revisit to maintain masculine virtues and powers that distinguish them from caged, artificial, feminized Europeans or, in the late twentieth century, from anemic, multicultural, antimasculine, elitist liberals.

But a quick glance through the history books suggests that, in fact, the United States has been more forcefully shaped by its industrial genius than by its love of the wilderness. In the mid-nineteenth century, American inventors were very much part of the extraordinary revolution in arms manufacturing that finally eliminated the muzzle-loading flintlock with its powder pan and in its stead introduced breech-loading, repeating rifles that used cartridges with percussion caps. Samuel Colt's single-action six-shot revolver was patented in 1836. Deringer's pocket pistol came out in 1848, about the same time as the ferocious Bowie knife. Americans Horace Smith and Daniel Baird Wesson developed a .22-caliber rim-fire cartridge in the 1850s and a revolver to fit it—all in time for the Civil War.

In fact, according to James J. McPherson, a Civil War historian, Americans first came up with the idea of producing everything from boats to locks with "machine-made interchangeable parts" when they set out to modernize small-arms manufacturing.[5] The mass-produced musket cleared a path for the assembly-line Ford. Foreigners were astounded in 1853 when a representative from the Springfield armory mixed the parts of ten mass-produced muskets in a box, then reassembled ten working guns from those parts. When the American Samuel Colt set up a revolver factory in England, the event "symbolized a transfer of world leadership in the machine-tool industry from Britain to the United States," according to McPherson, who goes on to quote a British industrialist praising America's inventive youths in 1854:

> There is not a working boy of average ability in the New England States, at least, who has not an idea of some mechanical invention or improvement in manufactures, by which, in good time, he hopes to better his position, or rise to fortune and social distinction.[6]

In short, while Romantic, nineteenth-century writers composed tales of lonesome hunters in a pre-industrial America, nineteenth-century firearms were being improved and manufactured by businessmen for a variety of uses, most of which had little to do with hunting deer. Despite all our stories linking guns and solitary hunters, guns were actually a key element in the industrial transformation that shifted Americans away from the woods, away from the rural farms, looms, and blacksmith shops and into modern factories and urban department stores loaded with mass-produced commodities.

It was during the second half of the nineteenth century that the legendary flintlock Kentucky rifle and the smoothbore musket, both muzzleloaders, were finally cast aside, replaced by breech-loading, repeating rifles—Springfields, Enfields, Spencer Repeaters, and in the 1870s, the Winchester Repeater, the "gun that won the West"—and, on the hills, by huge, trundling machine guns called "Gatling" and "Hotchkiss" (the Hotchkiss gun was a crank repeater capable of firing six hundred rounds a minute). With the aid of such weapons, the United States bloodied itself during the Civil War. After the war, U.S. armed forces, reconstituted with defeated Southern troops and equipped with repeating rifles, even buffalo rifles, turned their attention once more to their perennial opponent, the migratory native Indian. By the 1890s, Native American resistance across the continent was crushed. A Navaho chief, Cadette, spoke of guns in his message of surrender: "We have fought you so long as we had rifles and powder; but your arms are better than ours. Give us like weapons and turn us loose, we will fight you again; but we are worn-out; we have no more heart. . . ."

But America's frontier hero was not supposed to win battles just because he had a big gun—a technological advantage. He was supposed to win thanks to his own courage, canny quickness, and sympathy with nature. To revive this romantic hero, the Wild West entertainment industry offered the Victorian-American populace storybook cowboys and storybook Indians—painted performers, Sitting Bull on tour—because although Anglo-Americans had fought to contain and corral the Indian for 300 years, they required the *idea* of the native Indian to roam free. As the boundaries of the actual wilderness were pushed westward, influential citizens advocated the establishment of huge nature preserves that would allow Americans to visit the wilderness and brush up on their frontier spirit, masculine self-reliance, hardihood, resolution, and marksmanship. A number of men—including Henry David Thoreau—suggested that bands of Indians should be kept in with the bears and elk so people could look at them too. Like Daniel Boone before him, the explorer George Catlin climbed to a high overlook and sat down to meditate. He took out a map, and suddenly experienced an epiphany: a vision of a "magnificent park. . . . A nation's Park, containing man and beast, in all the wild(ness) and freshness of their nature's beauty!"[7] This would have been some zoo.[8]

Enter Annie Oakley. Annie Oakley gained her mythical status as a gunslinger largely because she rode into history at the perfect time, when the actual West was growing tamer and dreams of the West, as a result, becoming ever more gaudy. She was part of Buffalo Bill's Wild West Show from 1885 to 1901, in an era when actual buffalo were nearing extinction and America's all-important frontier dreams beginning to fade. She stands for her portrait in a brimmed hat and broad, straight skirt that reaches just below her knees. Her wavy hair has been gathered at the neck, but a portion falls forward over her shoulder. Her legs are heavily stockinged. The barrel of a narrow, no-nonsense rifle rests in the bend of her right arm. She looks short compared to the gun; if she set the butt between her ankles, the muzzle would reach past the collection of awards and badges on her blouse, to the throat button of her high collar.

Oakley was under five feet tall and weighed about 100 lbs. Born Annie Moses, she learned to shoot as a girl in Darke County, Ohio, where she sold game birds for cash to a shopkeeper who sent them on to hotels in Cincinnati; legend reports that hotel owners liked to serve pigeons, grouse, or quail provided by Moses because she always shot her prey straight through the head. Her childhood had been fractured. After her father's death, she was separated from her family and lived in a county home and then a brutal foster home for three years before running away. According to her autobiography, Oakley tramped back home to discover that her mother had remarried, and she could now rejoin the family. No further explanations are given.

She could really shoot. She was a marvel. With her rifle, she shot cigarettes from her husband's mouth and nipped spades off playing cards. Her photographs communicate the impression that she feels herself to be capable—and marketable. Contemporary journalists sent to report on Buffalo Bill's extravagant Wild West Show, a show that depicted violent western scenes with such glory that even the cynical Mark Twain was impressed, regularly photographed the inside of Annie Oakley's neat tent, which came outfitted with a Bible and crochet work. Oakley's rifle was a circus toy used in one of America's earliest traveling nostalgia fests, *and* it was a functional, everyday tool, worn smooth by this diminutive person's hands. She was a showgirl. She was for real. Contradictions. She recommended women take up shooting for exercise and concentration, and that they keep guns by the bedside and carry guns concealed in umbrellas to defend themselves. She might be called a proto-feminist, yet her social politics were conservative: she disapproved of Suffragettes and derided the "Bloomer" costume invented by female reformers eager to provide ladies with clothing that would give them more freedom of movement. However, she herself enjoyed freedom of movement, writing at one point: "Any woman who does not thoroughly enjoy tramping across the country on a clear, frosty morning with a good gun and a pair of dogs does not know how to enjoy life." And she liked to earn money through her work. Work constituted freedom: "Being just little Annie Oakley with ten minutes work once or twice a day, was good enough for me, for I had . . . my freedom," she said.[9]

In the United States, guns are at once solidly actual, portable machines developed over centuries to aim, spark, and fire reliably—and they are brilliantly fantastical tokens, radiant with patriotic and nostalgic significance. Most of a gun's actual power shoots forward, but its suggestive power flows backward, subtly altering the one who aims, for in this country a gun still completes a person's body—especially a man's body—matching it to a long procession of heroic, unfettered American shadows. The gun elongates the rebel's arm, accents the bend in a homesteader's knee, sharpens the focus of a frontiersman's eye. It is an extension, a clear line, a pointer finger, bigger and blacker than a cigar, but smoking and just as cinematically graceful, the masculine counterweight to the ballerina's toe shoe.

## Shooting Rats in the Parlor

As counterparts, possibly counterweights, to nineteenth-century tales of lone American explorers, there existed a body of stories meant for, and often written by, women. America's first two bestselling novels were written by female authors. The first, Susan Warner's *The Wide, Wide World*, was published in 1850 and sold an unprecedented number of copies; that same year *Moby Dick* appeared with little fanfare and less success. The next bestseller written by a female author, *Uncle Tom's Cabin* by Harriet Beecher Stowe, was the first American novel to sell more than one million copies. Contemporary readers acknowledged that the influence of that book on the nation was incalculable.

Looking over these popular women's books with new respect, the critic Jane Tompkins has discovered certain themes in them that, at the very least, illuminate American cultural assumptions about what traditionally constitutes a man's world and what constitutes a woman's world. Simply put, the man ventures outside the home; the woman's place is in the home. Tompkins has discovered a wealth of religious tracts, fiction stories, and "domestic novels" from the mid-nineteenth century that overtly preach what she defines as an "ethic of submission" for women. This ethic follows the Beatitudes in promising that, on Judgment Day, the first will be last, and the humble will be elevated to glory. In the domestic novels she studies most closely, mothers advise their daughters to be good, which translates as: patient, gentle, generous, forgiving, and, above all, uncomplaining. Confinement to the home becomes a kind of fulfillment and performing small duties in the home constitutes an act of religious devotion.[10]

Much of the American Victorian literature specifically aimed at women is (often rightly) dismissed as sentimental, and, consequently, as unrealistic. But a careful reading of these stories uncovers aspects of shared American experience that are terrifying. These stories speak repeatedly about patience in facing lifelong defeat, self-denial, and disappointment, and they often speak about death.

An American woman who lived concurrently with George Washington typically "spent almost all of her married life either in pregnancy or in nursing children, half of whom died before the age of ten."[11] One hundred years later, in the middle of the nineteenth century, things were not much easier for most women. Though in our classic adventure literature, male protagonists prove themselves to be real men by venturing beyond the artificial circles drawn to protect delicate little women from the real world, in fact, the average American woman knew the real world at close hand. She witnessed death repeatedly and came to understand its plain, voiceless nature. In sentimental novels, death scenes are typically writ large, and it's easy—following Mark Twain—to dismiss them as florid stuff and nonsense. Fair enough. But the death scenes experienced by American women have also been concisely rendered in memoirs, and these biographical voices significantly enlarge our understanding of the nation's history:

Albert caught it first, then Johnnie. Albert was terribly ill with it and Maggie realizing he had a very short time to live said, "Oh Albert, do you have to leave us?" He looked up at her and said, "Yes Mama, and Johnnie, too." Johnnie was not yet sick at that time, yet in five days both children were gone.[12]

Even a very brief review of frontier memoirs written by women illuminates the edges of a large, new territory, and challenges us, again, to think about Americans and guns in as broad a context as possible. The actual women who moved West, into the frontier, walked, doctored, hammered, spaded, and cooked, and some learned to aim a pistol. They were not safe even in their (rough) parlors. They claimed land and killed game, but we do not conceive of them simply as "gunwomen" because their weighty physical lives impress one in context, a varied context that includes guns and butter churns, childbirth, church, and attack. Thus each journal or letter written by an American pioneer woman acts as a corrective to simplified myth-making. The variety of their lives and their voices challenges not only the standard heroic myths about purely independent (because woman-free and child-free) male pioneers, but also the newly standard accusatory myths that assign gun-toting white men full responsibility for the rape of a new continent and ignore their resolute and ambitious female companions. These westering women were active, not passive. They actively took part in a long march fueled by courage, yes, and also imperial aggressions, land-hunger, and racism. Most of their reports come to us from the second half of the nineteenth century.

Some pioneer women liked to shoot. Some didn't. Sometimes women picked up guns to scare off Indians.

Barsina French's mother took turns standing guard with the men to protect the party's stock from Indians. Another woman defended her horses and mules by spending a long night on the roof of her stable shooting at a band of Pimas. Eliza Egbert guarded some wagons by brandishing an empty pistol in the faces of some Pawnee and ordering them to depart or be shot. Mary Ann Davidson threatened an abusive Indian with a poker. And when Susie Van de Weile's husband asked her if she was afraid of the Indians surrounding their camp she calmly replied, "No, give me a pistol."[13]

Other times they used their guns to shoot varmints, rats, and rattlesnakes. Aunt Fannie
(Mary Francis Baltzly) shot her own sitting room full of holes:

There was a make-shift of a log house on the place we bought, we made it our quarters for the first years as there were other improvements that had to be taken care of. . . . The house was a habitat for pack rats, they are a curious little animal, when everything is quiet they come out of hiding to investigate. If I was sitting quietly at my work I would keep the .22 rifle at my side, there were plenty of holes in the old house for them [the rats] to come in, at night they would run along the logs above the bed, it was a little too much for peaceful rest, I would get up and place a chair in the middle of the room, light the lamp and would wait for the rat with the .22 rifle across my knees, not long until I had my rat, the shot seemed to scare the others away, we had no fine furniture or plastered walls so it made no difference where the bullet hit. . . .[14]

Martha Stoecker got herself a rattler:

When I awoke there was a big rattler coiled up on top of the bank of dirt thrown up against the shack rattling like fury, about 10 or 12 feet away. I was frightened, got up and went inside and loaded my rifle. I took aim and fired, hit it in the middle and how it rattled and hissed. I waited a little while until I was calm and quit shaking and then fired again and blew its head to bits. I took the hoe and chopped the rattles off. There were nine. I still have them.[15]

Occasionally, girls who were raised by their fathers became avid hunters. Edith Stratton Kitt of Arizona described her days on the ranch:

When I was ten years old my grandfather presented me with a sixteen-gauge, single-barrel shotgun. I learned to shoot fairly well, but nothing fancy. I preferred to shoot at rest and never learned to shoot on the wing. The reason? I never had the ammunition. Dad did not go to Tucson often for supplies, and shells were expensive. I had only two brass shells, and when I went hunting I would carry a tin pail with powder, shot, wads, caps and the tools with which to reload my shells. . . . I have sat at a water hole for hours waiting for two or more doves to get in line so that I could kill more than one with a single shot. . . .[16]

Reading the journals of women like these, I turned through many, many pages uninterrupted by gunshots. Doctoring, cooking, and washing were more constant themes. Making soap was difficult on the trail. Lye made by pouring water and lime through ashes was kept for this purpose and mixed with leftover grease, then boiled and stirred—a stinking, hot, ashy job. Few guidebooks told women what they needed to know about buffalo chip fires, flea and mosquito repellents, alkaline water, and how to keep a supply of clean diapers available in a moving caravan over dry terrain. Nursing babies and doctoring children was hard; infant mortality ran as high as 25–30 percent. The usual childhood diseases could be deadly on the trail. Even more dreadful were pneumonia, cholera, smallpox, and dysentery—all threats immune to bullets.

Once the journey was completed and the homestead reached, women's work increased. On some days a homesteading woman might pick up a gun to eliminate a "pesky gopher" or bring down "5 little birds to make broth of," but on other days she would not. "Butter and egg money" earns more constant attention in women's diaries. "A dollar a pound for butter and fifty cents for cheese will do very well when you have eighty cows giving milk." Wasps and fleas are horrible, nearly sufficient to drive a strong woman mad. But fresh prairie flowers and two-day picnics on the beach must also be noted. Lantern light strains the eyesight. So do letter writing, weeping, and sewing. Tick beds and shrouds, ruffles and trousers are sewn; mountains of sheets laundered; and squirrels, quail, rabbits, chickens cooked for boarding house guests. Custard can be made without eggs, apple pie without apples, and hair oil whipped together from beef marrow mixed with clean lard. Snow drifts through the walls of plank houses, sod houses, and army tents. Letters from home never come soon enough. One woman gives thanks for her cheerful, cooperative husband. The next woman bemoans the weaknesses of her flighty, short-tempered husband, the lawless nature of her oldest son, and madness of her youngest daughter, who ran away young, got pregnant, left her husband, and then returned to perform a terrible cleansing ritual and then tear down her mother's house:

> She went out to the Well And drew Eighteen Buckets Full of Water and thru Water All over her self and striped Her Self down to her Wast And took A black Boll Brush And Some Sand And Scourd her head and Her Cloathes And Her Bodey All Over And scourd the Well And the ground In Frount of the Well. . . . Then She climed upon the Top of the House And Began to pull the Shingels off the House And Nearley tore the Hole roof All off. And then she Tore the top of the chimney down.[17]

A local place has weight. A woman living in a local place knows the weight of buckets filled with water, shingles, chimney stones and sand, kettles, cloth, shotguns, butter churns, dead calves, needles, thread, and rope. No mere gun can lever this figure free from the pull of gravity. Even if we hand her a gun, her silhouette refuses to fit inside the trim silhouette of the idealized male frontiersman. Supplemented by breasts, skirts, toddlers and pans, illuminated by her own will and shadowed by accident, this figure is substantial.

She is not *just free*. She's bigger than free, more complex than just free. And so is her husband or brother or son, and so is the Sioux who looks down on their farm from a distance. Seeing her, we must be provoked to reconsider them. Hear this story from Luzana Wilson, a 49'er (part of a large group of pioneers who sought gold after 1849) who lived for a time in a mining camp where armed men were as common as rats, as weeds, and not much more frightening to Wilson, who pitied them:

> Men plunged wildly into every mode of dissipation to drown the home-sickness so often gnawing at their hearts. They sang, danced, drank and caroused all night, and worked all day. They were possessed of the demon of recklessness, which always haunted the early mining camps.
>
> Blood was often shed, for a continual war raged between the miners and the gamblers. Nearly every man carried in his belt either knife or pistol, and one or the other flashed out on small provocation to do its deadly work.[18]

This writer doesn't think inside the categories we have come to expect. She never pauses to congratulate herself for her own feminine passivity or gener-osity, her own situation as a woman who carried no knife or pistol. On the contrary, she moves on to confess an action that she still remembers as shame-ful, for it allied her with two other frontier killers: neglect and Panama fever. Wilson describes the nameless young man she visited too late.

> . . . and when I heard his weak calls for water I never thought but some one gave it. One day the moans ceased, and on looking in, I found him lying dead with not even a friendly hand to close his eyes. Many a time since, when my own boys have been wandering in new countries have I wept for the sore heart of that poor boy's mother, and I have prayed that if ever want and sickness came to mine, some other woman would be more tender than I have been, and give them at least a glass of cold water.[19]

A mother weeps in sympathy for a dead boy's mother . . . and we are tempted to dismiss the scene as sentimental because it includes all the stock props: bedside discovery, lonesome dead boy, not just one but two sorrowing moth-ers, the usual references to weeping. But one plain detail will not be dis-counted . . . "at least a glass of cold water."

A real American woman cannot be liberated from the accumulated weight of memory and time just by throwing herself on a horse and galloping to-ward the horizon with a gun in her hand. Her narratives alert one to the fact that the same must be true of a real American man.

The twentieth century has introduced the world to gas-operated machine guns, semi-automatic pistols, bigger and bigger battleships, fighter planes, tanks, a variety of horrific new bombs, and fully automatic, repeating "as-sault rifles" like the Kalashnikov with its signature curved "banana" ammuni-tion clip, and the AR-15, which would become the M-16. Many of these weapons were invented by Americans: Benjamin Hotchkiss, Hiram Maxim, John Moses

Browning, Colonel John Thompson (the "Tommy" gun), and Eugene Stone (the AR-15). Our country has become home to a host of potent weapons. Yet in one way, Americans lack experience with the full range of this century's explosive havoc because for more than a century, since the Civil War, U.S. citizens have been spared the full terrors of invasion and bombardment.

Isolated from danger by two oceans and from heroism by a weapons technology that kills efficiently with little physical effort at a great distance, we begin to wonder about courage. Do we have it? Does America have it? The faraway air bombardment of Yugoslavia that was expected to break the will of Slobodon Milosevic in 1999 roused little jubilation or pride in the countries responsible for dispatching the planes. On-the-ground Yugoslav troops sustained more than ten thousand casualties, while NATO troops suffered fewer than a hundred. For a long time, NATO was unwilling to risk its own ground troops—its own men—and so used technology to fight the war. The pervasive sense that there was something shameful about this means of fighting hung over us and was compounded by simultaneous reports of well-armed American school boys staging surprise attacks on their unarmed peers: acts notable for their twisted theatricality and the profoundly self-deceived cowardice of the perpetrators, who apparently fancied themselves to be warriors.

Americans have worried that the nation was becoming "denatured" by its luxuries and technologies before, most notably, perhaps, during the boomtime at the end of the nineteenth century, when Frederick Jackson Turner announced that the United States had reached the Pacific and so could no longer send off its young men to the frontier for a proper American education. Buffalo Bill and Annie Oakley promised that the Wild West lived on in us. Questions about technology and courage will surely haunt the nation into the next millennium and shadow our public foreign and domestic policy debates. They already inform contemporary national debates about recreational hunters and the environment, discussed in the next chapter, and these debates tell us something about American tradition and nostalgia: the loneliness that comes from sensing that we have lost track of the road leading back home.

Faced with these dilemmas, I think we should not expect to banish our traditional heroes. I personally do not want to lose hold of Daniel Boone, Ahab, Henry David Thoreau, Jake Barnes, John Wayne in *The Man Who Shot Liberty Valance*, or Jack Kerouac. But it would be wise to enlarge our American pantheon and deepen our understanding of heroism. Let us also praise Aunt Fannie.

## Notes

1. See Leslie A. Fiedler, *Love and Death in the American Novel*, rev. ed. (New York: Stein and Day, 1966), p. 26.

2. Richard Slotkin, *Regeneration Through Violence: The Mythology of the American Frontier, 1600–1860* (Middletown, CT: Wesleyan University Press, 1973), p. 282.

3. Ibid., p. 316.

4. William Faulkner, *Go Down Moses* (New York: Vintage Books Edition, 1973 [original copyright 1940]), pp. 191–92.

5. James M. McPherson, *Battle Cry of Freedom: The Civil War Era* (New York: Ballantine Books, 1988), p. 16.

6. Ibid., p. 29.

7. George Catlin, *North American Indians: Being Letters and Notes on Their Manners, Customs, and Conditions, Written During Eight Years' Travel Amongst the Wildest Tribes of Indians in North America*, vol. I (Philadelphia: Leary, Stuart, and Company, 1913), pp. 294–95.

8. For a glimpse of our Victorian forefathers and their zoos, see the report of Ota Benga, a pygmy tribesman from the Free Congo who was exhibited at the St. Louis World's Fair in 1904, along with a number of Eskimos, Africans, and Indians. Among them was Geronimo, a prisoner of war and famous new exhibit who sold autographs and buttons to the spectators but was said to have "approached the pygmy huts and put a stone arrowhead into Ota Benga's hand" (p. 16). Ota Benga was later transferred to the monkey house of the Bronx Zoo. He shot himself through the heart in 1916. Geronimo had already died in 1909 after a drunken fall from his horse. See Phillips Verner Bradford and Harvey Blume, *Ota Benga: The Pygmy in the Zoo* (New York: Dell Publishing, 1992).

9. See Glenda Riley, *The Life and Legacy of Annie Oakley* (Norman and London: University of Oklahoma Press, 1994), p. 143.

10. See Jane Tompkins, *Sensational Designs: The Cultural Work of American Fiction, 1790–1860* (Oxford: Oxford University Press, 1985).

11. See Elizabeth Evans, *Weathering the Storm: Women of the American Revolution* (New York: Paragon House, 1989), p. 20.

12. The quote about Albert and Johnnie is taken from a recorded memoir of Mary Gose, the only child of Maggie Brown to survive into adulthood. Maggie and Charles Brown owned ranches first in Colorado, then in New Mexico. Letters describing their life are included in the book *Far From Home: Families of the Westward Journey*, ed. Lillian Schlissel, Byrd Gibbens, and Elizabeth Hampsten (New York: Schocken Books, 1989). Quote from page 164.

13. Stories of Barsina French and Eliza Egbert from *A Place to Grow: Women in the American West*, ed. Glenda Riley (Arlington Heights, IL: Harlan Davidson, 1992), p. 131.

14. See manuscript number 618 in the collections of the *Wyoming State Archives*, "Autobiography. Mary Francis Baltzly, 'Aunt Fannie,'" (1942).

15. From the journal of Martha Stoecker, homesteader in Montana, quoted in *A Place to Grow*, p. 236 [see note 13].

16. Story of Edith Stratton Kitt from *Let Them Speak for Themselves: Women in the American West, 1849–1900*, ed. Christine Fischer (Hamden, CT: The Shoe String Press, 1977), p. 291.

17. *Far From Home*, p. 77 [see note 12].

18. Story of Luzana Wilson from *Let Them Speak for Themselves*, p. 155 [see note 16].

19. Ibid.

# 3

---

# Fields Near Home

In America's Romantic myths, the hunt figures as an initiation ritual for men inspired to search out a reality too ferocious and mysterious for delicate women to understand. In practice, however, the hunt in America has traditionally been part of the business of living, and when it survives as an autumn ritual or a necessity, it tends to survive near farms. In households where family members have grown up hunting, guns are demonstrably functional tools. They're not seen as threats to family life, since at times in the recent past they have clearly helped sustain family life by providing food for the table. Any person trying to understand the place of guns as valued tools and prized family possessions in the United States would do well to begin here, with rural citizens who enjoy hunting because it gets them out into the woods and liberates them from the house, but who also understand (as their fathers and grandfathers understood) that their goal is *not* to disappear into those woods on some individual quest, but to haul the catch back home.

As family farms decrease in number, even its dirtiest tools acquire a nostalgic sheen and are adopted as props for fantasies; how many midwestern restaurants and bars come decorated with old harrows and scythes? Receding into the past, the landscape of the family farm can take on the same sort of tonic qualities that the receding wilderness acquired in the nineteenth century. We feel refreshed by collecting and surrounding ourselves with tokens of hard, repetitive, physical labor and physical challenges as they used to be encountered in the good old days.

Contemporary hunters with whom I've spoken give the impression that their firearms attach them to traditions that are simultaneously liberating and familial. Anti-hunters, in particular animal rights activists, don't see it that way, of course. For them, pursuits that conclude with the death of an animal don't liberate—they just kill—and hunts organized for pleasure rather than necessity aren't familial—they're repulsive. Thus we find, again, a contentious situation where people's perceptions of a certain figure—the gun hunter—diverge so far from each other that each side is astonished by the stubborn blindness of the other. The arguments grow passionate because they have to do with questions about how our country's past should be defined, and then employed, to reform the present and direct the future.

In the midst of this contention, the collective voices of women hunters sound predictable and derivative at some points, original and ambivalent at other points. Aware that their "sport" has lost status and attracted politically charged criticism, some respond to attacks in the same ways their male counterparts do, by accusing their critics of prejudice, by adopting rhetoric that includes exaggeration and euphemism, by citing tradition or nature, and at last, by defining all humans, male and female, as predators who belong in a natural world that teems with butchering and feasting. No surprises there. This standard pro-hunt rhetoric has developed to deflect animal rights critiques. But when these same women speak of hunting as an activity fitted inside a family context that includes trusted men, their statements are more interesting (in my opinion), even tonic, since American narratives common to the end of the twentieth century so *rarely* focus on happy alliances between young women and their male relatives or neighbors. Most women who hunt have enjoyed cooperative alliances with men who carry guns. They were not left behind to pour tea in the parlor.

## Karen, Esther, Becky

Karen Johnson works as a mid-level administrator at Ithaca College in the Finger Lakes region of New York. Her background is rural: her great-great grandparents settled in sparsely populated Tioga County, and her family has lived in the county since that time. She described to me a typical opening day of deer season: "I get dressed about 4:30, and I go to my Mom and Dad's—they live about five miles away—to have breakfast. . . . When November 15 or 19 rolls around, I know I will get up early that morning, pop into my clothes, go out into the woods and start in. I don't always feel I have to get a deer. To be able to go out and be in the woods and do something with my family that we've done for so many years, that's it. Over the course of the years, we've lost many members, and we all gather around the night before the opening day, and we talk about all the people that hunted with us, and 'Oh, you know, if Uncle Bob was here, he'd want to stand at that point.' So you feel like when you're going through the woods, they're still with you. I always feel that when I'm in the woods, my grandfather's with me. And even though my Dad doesn't talk about it, I think he senses the same thing, that his dad is with him and also his grandfather. One of us wears his dad's old hat; it has this bump on the top of it. The whole day reunites the family."

Johnson and her two sisters and brother all hunt. She uses a 12-gauge Remington Savage shotgun, an old gun with a long barrel and a hefty kick. She has also killed a deer with her great-grandfather's gun: "My mom's father literally built this shotgun. It's one where you flip a lever, and the barrel falls down, and you load the slugs into the barrel." She has watched deer die. "Once it stops running, it realizes what has happened, and it will just drop over and lay there. And if you stay back for about ten to fifteen minutes, it will have bled to death." She's seen a new hunter sicken at the spectacle of an injured deer. "This guy who was hunting, he was very young, probably eighteen, and he couldn't cope with it. The fact that the deer was sitting there under the trees, blatting. It sounds something between a goat and a sheep. It cries when it's been hit like that. He couldn't cope. He turned and walked away and got sick back in the woods." Johnson knows the snort, the rustle, the taste, and the weight of an actual deer. She freezes venison and packages the steaks. Once a massive doe slammed into her car windshield. "I was going around a corner, then here comes a big eighteen-wheeler truck. And out of the corner of my eye I saw this big deer running right down into the road in front of me. Well, it was either the deer or the truck. I hit the deer head on, and she was huge; she was over two hundred pounds. She hit my car, and her feet went into my radiator, and she flipped up onto the windshield, and all I could picture was she was going to come right in through the glass at me. But luckily, the glass didn't break, and she slid up over the top of the car."

When hunters talk about deer, they shift between describing an animal that is magically protean, and a carcass so heavy that it bends the nails of the garage block-and-tackle. Neither female nor male hunters spend time apologizing for the death of the animal, though they will often report that on certain occasions, facing particular deer, they chose not to raise the gun and shoot. Johnson said: "I just stand there and I watch the deer and I think. 'No, I can't shoot it today.'" More often, however, if there's a good shot, a hunter takes it, and later she and her family eat venison.

Esther Saunders, another female hunter and a native of central New York, grew up as part of the state's farm culture. A secretary who worked for the sociology department in the same college where Johnson works, Saunders is a frank woman with a big rough cough and judgment in her eye. Her father had always hunted and brought home meat for the family, and her husband had also been a hunter, but it wasn't until Esther had children of her own that she decided to go out with her husband and try to shoot a deer. She started target practice with a .22: ". . . and I got so I was better than him, so. . . ."

Like Johnson, Saunders also hunted with a convincing 12-gauge. "We had four children and meat's high, and the kids loved it. So I decided I'd get my hunting license, and we'd all go. . . . We cut our own wood for years and that's the kind of thing we enjoy doing as a family. Get away from the house, get away from the job, get away from everything. 'Cause we usually don't get away for vacations. Just let me out!"

Esther Saunders and her husband Lester both grew up on farms. "At my house, we raised our own pigs, chickens," and for many years they owned a farm house not far from the town where she grew up. But the number of working farms has decreased in the county. Saunder's brother-in-law gave up farming, though he kept a few cows. He used to grind his own feed, but "as a matter of fact, he just sold his feed grinder." Both the frame farm house where Saunders lived as a child and the farm house where she and her husband lived for years with their family have burned down. They moved into a double-wide mobile home after the fire destroyed their two-story house. The blaze started behind the chimney and was concentrated by asbestos siding. "When it got oxygen, everything just went at once. My brother-in-law was going to go in and let the dogs out, and we said: 'Don't do that, cause it'll knock you right off that porch.' So we lost three dogs and our house. We never did find that one dog. It was a pretty hard time."

"I miss my upstairs so bad. I loved that. It was hot in the summer, but I just loved it. I just loved going upstairs and looking up over by everybody else. We had to bury that house. Cost a lot of money," Saunders recalled. Bereft of her farm house, she expected that the messy job of butchering and preserving the extended family's three or four deer each autumn would move to her son's home, but tradition prevailed. "We still all do it at my house." Typically, four or five family members take their places in the small kitchen around the meat boards, massive cutting boards approximately three inches thick, and go to work in the usual way but with this new, shallower roof over their heads.

Bones and gristle accumulate. Fresh meat for winter is preserved. The antlers get thrown away. "You can't eat them," Saunders said. The tenderloin, two tunnels of high-grade meat tucked under the backbone near the rump, is wrapped carefully. There's neck roast. "Neck roast is wonderful." Also leg roasts. Rump roasts give the most meat. Ribs are whittled down to make "plate meat." There's the heart and liver ("I can't lead myself to eat the heart") and tongue ("You pressure-cook it, and then you have to peel the skin off it, slice it, make sandwiches out of it.")

The Saunders family makes venison sausage, and she cans deer meat, just as her mother used to can peas, corn, tomatoes, pickles, and fruits. "We used to have a huge garden. We bought as little as possible. There was five kids in the family when I was young. Things were rough." The technique for canning meat isn't much different than the technique for canning beans or tomatoes. "We take the venison and cut it up into stew size or smaller. And you pack it in a sterile jar, and we usually put a teaspoon of salt in. You don't have to. It makes its own juice; you don't put any water in it. Then you put it in a hot water bath for four hours. Oh, it's got a beautiful gravy. Makes wonderful sandwiches, and it's good with noodles. Lester's mother used to take some and warm it up and have it with pancakes in the morning."

The utilitarian farm culture that the Saunders have known is fading in New York State and across the nation. According to statistics, in Tompkins County, where Ithaca College is located, farm families represented 18 percent of the population in 1945, and that was in line with the national average. But by the mid-1990s, just over 1 percent of the population in Tompkins County was living on farms. People enjoyed more elbow-room in the 1940s: eighty-six people per square mile of land resided in the county in 1945, compared to 228 in the 1990s. But if they were rich in space, they were poor in standard "modern" comforts: only 75 percent of the farm houses in the county were equipped with electricity immediately after World War II, and only half had running water. This was actually better than the national average at the time, when more than half the farms in the United States lacked electricity and two-thirds lacked running water. Families were larger, but childbirth was riskier. Babies died more frequently. Though its population has doubled in the last fifty years, the public records of Tompkins County show forty infant deaths in 1948, compared to four in 1992, an indication that the *good* old days were rougher than acknowledged by nostalgic retrospectives.[1]

As thriving rural communities have faded, so has hunting. According to studies, 16 percent of the nation's population hunted in 1959, but the share was cut to 10 percent by 1989. Others put the percentage even lower, at around 7 or 8 percent. The trend continued into the 1990s. Research conducted by Cornell University's Department of Natural Resources discovered that only 14.1 million Americans aged sixteen or older hunted in 1993, approximately 2 million less than in 1985, when there were 16.3 million hunters—a loss of about 12.5 percent in less than ten years. What's more, as the number of hunters has steadily decreased, the amount of land "posted" against hunting and trespassing has increased, from 25 percent in 1963 in New York State to 61 percent in 1991.[2] America's fields are being closed to explorers with guns.

Enthusiasts who value hunting as a significant element in rural culture and believe that the activity teaches children patience, cooperation, responsibility, and respect for nature interpret these statistics as dire warnings. Cornell University's "Human Dimensions Research Unit, Department of Natural Resources" is funded by New York State to study hunting; members of the department have interviewed New York hunters, studied hunter apprenticeship programs, investigated why people quit hunting, compiled charts and graphs showing the cycles or stages individual hunters pass through, and published reams of articles describing their research. Across the country, wherever hunting yields revenues, other state-funded research groups are involved in essentially the same efforts. Some of their findings include:

> Fond and enduring memories of family-related hunting experiences were common for traditional hunting families. . . .
> Human-development specialists are increasingly warning us of the seriousness of the erosion of the family and the potential effects of this on familial values transmission. Interestingly, a traditional grass-roots activity like hunting shows evidence of being an effective vehicle for facilitating this process for many families. . . .
> Being a hunter is an embodiment of values, beliefs, attitudes, and behaviors that often have been passed on from generation to generation and comprise a significant focus of personal, family, and sometimes community life.[3]

Organizations that interpret the decline in hunting throughout the United States as a *loss* often write about how hunting might be marketed and its image refurbished in order to halt this alarming trend; the "Becoming an Outdoors-Woman" conference described earlier is a case in point. Advocates have become interested in opening the gates and trying to attract new populations of hunters: blacks and Hispanics (who now make up only about 3 percent of U.S. hunters), urban dwellers, and women.

Becky Stout studied wildlife management at the University of Missouri and Michigan State, then worked in the Human Dimensions Research Unit of Cornell's Natural Resources Department. She then moved from Cornell to pursue studies for a natural resources doctorate in Texas. When I spoke to her, she said she would like to see more women try hunting. Stout grew up in rural Jackson, Missouri, and she remembers that her uncles, who were farmers, would often make gifts of venison to her parents when their big freezers were overstocked, and that a deer head loomed on her cousin's back porch. "I'd look up, and I wouldn't think anything negative about it; I'd just think, 'That's interesting.'" Her own father never bothered to hunt as an adult, though he did shoot rabbits for dinner with his brothers during the Depression. He also trained as an army marksman during World War II, when he was stationed in Hawaii. He kept a deer rifle wrapped and stored in the closet, an insignificant, invisible presence, as Stout remembers it, and a BB gun behind the curtain "for those instances when there was some dog or cat in the neighborhood, and it was pestering our wildlife or pets. He would aim at the critter, and he would maybe flick one of the hairs on its back, and it would take off running. He was that good a marksman."

Stout and her brother enjoyed target practice in the back yard with BB guns and CO-2 pistols. "I did have dolls. I had that side of me with little tea cups and dolls, but then there was this other side of me that enjoyed doing things outdoors." She entered a few target competitions. She practiced her cello. She explored weedy Missouri paths with her mongrel dog. At no time did she feel that guns and hunting were sinful or unethical. Now she has encountered the accusations raised by anti-hunters, and as a "wilderness resource" professional, she adjusts her language accordingly. She corrects herself when she calls a gun a "weapon"; "Weapon is not the proper term here. Firearm is always a proper term for a hunter." She says she thinks of a gun as "a recreational tool, like a badminton racket or a croquet mallet. It's a tool for fun." She will also speak of "harvesting" deer rather than killing, shooting, butchering deer: "I've never really harvested a deer; I've harvested other wildlife species." Her colleagues in the Department of Natural Resources use these same semantic substitutes.

But Stout's professional euphemisms do not finally overwhelm her curiosity or her honesty. Her voice has a level foundation to it. She impresses one as an unfashionably humble person, a positively, substantially midwestern person. Describing her own approach to shot fowl, she keeps her eyes open and refuses to dodge:

> I think of the individual animal when I'm walking up to it on the ground, maybe seeing it thrashing around or shivering the life out of it. And I do feel sad. And then it's dead, and I pick it up and put it in my game bag or over my shoulder and talk about it with friends and take it home, and a few nights later, I'm looking at the animal again, but it's looking different. It's plucked. It's a piece of meat.

She bought her own first gun, a pump-action Winchester 12-gauge, after college when she returned to Jackson, Missouri, and attended an auction where some of Roy Atkins's household goods were being sold. Atkins had belonged to the same campers' club as her parents. He and his family were moving South, and he'd hardly ever shot the gun, so Stout paid a substantial price for it, only about twenty dollars under retail. Guns are passed down.

Her father had a pistol left to him by Bob,* another neighbor Stout remembers well. "[He was] one of my good friends, a neighbor man; when I was very young, we'd go on walks. He'd go fishing, and he often carried a pistol with him, so he could get rid of those snapping turtles that were ruining the fishing. He never got a turtle; they were always too fast. He was probably the most excellent fisherman I've ever seen in my life, and when he died, one of the things his widow gave to my father was his pistol. I associate that pistol with the memory of Bob, and it's a good memory."

When Becky was a girl, she walked alone into the woods with a man who packed a handgun and liked to take it out and shoot at turtles in the ponds. The situation didn't scare her. Bob was a neighbor, a trusted acquaintance of her father's, and now he's dead. Atkins has moved to Florida, and Stout herself has moved beyond girlhood and away from Missouri.

Karen Johnson, Esther Saunders, and Becky Stout have killed animals for food and for other reasons as well. Judging from their stories, they hunt to be part of a circle of present and past families, and those families include respected men. The slaughter of an individual animal sometimes makes them uneasy, but their attachment to a rural culture that appears in various forms— as an old hat, a feed grinder, a big vegetable garden, a stack of pancakes topped with deer gravy, water buckling over the shell of a snapping turtle— reassures them that hunters are not guilty or sinful people. On the farm, land is used; animals are used; people are used. Utilitarian ethics prevail. Animals live and die. So do men and women and children. In fact, many of the real farmers these women knew have died; similarly, corn grinders have been sold off, and hillside frame houses have burned to ash. The women hunt near home. They hunt in memory of home.

## Conservationists Versus Environmentalists

Voices associating the hunt with manhood and the "survival of the fittest" rose in volume at the end of the nineteenth century when, ironically, Native American resistance against white incursion had ceased and author Frederick Jackson Turner had declared the end of the American frontier. Rancher, "Rough Rider," police commissioner, and president, Theodore Roosevelt was certainly one of the loudest and most influential advocates for the manly gun sports, which he believed taught American white men "fighting, masterful virtues." Between 1885 and 1893, Roosevelt published a number of books— *Hunting Trips of a Ranchman*, *Ranch Life and the Hunting Trail*, the seven-volume *The Winning of the West* and *The Wilderness Hunter*—describing the

---

*Described by first name only.

hunt as an exercise that trained men in "the strenuous life" and so prepared them to become world leaders. Roosevelt had no patience with effeminate do-gooders who argued for the value of Indian cultures or the rights of the rebellious Filipinos across the seas; he derided sentimentalists who "make a pretense of humanitarianism to hide and cover their timidity," and who "cant about 'liberty' and the 'consent of the governed' in order to excuse themselves from their willingness to play the part of men."[4] And as one might expect, this president, who would elevate the hunting *man* as a model world leader, had set aside a little domestic corner for women. Teddy Roosevelt admired the American frontiersman for his spirit and the frontierswoman for her breeding:

> The man must be glad to do a man's work, to dare and endure and to labor; to keep himself, and to keep those dependent upon him. The woman must be the housewife, the helpmate of the homemaker, the wise and fearless mother of many children. . . . When men fear work or fear righteous war, when women fear motherhood, they tremble on the brink of doom; and well it is that they should vanish from the earth.[5]

Theodore Roosevelt loved to shoot animals—on one East African safari in 1909, he killed approximately 500 beasts with a Holland & Holland .500/ .450 Nitro Express Double Rifle presented to him by sixty members of the British elite. He was not a man to equate American independence with solitude or meditative, barefoot nature walks. He was an intelligent, confident predator near the end of an era that saw American market hunters eradicate immense native flocks of passenger pigeons and eliminate populations of beaver, moose, antelope, buffalo, and natural predators—wolves, big cats— in many of the forty-eight states. And Roosevelt was also an active conservationist. As a founder and leader of the influential Boone and Crockett Club, he helped press for legislation to protect Yellowstone Park and to grant the president of the United States power to "set apart and reserve public lands bearing forests. . . ." As president, he added almost 150 million acres of timber reserves to the public domain, initiated measures to increase the efficiency and power of the U.S. Forest Service, established the country's first wildlife refuge at Pelican Island, Florida, and then went on to create fifty more throughout the states, and spearheaded the establishment of state and national conservation commissions to oversee the preservation—and sustained use—of America's national resources.

The American Victorian legacy that drove so many species of native animals toward or into extinction, but which also led to the establishment of the first great national parks, plays a large part in today's pro-hunting and anti-hunting debates. Contemporary hunters, stung by accusations that they pose an ugly threat to the natural world, argue that the greedy market hunts of yesterday have been ended by this century's wildlife management agencies. Hunters whom I interviewed repeatedly spoke of the U.S. Pittman-Robertson Act, a piece of legislation passed in 1937 that levies an 11 percent excise tax on all hunting equipment and uses those revenues to improve and enlarge animal habitats. They also argued that sport hunting in the United States is well regulated and has not caused the extinction of a single species in the twentieth century. And they pointed out that populations of native species—notably deer and wild turkey—have increased substantially since the turn of the century (true) thanks to protective licensing restrictions and Pittman-Robertson fund monies contributed by hunters who maintain a strong tradition as "conservationists."

But critics of hunting are not convinced. They equate the American hunt with a generalized constellation of aggressive, imperialistic, invasive, escapist, environmentally destructive, and masculine habits. Though such critiques sound like recognizable products of the 1960s, in fact their history is longer; they've been aired for more than 100 years. In the nineteenth century, Charles Dudley Warner, a friend of Mark Twain's, equated attacks against buffalo with attacks against American Indians, declaring: "The business of this age is murder—the slaughter of animals, the slaughter of fellow-men, by the wholesale." And William J. Long, a contemporary of Theodore Roosevelt's, stung by the president's comment that he [Long] knew nothing about the "heart of the wild thing," responded:

> I find after carefully reading two of his big books that every time Mr. Roosevelt gets near the heart of a wild thing he invariably puts a bullet through it. From his own records I have reckoned a full thousand hearts which he has thus known intimately.[6]

The hue and cry against hunters has roared into the 1990s. Liberal feminist activists have argued that the hunt, a typically male initiation ritual that ends in blood and death, must train young men in violence, desensitizing them to other creatures' suffering and separating them from more cooperative, sympathetic feminine influences. Judged in this way, "the hunt" becomes psychologically distasteful and threatening to the community—especially to women. So one contemporary anti-hunting author argued that men hunt in order to kill off the female in themselves, and as part of his argument, he listed men trained to hunt deer who advanced—predictably—to become murderers of women:

> In his teens, Marc Lepin of Montreal massacred pigeons with a BB gun. On December 6, 1989, at age 25, he donned hunting fatigues, declared his intention to massacre "feminists" and killed fourteen female students at

the Université de Montreal with a semiautomatic rifle and a buck knife.

Whether or not hunters shoot deer to demonstrate sexual potency or out of sexual frustration, in symbolic lieu of raping and killing women, there can be little doubt that as a social ritual, much hunting is all about killing the feminine in the hunter's own self.[7]

In the same vein, feminist author Carol Adams equated all meat-eating people with dominant, aggressive masculinity; according to her theory, the patriarchy teaches a callous disregard for Mother Earth and engineers the oppression of all female living things—women, egg-laying hens, and milk-giving cows.[8] As for "wildlife management," it's all greedy mismanagement, according to the hunt's detractors. Author Joy Williams wrote of state fish and game agencies: "It's time for them to get in the business of protecting and preserving wildlife and creating balanced ecological systems instead of pimping for hunters who want their deer/duck/pheasant/turkey—animals stocked to be shot."[9]

Pressing this same logic, one of the most successful and visible animal rights organizations of the 1990s, People for the Ethical Treatment of Animals (PETA), musters celebrity allies and diligent volunteers in its efforts to expose and ultimately eradicate a broad constellation of perceived abuses against animals, from the slaughter of animals for fur and food, to the use of animals in circus performances and the torturing of animals in research laboratories. In its own on-line "Annual Review" of 1997, PETA reported that it had

- pressured the Fort Gordon Army Installation in Georgia to cancel its annual goose hunt;
- convinced Little Rock, Arkansas, to stop offering bounty rewards for dead beavers;
- insured that prairie dogs in Kansas were "saved from poison gas during the construction of a baseball field";
- convinced KLM Airlines, British Airways, and the Alfalfa Natural Food Stores to stop serving up *pâté de foie gras;*
- sent German Chancellor Helmut Kohl a vegan cookbook signed by Paul and Linda McCartney;
- prompted "horror icon" Clive Barker to submit an editorial to 100 national newspapers asking them to "put hunting and fishing columns where they belong: on the obituary pages";
- organized school presentations asking kids to abandon fishing for "compassionate pursuits like biking, snorkeling, and hiking"; and
- challenged Interior Department Secretary Bruce Babbit to "remain true to the National Park Service's credo of conserving wildlife by banning fishing in national parks."[10]

Men and women sympathetic to such arguments—referring to themselves as "environmentalists" rather than "conservationists"—generally charge that sport hunting contributes substantially to the destruction of the environment because an enormous bureaucracy of state fish and game agencies eager for licensing revenue manipulates park lands and bag limits to maximize hunting opportunities, so the bureaucracy repeatedly upsets the ecological balance of the wild sanctuaries that their agencies ought to be struggling to preserve. Habitat programs funded by excise taxes on hunting equipment only benefit game animals, they contend; the Pittman-Robertson monies are never used to preserve appropriate land for threatened creatures that are unappealing to hunters. One researcher has found that in forests vulnerable to hunting, deer reproduce at an unnaturally frantic rate, thus actually increasing the pressures on the habitat, which hunters claim their "harvest" diminishes.[11] In short, these critics oppose one of Teddy Roosevelt's first premises: that America's wildlife and wildlands are renewable resources owned collectively by U.S. citizens and available for their use. They do not believe wild animals can be owned or should be "harvested" by anybody.

Both anti-hunters and hunters tend to perceive each other's forces massed and on the march; an NRA Internet report praised Executive Director Tanya Metaksa for her efforts advocating legislative measures to "protect hunters, anglers, and other sportsmen from harassment, intimidation, and attack by animal rights extremists." Each group has reserved some territory that it wishes to protect from the intrusion of the enemy. Speaking generally, for the leftist environmentalist, this territory is a vast wilderness ideally untouched by man. Blood spilled by resident predators in such a place is cleanly spilled because nature has worked out a balanced system for the good of all. Modern man's invasion of any such balanced ecosystem is therefore unethical because humans can no longer take part in the complicated exchange fairly. Thanks to technological innovations, they are grossly overequipped, overprotected, and prone to blunders; even their well-intended efforts backfire. Aliens on earth, they have proven themselves to be destructive and virtually unassailed, especially if they're male. A liberal interpretation of American history highlights the disasters that result when European or Anglo-American men establish dominion over a new piece of the earth: resident animals and indigenous peoples are killed.

For hunters, "conservationists," the territory they wish to protect seems to be more local; it may include their own homes, the reputations of their fathers, and eighty acres of woods upstate. To them, the leftist's vision of a delicately balanced, harmonious wilderness is nonsense, a pipe dream concocted by elitists who have lived so long in air-conditioned, sanitary rooms that they can't imagine the rough, muddy, sodden real world outdoors. The hunter does not believe he is crueler than a rattlesnake or puma when he kills prey. There's a lot of predation going on in the world, and humans are part of it. Even vegetarians consume natural resources; present-day environmental dilemmas are as much the result of suburban sprawl and fertilizer run-off as anything else.

Both these arguments rely on subtexts that involve assumptions about gender and about a person's ideal relationship to "Mother Earth" or "Mother Nature," who is personified as a female with a personality, variously maternal or brutal. Nostalgia tells us that we no longer have the sort of contact with this entity that our ancestors enjoyed—or suffered. Residents of a post-industrial nation, we live surrounded by convenient machines now rather than horses, cattle, sheep, and chickens. We have been liberated from a great deal of the physical exertion and plain, dirty, bloody business performed daily by our forebears, who butchered their meat behind the house and visited doctors and dentists equipped with blunt instruments and no anesthetics. In response, we feel grateful, but also troubled by the suspicion that we have lost touch with something important and that the nation is growing "sicker" because of this loss.

In order to regain contact with the earth, some choose to make a peace offering. They promise to leave more land undisturbed and hope this will allow the Earth, which has been "raped" by man, to begin recovery. Others choose to throw themselves back into Mother's rough arms by practicing the seasonal disciplines required of a predator. The first option is more courteous and peaceful—classically feminine. The second is aggressive, even sexual—classically masculine. People who choose one approach or the other seem to feel that they can define the nature of the Earth clearly: she is in sympathy with their mode of action. But ideological categories that depend on unmixed interpretations of man's nature, woman's nature, or nature's nature breed rigid and repetitive squabbles. They generate nostalgia for an uncontaminated, lost world that never existed, whether it be a real man's fighting world or a woman's peaceful, cooperative world. In ideological houses built to satisfy nostalgia, the windows all face in one direction, away from a particular irritant.

## Hunting Under the Sign of Artemis

Mary Zeiss Stange, writer and academic, director of the Women's Studies program at Skidmore College, hunts mule deer, elk, and pronghorn antelope in Montana with her husband. She is author of the book, *Woman the Hunter,* a detailed critique of anthropological and eco-feminist theories that characterize hunting as a traditionally masculine pursuit, theories that consequently assign women gentler roles as stay-at-home gatherers and nurturers and move from that point to define woman's inherent nature.[12] Stange's book challenges these theories and their portraits of pre-agrarian hunter-gatherer cultures, and then moves on to challenge ". . . the conventional view of nature that has developed in American civilization and, arguably, has reached its quintessential expression in such movements as animal liberation and radical ecofeminism [which] insists upon two assumptions: that humans are not really part of nature, and that our primary way of involving ourselves with the natural world is to destroy it."[13]

As a woman who considers herself a feminist and who advocates for hunting, Stange must follow a careful, zig-zag path to explain which elements in the standard texts she acknowledges and which she rejects. At last, she argues that it was the shift toward agriculture that ultimately facilitated the development of acquisitive patriarchal cultures and humans' subsequent alienation from nature, for "ethnographic studies have shown that hunter-gatherer societies tend to display relatively more egalitarianism than do agrarian or industrialized societies."[14]

> With a settled agrarian lifestyle, property and possessions take on significance quite inconceivable to the relatively unencumbered hunter-gatherer. So, too, does the need to defend one's territory against attack, one's goods and animals against plunder. . . .
>
> In agrarian societies, women's reproductive role is all-important: Women provide the labor (in more ways than one) to run the farm. Wives (or more strictly speaking, their procreative abilities) are thereby among the farmer's most important possessions, and daughters—along with herd animals—among his most lucrative mediums of exchange.[15]

Along similar lines, the author defends contemporary hunters against the usual critiques by asserting that the harm or environmental destruction caused by hunting is minimal compared with the harm and destruction wreaked by farming:

> One may argue the immorality of hunting wild animals, for example, on the grounds that domestic animals are raised especially for the purpose of human consumption. Yet the factory farm, feedlot, and slaughterhouse are scenes of untold animal suffering, in comparison to which the death effected by a skilled hunter is arguably infinitely more humane. One may argue for a vegetarian diet and abhor all meat-eating on the grounds of cruelty. But in a single sunny afternoon, a farmer plowing a field wreaks more carnage, in the form of outright killing and the destruction of nests

and mating areas, not to mention the impacts of pesticides and herbicides on wildlife, than the average hunter does in a lifetime.[16]

Stange's interest in the wellsprings of human culture and her impatience with contemporary environmentalist, eco-feminist, and anthropological portraits of woman pressed her to search for a new mythical figure to recenter the general picture and refocus feminist debates. In the concluding chapters of her book, she reaches back to ancient Greece for that mythic figure and chooses Artemis, Greek goddess of the hunt and of childbirth: ". . . a goddess of sacrifice and transformation, death and renewal, of boundary situations." Stange's penultimate chapter explores the significance of Artemis, for it is the author's opinion that: "an Artemesian sensibility with regard to women's and environmental concerns thus appears to be precisely what feminism needs, as a necessary corrective, at this point."[17]

*Woman the Hunter* is interspersed with autobiographical stories, "prologues" to the analytical chapters, describing the authors' own experiences in the field. All the stories describe Montana hunting expeditions that the author took with her husband, Doug. ("Forest Reflexes," the final story, refers to "my partner" and "my companion" rather than "my husband," but this partner, a patient, expert, companionable hunter, appears to be Doug.) These stories are meant to illustrate how the author's perceptions of life, death, landscape, and companionship have been reshaped by her hunting experiences. In one of the stories, "Diana's Portion," Stange shows how an "Artemesian sensibility" might be brought to bear in comprehending and confronting a hunter's nightmare: the moment after the shot when an animal, clearly hit, gets back to its feet and runs off. She describes her own search for an animal she herself had shot, in this case a failed search for a wounded mule deer buck. Stange concludes this story by calling on the goddess Artemis, or Diana (the Roman name for Artemis):

> The weekend's experience had been bittersweet, in the deepest and most complex sense of that term. I had not wanted to leave that hunt as I did. And yet, I knew—with an inner, unshakable conviction—that if I had all the time in the world, I would never have tracked down that buck. In his seemingly magical appearance, Diana had offered the deer, and in his near-mystical disappearance she had reclaimed him. Recrimination was pointless now. It had not been bad shooting. It had not been bad judgment. It was not even bad luck. Tonight, the coyotes would feast. Diana provides for her own.[18]

One story the author does not include in her own book, but which she published in the early 1990s, had to do with the significant killing of "Winston," a pronghorn antelope she and her husband discovered on their five-thousand-acre Montana ranch in 1988, the first year they owned the place. In an article for *Game Country*, Mary Zeiss Stange described her first sight of this particular animal's big horns and referred to his "noble air."[19] The drought of 1988 had devastated the "prime antelope country" that the new ranchers hoped to conserve, but when this pronghorn buck appeared in the midst of the ranch, his presence impressed them as a good omen. Stange's husband kept an eye out for the animal and even nicknamed the beast "Winston" during the months when his wife was away in the Midwest, teaching. That October, they tracked it. Stange shot it with a Sako .270. Then she sat down on the hill next to the dead buck. "Confronting these feelings, the paradoxical counterpoise of life and death, loss in the midst of capture, is fundamental to how and why I am a hunter," she wrote. And about Winston's subsequently mounted head:

> This antelope seemed also to embody what an older religious tradition would have called the "familiar spirit" of our new home. That he would make a fine mount would have been clear to any objective observer, but there was something almost magically appropriate in the idea that his countenance should grace our livingroom wall, as his meat would our table.

Explaining why she and her husband decided to shoot their good-luck spirit, Winston, rather than let it go free, she wrote: "If I did not shoot Winston, someone else most likely would." Beyond that pragmatic justification, she speaks of mysteries, magic, religion, love, and essence and suggests that all hunters, ancient and modern, invoke "the primal notion of partaking in the 'essence' of one's prey."

Stange's interpretations of her own experiences as a hunter point out a fact about human predators. Even before they take aim at an animal, they have already netted it into a context, into a narrative, and asked it to perform a role in their scheme of things. Renaissance hunters singled out the red stag as ideal prey for the aristocrat. When a contemporary Montana hunter kills a "noble" antelope, she kills a designated king crowned with horns by nature and crowned with significance by her. Stange perceived Winston's mounted head to be meaningful and beautiful, but she would not find the severed, mounted head of a golden retriever or Siamese cat to be beautiful. Inside her narrative, the mounted head of a wild animal acts as a token signifying communion between the homeowners and the purchased, wild land surrounding them. Outside that narrative, however, the head shows what happens when a Sako .270 with a 2x7 Leupold scope is aimed and fired accurately broadside at a mature antelope.

Stange's reshaping of the canon of texts and the gallery of heroines used to define woman's history is kin to other feminist efforts of the same kind, and those efforts are of course kin to any reshaping of a historical narrative. If Theodore Roosevelt can establish a Boone and Crockett Club for sportsmen, Stange can certainly lay claim to Artemis. Stange's efforts to create a new story of *Woman* with Artemis at the center may show itself to be most challenging, however, not when it confronts the paradox of killing to live, but when it engages the conflicting demands of complex personal, religious experience and contemporary politics. *Woman the Hunter* is in part guided by the author's contemporary political allegiances. It begins and ends with assertions that more and more American women are hunting, describes this increase a few times as "exponential," and cites the National Shooting Sports Foundation, a hunting advocacy organization, as the prime source for the information. It applauds the expansion of the Becoming an Outdoors-Woman program. This ultimately means that certain stories are left out of the author's theories about the comparatively egalitarian situation of women in hunting-gathering cultures and their oppression in agricultural cultures.

In fact, it's not necessary to reach all the way back to the dawn of history to discover something about societies that lack metal tools and the general situation of woman in hunter-gatherer as opposed to farming cultures. One can look instead to the first dawning of the United States. The Native American groups settled throughout the tidewater area of coastal "Virginia" (now Virginia and North Carolina) at the turn of the seventeenth century, in the early-Contact period, when the English explorers and colonists first arrived, were functionally "Old Stone Age" people (they had no metal tools) that lived three parts of every year as hunter-gatherers, but also practiced agriculture and supplemented their diet with harvests of corn, pumpkins, and squash when they could. Though their culture has vanished, they remain part of America's broadest history. Examining the situation of women among the Algonquins under the rule of Powhatan (father of Pocahontas), one discovers lives difficult to categorize as either passive or active, oppressed or forceful. Algonquin culture was matrilineal, which meant that the daughter of a chief could rule if all her brothers died, and also meant that the offspring of the chief's eldest daughter inherited power in the next generation. *And* young women were offered as sexual gifts to respected visitors. Women were responsible for constructing the sapling-and-mat long houses, planting and tending the fields, making pottery, foraging and preparing food; according to anthropologists, this work was "not much less prestigious than men's work." *And* women did not spear fish, construct fish weirs, go to battle, or hunt bear and deer. It was men, exclusively, who gained prestige when their "great personal exploits in hunting and war" were recognized by their leaders and peers.[20] Following a battle, women and children were claimed as booty by the victors. Women did take part in some acts of war, however. When torture was called for, they assisted in the flaying and dismembering of bound prisoners using sharp shells, and if the prisoners cried out in pain, they sang "shame" songs at them.[21]

Moving farther west across the continent, focusing about one century later, one can trace the story of what happens when a relatively egalitarian "Stone Age" hunting culture is introduced to firearms. The hunt as it was conducted by Plains Indians before the eighteenth century, before the horse and then the gun were introduced to the prairie by colonial traders, required the cooperative work of all able-bodied individuals to help construct the "pound" into which buffalo would be decoyed.[22] After a successful large-scale "pound" hunt or cliff drive, the kill was equitably distributed among all members of the tribe, men and women included.

This situation changed with the introduction of the horse and then the gun to the central plains in the mid-eighteenth century, innovations that allowed individual hunters to chase and bring down animals more easily. The nineteenth-century Plains hunter used special arrows as property markers and had a right to the hide, tongue, and choice cuts of meat from the animals he killed. Women lost their place in the actual pursuit of game. "The absence of women from the nineteenth-century hunt was conspicuous. It was now the domain of men. . . ."[23] Meanwhile, the stacks of buffalo hides that women were expected to tan mounted as their men became increasingly efficient killers; this increase in women's labor coincided with a loss of their economic power.

There are very, very few tales of nineteenth-century Native American women shooting guns. Those times when they did ride with the war parties, they were more likely to be involved holding or stealing horses. It appears that the introduction of European gun technology[24]—the technology that ultimately led to the creation of Stange's Sako .270—worked to alienate Plains men from women, for it empowered the galloping, shooting men who showed "youth, daring, and self-concern,"[25] thus decreasing cooperation and encouraging a kind of individualism inside the tribal circle. At the same time, it should be added that Native American women were never alienated or shielded from predation. Their oldest traditions included them as participants not only in processing dead buffalo, but also in preparing enclosures and cliff drives where the huge beasts would meet death.

And yet we oversimplify the picture, again, if we focus on the gun as an icon that invariably identifies the key oppressor or leader. Anthropologists have argued that the status of Plains Indian women was consistently underestimated by biased Western observers because Westerners perceived guns as key tokens of power, and the Plains Indian women didn't carry the guns or trade buffalo skins with the white man. Yet while it is true that Plains women in the nineteenth century reaped few benefits from the cash trade that grew out of an increased white demand for buffalo hides, still they retained ownership of hides processed for domestic use, including the hides that made up the tipi [also spelled tepee or teepee], and earned respect through their abilities to grow and prepare food. One researcher argues that among the Blackfoot, women sometimes engaged in the hunt and rode with the war parties, but generally they "were less likely to seek the glory road" than men because they didn't *need* to. "Their families and tipis were constant mute witness to women's capabilities, whereas men had to recount again and again their ephemeral deeds in war lest they be forgotten."[26]

The history of woman is various.

## The Woodchuck Bucket

Pro-hunters who accuse their ideological opponents of being detached from the elemental, predatory nature of the natural world also tend to perceive these same opponents as being detached from the practical necessities that drive certain hunters to kill prey for meat, necessities of the kind that pressed on Esther Saunders's parents when they were trying to raise five children on a family farm. Thus, hunting advocates will often complain that privileged, twentieth-century Americans have been so comfortably swaddled in modern conveniences—read "packaged food"—that they've forgotten what "real life" is like. Accused in this way, critics of the hunt quite sensibly respond that few of today's *sport* hunters shoot deer or turkey because they need the meat to keep from starving, and that sophisticated shotguns and rifles outfitted with telescopic sights figure poorly as tools for rediscovering and recreating self-reliant life in the good old days. Reading between the lines of such debates, looking for the assumptions and allegiances that undergird them, one discovers not only marked assumptions about local culture (rural farm culture vs. suburban or urban cultures) and about gender, but also about class. One woman who spoke to me most clearly about this last distinction had shifted from associating with one "class" of people to associating with another as a result of her alliance with a rural hunter.

Joy Veverka grew up in the city of Boston with her mother and grandmother; she did not know her father. She did not know any hunters. When I interviewed her, she lived in the country south of New York's Finger Lakes, where she owned approximately fifty acres of woods and the hilltop mobile home in which she lived with her partner, Gordy Gabaree, a hunter and trapper, who worked as a "nuisance wildlife control" professional when she met him. Veverka had shot or trapped woodchucks, raccoons, mangy coyotes, diseased foxes, rats, bats, and even feral dogs. She has hunted with guns and bow. Her hunting bow was stiffly set and impossible for a novice to draw, but she took a ready stance and pulled the tiny "kiss" button on the bow string directly to her lips.

Veverka was introduced to hunting by her husband's father. When I interviewed her, she was divorced from her husband, the father of her two sons. His father, her father-in-law, had fled from Czechoslovakia to settle in Canada, where he started an outfitting business on leased wilderness land in northern Ontario. Her first kill took place with him.

> It was just me and my father-in-law. And that was the first time I actually killed, consciously killed, an animal. It wasn't even a conscious decision. I saw the doe. We had a doe permit. I remembered what I'd learned in class and rehearsed it in my mind, just as I used to do when I'd take a test in swimming, rehearsed what my body needed to do, and I just followed through with that, and I shot her. It was actually a hard shot. There was a lot of stuff in the way. I was in a tree stand, and she was a fair distance from me. My father-in-law heard the noise, and he got to the deer about as quickly as I did, and he was just, oh, he was so proud. He was just delighted.

Veverka's father-in-law is no longer alive, and she separated from her husband in 1990. During her marriage, her life was more materially secure than it is now. She and her academic husband, a tenured Ivy League professor of astronomy, were able to entertain handsomely and travel to France, the South Pacific, Hawaii, Mexico. But she didn't always feel at ease or competent alongside her husband's colleagues, whom now she habitually calls "privileged." She described a cruise to New Zealand and Australia organized for well-heeled travelers who wanted to follow the tail of Halley's comet across the globe in the company of expert astronomers, geologists, and psychologists. Navigating in league with the stars, they stopped at an island in the South Pacific:

> . . . and the ship usually arranged ahead with the people of these islands so that we would be treated. This particular place traditionally gave a feast to honor the people on the ship. Well, it was a holy day for them, and they're not supposed to cook or work on this day, but the ship was planning on stopping. My husband knew about it because he was on the staff. So the ship was [passengers were] angry at the islanders. "You know: 'Hey, we pay you a lot of money; how dare you say you're not going to put on a feast.' " And these people were intimidated enough so that they did. They dropped everything, including their holy day, and they put together the

most amazing feast within very short notice. And these rich, spoiled, ignorant passengers that were on board ship had the balls to complain about the
food, how they'd rather have a hamburger!

Since her divorce, Veverka has become acutely aware of class divisions,
especially divisions that encourage privileged urban or academic professionals
to denigrate rural culture. As a woman who abandoned a college town and
moved in with a hunter, she came to divide the world her own way, elevating
individuals who had "scope" and dismissing those who lacked it, some of
whom happened to be poor and uneducated, some of whom happened to be
rich and hold advanced degrees. Though she praised her former husband as
a sensible, admirable, broad-minded man, she passed critical judgment on
many of his colleagues, scientists who had probably forgotten her name. In
her book, people who lack scope tend to be intolerant, self-occupied, and
confident in their dismissive judgments of others. Regardless of their educational advantages, they remain steadfastly ignorant.

During the interview, Veverka often said that the people she came in contact with in rural New York, many of whom lacked much formal education,
some of whom hunted deer or rabbit or squirrel because they needed the
food, were *real*, and that this place—Alpine, New York—where she was
living with her new partner, was real. For her, the real was pragmatic, uncomplaining, alert, and embodied in people she has actually met. She described one woman she had come to know in the nursing home where she
worked.

> This woman and her husband owned a chicken farm at one time and shipped
> about two hundred cases of eggs a week, but after her husband died, there
> were these woodchucks that got into the chicken house. Now this is her
> livelihood. She had to get rid of these woodchucks. She didn't have a gun,
> didn't know how to kill them. So what she did was she got this old fork and
> she stabbed this woodchuck in the back of the neck, somehow managed to
> heave this writhing woodchuck into a bucket of water, put a lid on the top and
> sat on it until the thing stopped kicking. She had to do what she had to do.

Veverka follows the pattern of an established American tradition when
she bypasses the aristocracy and selects, in their stead, a few hunters and a
poor widow to represent native nobility. She enthrones the widowed chicken
farmer on a bucket full of churning, bloody woodchuck and recognizes in
that woman the pitiless determination that marks a queen, an absolute ruler
who has learned authority through necessity.

When we spoke, it was very clear that Veverka felt a kinship with this
blood-spattered older woman since her own life had been reshaped by con-

frontations with necessity. "I stack wood, I sweat, and I'll take the tractor way up back, and I was scared to death of tractors, all that power, and these tractors aren't very good; they're old, not very safe." At that time, she and her partner together earned annually about a quarter of her former husband's salary; complications drove Gabaree out of the nuisance wildlife business, so when I interviewed her, he was driving an armored truck, he worked unpredictable hours, and he had no benefits. For years, she worked two jobs, mornings in a daycare facility, afternoons in a nursing home. Busy trying to earn a living:

> I can't exercise, I can't go take aerobics, and I used to do that . . . I don't even go out. We do eat out once in a while, but we really can't afford it, so there's this experience, you're enjoying your dinner and at the same time you know you shouldn't be going out to dinner. I haven't bought myself clothing in a long time. And the things that are important: I haven't been to the dentist's for about a year to have my teeth cleaned. I need a mammogram. I haven't done that because I don't have health insurance.

When we spoke, she and Gabaree had been trying out a few assignments as private investigators to earn some money. All this, but she called her present life less restrictive than the one she lived before.

When turkey hunting, Veverka used one of her partner's guns and either took the tractor or hiked to the sloping field beyond the stream gully south of the pond. Just down the hill from the mobile home where they lived was an abandoned farm house, humid, dark, and peeling. On the southern hill where she sat for turkey, the foundations of another lost homestead rest underground someplace. The couple hadn't discovered the spot, though they knew from old maps and from a few obscured apple trees, now entangled in the woods, that a family once lived there.

Gabaree himself came from a New York farm background, but not a pretty one. Passed from the hands of one unpredictable, even threatening, relative to the next, he made do by eating blackberries in season when food was scarce ("His sister to this day can't stand blackberries") and spending days out in the woods with his gun. Veverka told stories of Gabaree's uncanny instincts in the woods. When I visited, she and her two sons were living in a house where the drawers and cabinets were stocked with her partner's guns. At last count, there were three rifles, five shotguns (three 12-gauges, a 10-gauge, and a little squirrel gun), four handguns (a .22 automatic, a .22 revolver, one .44 magnum revolver, and a .38 revolver), some pellet guns, and also the .22 that her eldest son often took back and forth from her house to his father's house. She and her sons weren't nervous inside this thicket of firearms. In the south bedroom that the boys shared, the older teenager kept his growing supply of reloading equipment, boxes of slugs and shot, metal presses that resembled hand-juicers, and careful records of the loads each recycled shot-gun cartridge could safely hold. Next to the desk where the reloading equip-ment stood was a chest of drawers crowned with a Lego construction.

Veverka dressed for the hunt and took me up the hill with her. When we reached a good place, she settled down and propped her shotgun against a tree stump located just inside the woods. Then we sat there for a long time, looking out through the trees into the grass field, hoping to spot or even hear a wild turkey. She was dressed in green and brown camouflage gear, for wild turkeys are reportedly spooky, sharp-eyed, and totally lacking in curiosity, unlike deer, who often stamp or snort if they see anything odd. The glitter of an eyeball, a glint of flesh, will alert a turkey, so she took out small tubes of thick green and brown camo paint and began to smear it over the backs of her hands. She once observed a privileged woman on a Hawaii beach sit grooming her feet for an hour with expensive creams. Watching Veverka paint her own hands camo green, I thought here was a belated response . . . "You don't see me, you don't remember me, but in this place I am real."

## Shirley Grenoble: Hunter/Prey

Shirley Grenoble had placed herself on the edge of a low ridge, overlooking a sparsely wooded valley floor that provided quick passage for deer running between two hills. It was doe season in Pennsylvania, and this was an arena for does, not bucks. The hunter knew her territory. She stood against a tree with a rifle under her arm. Unlike New Yorkers, Pennsylvanians are allowed to hunt with rifles. If necessary, Shirley could shoot clear over the small valley below and across the ten-acre field behind it as well.

It was very, very cold that morning.

One hour later, Grenoble moved her gun. There was the steady rustle of an animal walking through leaves. Instantly, the hunter raised and planted her rifle on her shoulder and snapped herself into ready position—an agile, automatic action. But then the rifle sank. Her scope was fogged. With prac-ticed speed she cleared the lens and raised the gun again. The rifle blast exploded into the world solidly and rained sound. She didn't hear it. She put down her rifle and set off running toward the sad bleat over the ridge. A bad sign. The deer was small, about the size of a large dog, and the shot has not been perfect.

Grenoble sprinted back to the tree for her rifle. In the leaves there lay a markedly pretty animal with big eyes and delicate bent legs, moving its jaws, trying to get air.

Returning, Grenoble shot the fallen animal in the neck. The blood issuing from the first bullet hole had made a sticky path down its coat. A small procession of blood drops continued to follow the path even now that the animal was dead. She had to gather herself before field-dressing this little catch. The imperfect shot and the pained bleat of the animal made her miserable. I was there, dressed partly in my own clothes and partly in insulated overalls that Grenoble had brought to my motel room before 5:00 that morning, and she explained to me that *this* wasn't a typical shot for her, she expected better from herself.

In a minute, she got down to work. Clumps of brown, digested roughage fell from the stomach. Soon there was a blue and red gut pile in the leaves and bright red blood spots on the fallen leaves and on the hunter's cuffs. She had a plastic bag in her fanny pack for wrapping the edible organs. The empty deer was dragged, slippery as an otter, over the forest floor to the truck and hauled into the truck bed on top of an old flowered shower curtain. Grenoble had invented a hip sling that enabled her to drag out even huge deer alone, without a man's assistance. Once she shot a buck weighing nearly 200 lbs. in difficult terrain at 8:00 in the morning and didn't finish hauling it out of the woods until 4:00 that afternoon. With a big animal, she takes four steps leaning forward from her hips, then rests, then a few more steps and rests, until she sees her parked truck.

When I met her, Shirley Grenoble had been hunting for more than forty years, since the day she followed her broken-legged husband and his beagles into the field and predicted, correctly, where the flushed rabbit would emerge after it circled. She was nineteen years old then. The next time out, she stood at the conclusion of the circle with a gun and shot her rabbit. "Blew it to smithereens."

> All this time, I was standing there wondering whether I could really kill something. But when you get out into the field and realize how tough this is, and how the animals win more often than you do, they get away more often than not, a lot of that "poor brown-eyed syndrome" goes out the window. These wild animals can run faster than you can, they can climb down in holes, they can see you, they can hear you, they can smell you, better than you can see or hear them. They can fly. So when every once in a while, you figure things out right, and there he comes, it's time to shoot him, knowing you're killing that individual rabbit, but you're not wiping out the rabbit population. You clean it, take it home, cook it, have rabbit stew.

Grenoble was an avid hunter. She identified years past according to deer seasons, and her reputation as a turkey hunter and specialized magazine writer had earned her invitations to promotional hunts in a number of states. When she was younger, she would go out into the woods alone two or three days a week, always protected by a gun, which she used a few times to kill rattlesnakes in high grass and once to scare open a path through an aggressive crowd of drunks gathered near a creek: "I just pulled my pistol out of the holster, and I just had it like this, resting against my chest near the steering wheel, and this one came around and looked in and saw it. And he YELLED something, and the biggest hole you ever saw opened up in that gang of men, and I just drove through." If she's out on a trek alone and has to sleep in the car, she dozes with shotgun shells in her hand. But a financially messy divorce forced her to pull up stakes and start a modest used-paperback store to support herself, so that when we spoke she said she rarely escaped to the woods on weekdays anymore—except in deer and turkey season. Like Veverka, Grenoble owned her own house, a small brown house fronted right on the sidewalk and packed inside with hunting trophies, antlers, turkey tail fans, plaques, and family photos. There was a time when she feared her property would be seized to pay her ex-husband's debts, but she confronted the IRS and then an insurance settlement helped keep her afloat after she was shot in the face and body by two brothers carrying semi-automatics who thought she was a turkey.

Grenoble couldn't explain precisely why she had become such a committed hunter: "It's like trying to say what's so great about sex, or how you know when you're in love." She began hunting in the 1950s when it was not at all fashionable for a woman and encountered predictable resistance from some men. "They'd say: 'Well, what are you out there shooting a man's deer for?' But my hunting was in no way any kind of women's lib statement. It was what I wanted to do because *I liked it*." She didn't think she would have taken up hunting if her husband hadn't gotten her started, but she expected that she would have found *some* activity to get herself out of the house. "If I'm in this house very long, pretty soon I feel like it's all falling in on me." Her former housemate, Ron,* was an experienced hunter, as was his son and Shirley's grown son.

The resistance Grenoble had encountered more recently came from anti-hunters rather than from fellow hunters. As a magazine writer and local newspaper columnist, "I get a lot of hate mail. 'You dumb broad; you bloodthirsty wench,' all kinds of stuff. They say: 'It's too bad the deer can't shoot back,' and 'I hope you die in a groundhog hole.'" Asked if she ever met an anti-hunter she liked or whose arguments made sense, she responded: "No. They haven't lived with hunting, and they try to paint us all as ruthless slaughterers and assume that if they could just get the hunters out of the woods, the animals would live happily ever after." To Grenoble, this was cartoon nonsense. In support of hunting, she quoted studies that showed the winter survival rate of turkeys in West Virginia remained steady whether the hens were hunted

---

*Described by first name only.

in autumn or no. Like many other hunters, she spoke of overpopulated deer herds starving in winter, saying that Mother Nature is a "ruthless old gal," which most people don't realize because they get their information about the woods from *Bambi.* "If there's anything I hate, it's Bambi. When a Bambi book comes into my bookstore, I burn it. I don't let it go out into the public."

Grenoble laughed. She is a small woman with a face defined by clear, compact features, though in certain light she appears worn and grandmotherly and lacks color. She told me her life had not been easy lately. She kept the details private but added that she was glad she knew how to shoot a gun.

Turkey hunting is more risky than deer hunting because the turkey hunter wears camouflage gear—not blaze orange—and in spring she imitates the call of a wild hen turkey in order to lure the aroused gobbler into range. To make the proper noises, a turkey caller will use a variety of devices: circles of black slate scratched with a wand, reverberating wooden boxes scraped with a paddle, or the more difficult diaphragm calls, little plates of latex equipped with thin reeds and shaped to fit behind the teeth, up against the roof of the mouth—an experienced caller can keep two or three of these contraptions in her mouth at a time and switch them with her tongue. Experts distinguish between a variety of turkey calls, from the "ki-ki run," the distress cry of a young, lost turkey, to the "yelp," the "cut," the cluck, and the raspy assembly cry of the mature hens. The "yelp" sounds like a crow's caw mixed with the barking of a little dog in a tight collar. The "cut" sounds like air being released from a balloon; with it a hen challenges her competitors. The favored hen mating call rises in pitch hungrily before dropping off. "Ik, ik, ik, IK, IK, IK!" The purr of a contented hen is said to be lovely.

Shirley Grenoble, her son Mark, and her former partner, Ron, all hunted turkeys and had all managed accidentally to lure in hunters with their convincing clucks and yelps. These hunters approached with guns blazing and eyes shut. A heavy peppering of metal shot remained in Grenoble's scalp and her son's head. When we spoke, she still had twenty-seven pellets in her body. Occasionally, a little blister would appear on her arm when another tiny globe of shot surfaced; she would squeeze it out. Ron's experience was terrifying; his attacker was a "hit-and-run" man who left him alone, bleeding in the woods. Yet Grenoble defended hunters passionately and told me that her son wanted to carry his young daughter into the woods in a backpack just as soon as she was ready. His wife would likely protest. She was present as a witness the day her husband took a full blast to the head.

It was the first time Mark had taken Debbie up into the woods on a hunt. Grenoble came along without a gun. They tried to call in turkeys but had no success.

So the three of us came down off this hill with a big green field at the bottom of it. We were just talking to each other, not hunting any more. We were just laughing and talking. Sunshine was out and the birds were singing. It had just been a great morning. And Mark was in the lead because he knew the way, and we were just cutting across the corner of this open field when KAWAHMM. They shot Mark, my son, right square in the face. And he fell right down on my feet. And I thought he was dead. And I went down, I knew what had happened, and he rolled around like this, both hands clapped over his face, and the blood was running down his fingers. . . . The minute he went down, I remembered he had a side pocket on his pants and in it had a wad of toilet paper, and I immediately dug it out and began to wipe the blood from his neck because I was afraid of these arteries in his neck. You see, shotgun shells it's not like one bullet. They're just all over you, and blood is coming from all over you, and it's difficult to tell exactly where you've been hit or what would be the worst wound among many. . . .

It was three men hidden in some thick brush who had just decided that because they'd heard us calling turkeys up on top of the hill and then they heard us walking, they just decided it was a flock of turkeys coming, and they didn't wait to see if it was turkeys or what. Just as soon as they saw the first movement, they pulled the trigger, and the movement turned out to be my son.

When these three men emerged out of the brush, we yelled at them, and it turned out that my son knew one of them because we were on private land. Here one of them was the landowner. They came up and saw. And they had one of these old boxy army-type Jeeps that just has one seat in the front. And one guy ran up and got it and drove it down in the field. They loaded Mark and Debbie in it. Debbie was hysterical.

They tore out through there with him, and I'm left standing there with the man who's just shot him. I don't know what his name was. I never asked what his name was. We had quite a conversation. Of course he immediately began to justify himself. "Well," he said, "you know you people are damn good callers."

I didn't want to mess with this guy. I just wanted to get out to my truck and get on the road, get to the hospital. But we were both back in the woods, so we walked out together.

Mark still has one pellet that is bucked right up against the optic nerve and has to be watched continually because if it should move, it could cause him to lose his sight.

Less than three weeks after her son was shot, Grenoble went turkey hunting again.

And just two and a half weeks after he was shot, I went out around here, around Racetown Lake, and I'd been hunting all morning; hadn't heard anything. About 9:00 in the morning—there's a big open gas line coming down over the mountain in this place, so I thought I'd just sit by this gas line and do some calling. Turkeys like to come out into open areas. So I'm sitting there, calling, and I'm calling off and on for about thirty minutes, and I didn't hear anything so I thought: "No use; I'll go someplace else." So I stood up. And I was just getting my gear together, buckling on my waist pack, picking up my shotgun . . . doing a lot of stuff like that in the brush. Well, apparently, what happened was two guys in the woods, two brothers, forty and forty-two years old, had heard my calling and decided they were going to sneak in. They circled and came in behind me, and I never saw them. And apparently they saw my moving and mistook me for a turkey, or just decided it had to be a turkey. So they started shooting. Now they had 12-gauge semi-automatics, which means all you have to do is keep pulling the trigger, and it keeps going. These were BB loads, which is the largest. That size is outlawed in Pennsylvania now, but it was legal then. Anyway, they emptied their guns at me, which means they each shot at me three times. I was hit first time smack in the face, from the left side, like this. Then in the arm and both legs. I was screaming the whole time, but the noise of their guns in their own ears . . . they were firing simultaneously, and they could not hear my screams. Of course, once their guns were empty, and they stopped shooting, then they could hear me.

Grenoble had been forced to wait alongside the man who shot her son. Now she was forced to lean on the man who shot her. The brothers wanted her to lie down; she refused. "I said to myself and to them: 'No. As long as I can put one foot in front of the other, I'm walking out of here.'" One brother sprinted to get her truck. The other supported her, "put his arm around my waist, and I put my arm around his, and I walked." She told him her phone number and made him repeat it back to her. She didn't know the extent of her injuries. "The blood is running down my face, spreading out over my chest and arms; I think I'm going to die any minute. I truly thought I was going to die. . . . All this time I'm hanging on this man, and he's hanging on me, I'm thinking, 'You cannot pass out. You must not pass out.' And he kept saying, 'How could this have happened?' Noncommittal. I said something like, 'Well if you'd made sure of your target, it wouldn't have.' But believe me, you are in no frame of mind to be arguing with them. All that was on my mind was to survive. I figured we could sort it out later. And the most incredible thought kept going through my mind, which was, 'Wait 'til Mark hears this.'"

Later in court, ". . . immediately their lawyer attacked me, as to what had I done to make these two men shoot at me. Well . . ." Hunting accidents do not qualify as crimes in Pennsylvania. The brothers were fined by the game commission and had their licenses revoked for five years. Grenoble's civil suit took two years to settle. The settlement covered her medical expenses with little to spare.

When Shirley, Ron, and Mark were shot like turkeys, they did not learn the simple lessons that some people would urge on them: they did not learn that hunting is unacceptably violent and dangerous, and everyone who hunts should give it up. Grenoble said she *is* more afraid than she used to be. When she's climbing down a Pennsylvania mountain and just coming over a bench —"Mountains aren't one big smooth piece; they're actually made in benches; they go up [and] then they level off"—her spirit freezes. "When you get to that place where you're just going to reveal yourself, step out over an edge, I think now: 'I don't want to do this.' Every muscle tenses because you think you're going to get shot again." But she takes a breath and steps over the edge.

This woman had watched the blood spread down her own chest and arms. With a handgun tucked over her left breast, she had sailed through a flock of drunks in her pick-up. Gobblers had danced for her, their shiny, charred wing feathers dragging on the ground. And then she had shot their heads off. She knew her son might go blind if the pellet shifted into the optic nerve, yet she hoped her granddaughter would be introduced to hunting. Trophy caribou antlers dominated her front room. She had stalked animals. And she had been stalked like an animal. She thoroughly enjoyed hunting as a comrade alongside men. Men had caused her much trouble. Blood-stained, stubborn, maternal, predatory, sad, and lively, she had grown a personal history forked with contradictions.

In fact, a notable quality in many women hunters is their enjoyment of managing two or three lives without much fuss. They change costumes according to the weather and the occasion and keep thick camo clothes in the basement near their washer-dryers. There's a gamey tranquillity in the body of a woman who has outfitted herself in clothes more often worn by a man and who has picked up a hunting gun. The fact that she remains a mother who could, with a little effort, bend down in all her gear and speak in her normal voice to a child is disconcerting.

Contemporary American female hunters are certainly aware that they've adopted a multiplicity of costumes and therefore a multiplicity of identities. Paradoxically, this experience convinces them that deep down they have selves that survive through the costume changes. In many cases, experience in the hunt convinces a woman that her self is more happily independent than she had realized previously; it is clear that the decision to join men in the hunt was liberating for a number of individual women—I think of Joy Veverka and Shirley Grenoble particularly. Carrying a gun into the woods allows a woman to appropriate or accept certain appealing "masculine" qualities

—the confident handling of tools usually associated with men's work, the willingness to endure some physical hardship and get dirty, the stoic acceptance of death and one's part in killing to eat—and then, possibly, to redefine what constitutes "masculine" and "feminine."

But there is a last darker turn to this road. Women who use guns in pursuits that outsiders critique as brutal or vicious naturally defend themselves by relying on their personal knowledge of others who follow these same pursuits and are fundamentally decent: paternal, maternal, honest, plain, kind. In the process, they necessarily defend and define themselves as decent. This process of self-discovery and affirmation can be altered by political disputes to the point where it hardens into self-assertion.

The impulse to *self*-defense has been an important force in the contemporary American gun debates of the 1990s. Many gun owners share the conviction that liberal elitists malign them from a distance without ever bothering to visit their homes, meet their families, or listen carefully to their stories. The conviction that traditionally acceptable, even laudable rural activities have been stigmatized by liberal misinterpretations is directly related to the broader conservative conviction that pacifist liberals have demeaned all their fellow citizens who keep or use guns, including not only hunters, but also soldiers and homeowners. When we begin to speak of guns that are aimed not at animals, but at humans, the rhetoric grows harsher and the targets dimmer. Women who stereotypically figure as prey, not predators, naturally attract more sympathy than men when they choose to purchase handguns for self-defense. Attempts to calculate just where an American woman ought to stand relative to this issue are perplexing and therefore revealing, for they tell us a great deal about the dangers that people in the 1990s have imagined threatening not just themselves, but America.

## Notes

1. Demographic statistics for Tompkins County were reported in Claudia Montagne, "Family Portrait: The Facts, Figures and Faces of Tompkins County," *Ithaca Child,* 5, no. 2 (Spring 1995): 12–13.

2. Jeff Stimpon, "Study: Hunters Are a Dying Breed," *The Ithaca Journal*, October 21, 1993, p. A-1, A-4.

3. See Daniel Decker and George F. Mattfeld, "Hunters and Hunting in New York." Pamphlet, HDRU Series No. 88–7, June 1988, Human Dimensions Research Unit, Department of Natural Resources, New York State College of Agriculture and Life Sciences, Ithaca, New York, esp. pp. 15, 24.

4. Theodore Roosevelt, "The Strenuous Life," in *The Works of Theodore Roosevelt*, vol. XII (New York: C. Scribners' Sons, 1926), pp. 7–8. See also Richard Slotkin, *Gunfighter Nation: The Myth of the Frontier in Twentieth-Century America* (New York: Atheneum, 1992), p. 53.

5. Roosevelt, "The Strenuous Life," pp. 3–6.

6. Quotes from Charles Dudley Warner and William J. Long taken from Matt Cartmill, *A View to a Death in the Morning: Hunting and Nature Through History* (Cambridge: Harvard University Press, 1993), pp. 143, 154.

7. Merritt Clifton, "Killing the Female: The Psychology of the Hunt," *The Animals' Agenda,* September 1990, p. 29.

8. Carol Adams, *The Sexual Politics of Meat: A Feminist-Vegetarian Critical Theory* (New York: Continuum, 1992), throughout.

9. Joy Williams, "The Killing Game," *Esquire*, October 1990, pp. 113–28.

10. "Annual Review 1997," http://www.manatee.envirolink.org/arrs/peta/index.html. Produced by People for the Ethical Treatment of Animals, 501 Front Street, Norfolk, VA 23510. 757–622–PETA.

11. Ron Baker, *The American Hunting Myth* (New York: Vantage Press, 1985), pp. 30–36.

12. Mary Zeiss Stange, *Woman the Hunter* (Boston: Beacon Press, 1997).

13. Ibid., p. 126.

14. Ibid., p. 47.

15. Ibid., pp. 46–48.

16. Ibid., p. 120.

17. Ibid., p. 137.

18. Ibid., p. 135.

19. Mary Zeiss Stange, "Winston," *Game Country*, January/February 1990, pp. 52–59.

20. According to a 1992 cross-cultural anthropological study, there are few occupations so gender-specific as the related occupations of warfare, hunting, metalworking, and the manufacture of weapons. "The male monopolization of warfare had enormous consequences for all subsequent human history . . . it extended from warfare itself into the monopolization of the tools of war, which meant a monopolization of big-game hunting and metalworking." See David Adams, "Biology Does Not Make Men More Aggressive Than Women," in *Of Mice and Women: Aspects of Female Aggression*, ed. Kaj Bjorkqvist and Pirkko Niemele (New York: Academic Press, Harcourt, Brace, Jovanovich, 1992).

21. Helen C. Rountree, *The Powhatan Indians of Virginia: Their Traditional Culture*, The Civilization of the American Indian Series (Norman and London: University of Oklahoma, 1989), pp. 79, 84, 89, 91, 93, 109, 121 and throughout.

22. Alan M. Klein, "The Political Economy of Gender: A 19th Century Plains Indian Case Study," in *The Hidden Half: Studies of Plains Indian Women*, ed. Patricia Albers and Beatrice Medicine (Washington, DC: University Press of America, 1983), pp. 143–73.

23. Ibid., p. 153.

24. For a much fuller examination of the consequences that resulted from the introduction of European gun and metalworking technology—along with European contagious diseases—into the Americas, see Jared M. Diamond, *Guns, Germs, and Steel* (New York: W.W. Norton, 1997).

25. Klein, "The Political Economy of Gender: A 19th Century Plains Indian Case Study" [see note 22].

26. Alice Kehoe, "The Shackles of Tradition," in *The Hidden Half: Studies of Plains Indian Women*, ed. Patricia Albers and Beatrice Medicine (Washington, DC: University Press of America, 1983), pp. 53–73.

# 4

---

# Self-Defense, Part I:

## Combat by Story and Statistics

**Combat by Story**

The female hunter is not a common visitor in American stories. The hunted female victim is. Even women who take precautions to avoid her fate inevitably join her in our imaginations.

"It's like you're standing there with no clothes on, completely vulnerable. No clothes on," said Ann Wexler, a social therapist who divorced when her children were young and raised her family alone in Highland Park, New Jersey. "There were times, many times, when I would wake up at night and hear noises and lie awake with my heart pounding wondering whether I'm hearing something or am I not hearing something and realizing that I have no protection whatsoever. It's terrifying." Once, panicked by the sound of pounding and screams in her attic, she dialed the police emergency number. "And the voice goes on: 'EXCUSE ME MA'AM, could you repeat that, MA'AM?' Five minutes passed; I could have been dead. I said: 'Look, there's some noise in my attic. I think there's somebody up there.' 'UH, WHAT IS YOUR EXACT . . . COULD YOU SPELL YOUR NAME?' I'm trying to say here's my address, 'UH, COULD YOU TELL US . . .' not, 'We'll send somebody right over.' And that really scared me because I realized that they don't just . . . arrive."

As it happened, the shrieks that Wexler heard in the attic came from a female raccoon raising hell to defend her young against the returning male. In the night they sounded like the screams of a lunatic. "I remember really lying there and realizing—I have nothing. I have no protection. I used to think: 'What would I do? Could I get out my window? Would it be too far to jump? If anybody came in, could I lock my door and stand on the roof and yell?'"

Wexler does not keep a gun in her house. The majority of women in the United States live through the night as she does, in houses equipped with telephones, beds, windows, but no pistols, rifles, or shotguns. According to a poll conducted by the National Opinion Research Center (NORC), University of Chicago, in the mid-1990s, only about 11–12 percent of America's women owned their own guns, and only about 7 percent owned their own handguns. Tom Smith, who conducted the General Social Survey published by NORC, argued that these proportions had remained basically steady since 1980 and that media reports in the early 1990s describing American women swarming to buy guns for self-defense were unreliable, for a number of journalists based their information on a 1986 Gallup poll sponsored, and then misrepresented, by the Smith & Wesson Company.[1]

Judging from responses tabulated by the NORC survey, less than half of the adult women in America, 39 percent, live in households with guns. According to a 1998 survey by the Center to Prevent Handgun Violence, 43 percent of American households with children had "a gun somewhere at home," and 23 percent kept the gun loaded at least part of the time.[2] According to a 1998 University of Chicago, National Gun Policy Survey, about 39 percent of the households in America contain guns, a decrease from two decades earlier—in 1973, 47 percent of American households surveyed had guns in them.

But the types of guns that Americans keep in their homes seems to be changing. As hunting wanes, a greater proportion of the firearms purchased are handguns. Handgun ownership reportedly increased proportionately from 1973 to 1998, rising from 20.3 percent to 24 percent of the "gun stock"—placing handguns in nearly one out of four households. Yet gun sales have slipped in the second half of the 1990s, dropping from 5.2 million in 1993 to 3.7 million in 1997.[3]

Those women most likely to own their own firearms or live in households with firearms tend to be either married or widowed and associated in some way with a hunting culture, according to the NORC survey. Generally, these women reside outside large metropolitan areas and live in the South or West, rather than the Northeast. Young, unmarried women sojourning in big cities are among the least likely handgun owners. Past victimization and even fear of crime showed up as relatively insignificant factors influencing gun ownership by women in the NORC surveys; alliance with a hunter had a lot more impact.

But when reports of random gun violence in the nation increase, interest in self-defense expands: at these times it may not even matter *how many* women own handguns. A glance back into recent history shows that the debates over use of handguns for self-defense were at their height around 1994, the year when Republicans won control of Congress following a broad conservative campaign that received significant support from pro-gun organizations, and in 1995, the year when Newt Gingrich and his allies reigned over Congress. An NRA posting on the Internet marks 1995 as having been "the most successful legislative year in the 20-year history of the NRA-ILA [Institute for Legislative Action]."[4] That was the year Suzanna Grazia aimed her long finger at the head of a reluctant Texas state senator to underscore her point that if she'd been allowed to carry a concealed pistol, she might have saved her parents from being gunned down (along with twenty-one other victims) by a lunatic in Luby's Cafeteria.[5] The Texas concealed-carry bill, SB-60, was signed into law by Governor George W. Bush in the summer of 1995. Suzanna Grazia-Hupp (newly married) was elected to the Texas House of Representatives in 1996.

The image of Suzanna Grazia or of Sharon Jo Ramboz, who testified in 1995 before a House subcommittee that she had saved herself and her children from an intruder by merely loading her AR-15 semi-automatic rifle loudly at the top of the stairs, imitates archetypal American images of armed male heroes, while adding an element distinctly female. These women asked to adopt a traditionally virile weapon in order to oppose a repugnantly virile enemy: the male killer or rapist. They asked to be allowed to fight fire with fire. Facing legislators, their stance could be variously masculine and feminine. Grazia aimed her pointer finger at a senator's forehead. Ramboz wore a neat red skirt suit for her appointment with Congress and displayed a framed picture of her children.

Ramboz argued for the right to keep her AR-15 semi-automatic rifle, an "assault weapon" outlawed by the Violent Crime Control and Law Enforcement Act of 1994 (commonly called the "anti-crime bill of 1994") in order to protect those children. Behind her, another woman in a red suit waited her turn to testify. Her son had been shot in the back and killed by an obsessed Eagle Scout carrying an AK-47. Byrl Phillips-Taylor said that listening to Ramboz argue in defense of semi-automatic weapons "made me physically sick." She continued: "They're saying they want to arm themselves to protect themselves. . . . So do you arm seventeen-year-olds to protect themselves? Do you arm fifteen-year-olds to protect themselves? When the hell is it going to stop?"[6]

Four years later, in the wake of the April 1999 Columbine High School shootings in Littleton, Colorado, newspaper reports focused on people who argued for tighter gun-control restrictions. Byrl Phillips-Taylor would address the House Judiciary Committee again in May 1999, speaking in support of new gun-control legislation. Embarrassed by local protests, the NRA scaled down its 1999 annual meeting, which was, by chance, scheduled to take place in Denver. The Republican majority in the Senate, surprised by a heated public reaction after the Columbine tragedy, approved a gun-control measure that would have required background checks of individuals purchasing firearms at gun shows or pawn shops (the Republican leadership had opposed the bill earlier). Since virtually no new gun-control legislation had passed through Congress since 1994, anti-gun advocates, heartened by the shift, spoke of a "sea change" in American attitudes toward firearms. But a short while later, this legislation died in the House, killed in part by opposition from liberal Democrats who considered the House version of the bill to be weak and riddled with loopholes. The heat from Columbine had not been strong enough to forge a coalition that could move the House. Currently, prospects for introducing and passing new national gun-control laws do not look promising, and anti-gun advocates are pressing their cases in the courts, through lawsuits, with more success.

The publicized shooting and murder of a six-year-old girl, Kayla Rolland, by a six-year-old male classmate in March 2000, revived the struggle for passage of additional national gun-control measures, but by this time the reactions of the usual parties to the debate had become so familiar that they were disheartening—in part because none of the laws being advanced would have prevented the six-year-old boy from getting his hands on a stolen gun in a functionally lawless household: the political battle had little to do with the individual case. All parties were obviously energized by their interest in the ongoing contest between Al Gore and George W. Bush, newly selected presidential candidates. Wayne LaPierre publicly lambasted President Clinton, claiming that "he's willing to accept a certain level of killing to further his political agenda." Clinton returned fire. ". . . this sort of wounded rhetoric by the NRA . . . you know, these crocodile tears—I don't think it'll wash with the voters." In the midst of it all, a significant development did take place. The revered Smith & Wesson Company reached a compromise agreement with its critics and promised to re-engineer its guns and enforce certain restrictions on their sale for safety's sake; the company adopted these measures in order to save itself from devastating city and governmental lawsuits.

Although gun-control controversies staged in Congress invariably attract attention—with good reason—many of the most telling battles in the pro-gun/anti-gun war have been fought at the state level. From 1994 through 1997, state legislation insuring citizens the right to purchase and carry guns passed in fourteen states; many interpreted this avalanche of pro-gun activity as part of the successful Republican backlash against the Clinton administration, particularly against that administration's gun-control successes, including passage of the 1994 anti-crime bill (prohibiting certain "assault weapons") and the Brady Bill (mandating background checks and waiting periods for gun purchasers). From 1977 to 1992, ten states had passed concealed-carry laws; then in 1995 alone, ten additional states adopted new right-to-carry laws. By the end of the decade, thirty-one states had right-to-carry laws on the books. "Concealed-carry" or "right-to-carry" legislation prevents local law enforcement agencies from imposing their own restrictions on citizens who request permits not only to purchase guns, but also to carry concealed handguns on their person in public. The laws are meant to insure that qualifying citizens—adults who are not prohibited from owning guns because of a criminal record, certified mental illness, or history of spousal abuse—can legally purchase and carry guns if they elect to.

Women were often invited to join in and speak up in favor of these laws for rather obvious reasons. First, they created attractive stories for journalists. Second, women could pose convincingly as family caretakers. And last, they look like people who would use guns responsibly (even reluctantly), and this rendered their message more palatable to an audience. The general public has little fear of armed women, who tend to be identified as victims rather than aggressors. This last factor especially empowered female citizens who pressured legislators to repeal gun-control legislation or to ease concealed-carry restrictions so that they could carry concealed handguns on the streets to protect themselves.

One of the most powerful and public spokespeople for the NRA in this decade was Tanya Metaksa. From 1994 to 1998, the NRA foregrounded Metaksa, whose public letters and numerous contributions of short "Backgrounder" articles posted on the NRA's website were notable for their angry attacks against Bill Clinton, Janet Reno, and the Centers for Disease Control.[7] Metaksa was variously described in her posted 1998 bio as "chief lobbyist," "executive director of the NRA Institute for Legislative Action," the director of "CrimeStrike," a division of the NRA occupied with "victims' rights," the founder of the NRA's woman-oriented "Refuse To Be a Victim" program—and "a mother and grandmother." In October of 1998 the NRA announced that Metaksa would be stepping down as NRA-ILA executive director, to become senior advisor to the executive vice-president, and that she was being replaced by Jim Baker, her predecessor, the man who had directed the NRA-ILA up until 1994. It appears that the NRA's loss of membership through the late 1990s had something to do with Metaksa's demotion, along with the organization's discovery that its efforts to attract women by highlighting a female spokesperson had not proven as successful as expected. By the middle of 1999, it was difficult to find any postings on the NRA's website that concluded with the name of the formerly ubiquitous firebrand, Metaksa.

At the height of her power as an NRA representative, Metaksa had lobbied vigorously for "right-to-carry" legislation of the kind that Grazia successfully advocated in Texas. When she addressed the NRA's 1998 annual meeting, Metaksa called up on stage a gardener, Gene Case, whom she identified as an "armed citizen" from Oklahoma. Case had witnessed the kidnapping of a little girl, chased the kidnapper with his gun, "saved the little girl, and held a monster at bay for police." Metaksa announced triumphantly: "Gene Case had a carry permit."

The movement to pass state laws liberalizing restrictions on concealed weapons and granting citizens broad powers to carry handguns attracted enormous media attention from 1994 through 1996, and for a few years afterward the two best-known organizations engaged in this political struggle—Metaksa's NRA and Brady's Handgun Control Inc.—made it a practice to tally up and report on concealed-carry legislation nationwide. Of course, their judgments of the results directly contradicted one another. At the end of 1997, Handgun Control Inc. posted a "Year-End Report on U.S. Concealed Weapons Laws" that unhappily acknowledged a total of thirty-one states "have now denied their law enforcement officers discretion in the issuance of concealed weapon licenses." The posting included a "report card" showing which states most effectively restricted the carrying of concealed handguns through a system of licensing, just plain banning, and training requirements; the states where restrictions were most tough earned the highest marks.[8] Simultaneously, the NRA posted its "NRA-ILA Victory Report from the States, 1994–1997" celebrating the fact that ". . . since the beginning of 1994, we've passed new right-to-carry laws in 14 states and improved 24 existing right-to-carry laws."[9] The NRA also re-broadcast Handgun Control, Inc.'s report card and advised its members simply to reverse the marks in each case—drop the grades for Illinois, Missouri, Nebraska, Ohio, and Kansas from A to F, and elevate Georgia, Vermont, New Hampshire, Pennsylvania, South Dakota, North Dakota, Washington, Montana, and Idaho from an F to an A—if they wanted to measure the current state of the nation and its liberties.

## Combat by Story and Statistics

In the mid-1990s, one "pro-carry" group that attracted frequent media attention was Safety for Women and Responsible Motherhood (SWARM) in Colorado. SWARM was organized in 1994 to support the passage of concealed-carry legislation in that state, and by early 1998 it was still post-ing its position papers on the Internet because its efforts had not yet met with success; in January of 1998, the state Senate Bill 81, the Carrying Concealed Weapon (CCW) bill, was squashed in Colorado's Senate Judiciary Commit-tee. In the wake of the 1999 shootings at Littleton, Colorado, two pro-gun measures being considered in the Colorado legislature were pulled from the schedule by the Senate, with the support of the governor. One would have prohibited cities "from enacting any gun violence prevention laws" (i.e., law-suits against gun manufacturers), according to Handgun Control, Inc. The other was a concealed-carry bill.

As pictured in news and magazine reports during the heyday of these debates, Rebecca John, president of SWARM, appeared to be a very slim, worn woman who wore dark clothing. When I contacted her by phone, John explained that she had been drawn to the right-to-carry issue and ultimately politicized by her own experiences as a victim. While living in a large city in Colorado, she was attacked two times. She refused to name the city or to describe details of those attacks to journalists: "I don't go into details be-cause I really want to try to focus women on the solution, as opposed to perpetuating us in the women-as-victim roles."

She received counseling after the first attack: "They told me, 'whatever you do, don't get a gun; it will only add to the violence.' . . . I was told I could use awareness and safety instructions and lights and locks and do all these things and that's how I would prevent being attacked, and I *did* all these things, believe me, I did all those things, and it did not work. I was attacked again. The bottom line is, when a criminal is there and wants to do harm to you, he doesn't care about all the lights and the locks you've used and all the other precautions you've taken *unless* they present a danger to him. Then he starts caring."

After the second attack, one of her friends, a man, lent her a gun and gave her some training with it. Daughter of an insurance executive, raised in a home where she hadn't had access to guns, John was uncomfortable with the weapon at first. "Before I knew it, though, I started realizing how much clearer my thinking was when I would hear a creak in the night; my thinking was clear because I knew all I had to do was get to that gun, and I would at least have a fighting chance." She enrolled in the NRA Home Firearms Safety Course and purchased a Smith & Wesson revolver. She dated a policeman, who had since become her "ex-boyfriend," who informed her that "the street cop is largely in favor of the private citizens being able to carry on the street, concealed, but the top brass, they're very political, and they have their own motivations, and they don't want to see private citizens carrying no matter what." And she began talking politics, discovering allies, networking.

Rebecca John did not think individuals should depend on the government. She had nothing positive to say about welfare. She had followed court cases, like *Deshaney v. Winnebago, 1989,* that determined law enforcement agencies cannot be judged guilty for violating an individual citizen's Fourteenth Amendment "due process" rights by failing to protect that individual from violent attack. In short, according to John, the courts had decided "that our government and the police department, separately, together, are not responsible to protect us individually." In this conclusion, conservative Rebecca John agreed with the feminist author Ann Jones, who has written at length about the legal system's abdication of responsibility toward battered women in her book, *Next Time She'll Be Dead.*[10] Both see that such court interpretations of "due process" left female victims powerless to seek retribution against police officers and social agencies that failed to respond when these women begged for protection. But whereas Jones advocated for extensive changes in the legal system, John advocated for personal firearms.

> Like you get a gal, her boyfriend has battered her, and she begs the police, begs them: "Can I carry a gun? Can I carry a gun?" "No you can't." And then her boyfriend comes up and kills her or comes up and throws lye in her face. What the court has held is that the police are responsible to protect the community as a whole and not the individual. The reason—they can't guard you twenty-four hours a day; that would be silly. There's no way. They're not psychic.
>
> The way I see it, we're responsible to bathe ourselves, we're responsible to feed ourselves, and we are responsible for our self-defense.

In Rebecca John's arguments one recognizes significant conservative themes: the distrust of government and the admiration of American self-reliance. I would hear these same themes evoked by other women who had taken up guns not only to defend themselves against individual attackers, but also against the perceived threat posed by an increasingly invasive, liberal government. I was interested in those places where contradictions and inconsistencies set in, often because the personal lives of women—so many of which involved children—raised dilemmas that could not be solved by one neat solution or another. I always attended to these stories because women who were convinced that they had found clear answers to their problems fascinated me, and those who were more confused impressed me.

But I was also aware of the proliferation of stories, the deployment of personal stories. In the gun debates of the last decade, dramatic personal vignettes, often related by women, were packaged to influence legislative decisions. Rebecca John, Byrl Phillips-Taylor, Sharon Jo Ramboz, Suzanna

Grazia, Sarah Brady, Tanya Metaksa, and many, many others understood the function of women's autobiographical narratives in this political context. In order to attach these personal narratives to a larger picture, however, and thus establish their significance, advocates from both pro-gun and anti-gun camps have always found it necessary to offer broader, more purportedly objective information about the nation, and for this they commonly turned to statistical reports, such as published surveys or government tallies (e.g., FBI Uniform Crime Reports or the National Crime Victimization Surveys). One might expect that the personal stories would flesh out the statistics and the statistics would locate the stories in a broader context so that broad swipes between personal narratives and national percentages *would* create a whole portrait of America, but, in fact, this expectation is repeatedly frustrated. Somehow even the most moving and terrible stories lose authenticity when they come retrofitted to impress a committee or fit into a magazine article, and statistics cease to register as objective once it becomes obvious that the experts generating the numbers have divided up into antagonistic teams. Ultimately, I came away with the impression that these narratives and numbers weren't actually part of a vigorous exploration to discover something about the composition of America but part of a battle, and that few people in the audience were attending to the whole expanse of data. Instead, most people were out shopping for evidence to restock their own arsenals and defuse their opponents'.

So, let me discuss statistics. When I spoke to Rebecca John and Diane Nicholl, co-founders of SWARM, both of them referred me to Gary Kleck's studies. Gary Kleck's research was used as key source material by pro-gun advocacy organizations throughout the 1990s. In his book, *Point Blank*, published in 1991, Florida State University criminologist Gary Kleck extrapolated from survey data to conclude that Americans used guns to defend themselves approximately 1–2 million times a year and that guns saved lives approximately 400,000 times a year. Another study published by Kleck and a coauthor, based on a 1994 telephone survey, basically confirmed these numbers, though this article estimated national defensive gun uses (DGUs) at 2.5 million per year nationally and concluded that in America the efficacious use of firearms for self-defense outnumbered criminal use of firearms by factors of three to five. Then in 1997 Kleck updated and refined his argument once again, critiqued the methods of the gun-control and public health writers who had questioned his research, and essentially reasserted his 1994 conclusions in the fifth chapter of that book. Kleck's findings were prominently cited in the NRA's "1997 NRA Firearms Fact Card" posted on the Internet and in a number of NRA postings still on line in 2000, including a long article entitled "Armed Citizens and Crime Control," which offers a detailed defense of Kleck and Gertz's 1995 article.[11]

In response to the enthusiastic promotion of Kleck's studies by pro-gun partisans, a host of gun-control, public health, and even government organizations declared that Kleck's methods were badly flawed.[12] The National Research Council of the National Academy of Sciences argued that Kleck's definition of "self-defense" was so ambiguous that many of the anecdotes accepted by his pollsters as DGUs could well be based on people's confrontations with imagined threats. The National Institute of Justice (NIJ), an arm of the U.S. Department of Justice, published a "Research in Brief" paper in 1997 titled "Guns in America" reporting that the department had conducted a telephone survey similar to Kleck's 1994 survey and had come up with an equally astonishing number of reported DGUs. But the NIJ had concluded that these numbers were the results of "false positives" from the respondents: "This surprising figure is caused in part by a few respondents reporting large numbers of defensive gun uses during the year; for example, one woman reported 52!"[13] This debate over the validity of Kleck's studies continued unresolved through the 1990s and reached into 2000.

After Kleck's articles, the most influential pro-gun statistical analyses published in the 1990s were authored by John Lott. In 1997, John R. Lott, Jr., and David B. Mustard of the School of Law and the Department of Economics, respectively, at the University of Chicago, published a study finding that the rate of person-against-person crimes decreased in states that passed right-to-carry legislation. According to these researchers:

> We find that allowing citizens to carry concealed weapons deters violent crimes and it appears to produce no increase in accidental deaths. If those states which did not have right-to-carry concealed gun provisions had adopted them in 1992, approximately 1,570 murders, 4,177 rapes, and over 60,000 aggravated assaults would have been avoided yearly. . . the estimated annual gain from allowing concealed handguns is at least $6.214 billion . . . when state concealed handgun laws went into effect in a county, murders fell by 8.5%, and rapes and aggravated assaults fell by 5% and 7%.[14]

The web-posted "1997 NRA Firearms Fact Card" introduced its "Right-to-Carry" section with this array of numbers from Lott and Mustard's study. A year later, Lott published a book entitled *More Guns, Less Crime*, that, like Kleck's book, refined his earlier arguments, answered the criticisms leveled against those arguments, and then defended his earlier study, its methodology, and its conclusions. The NRA promoted this book as well on its web-site, quoting Lott's statistics regarding the measurable benefits of concealed-carry laws for women: "Murder rates decline when either more women or more men carry concealed handguns, but the effect is especially pronounced for women," Lott notes. "An additional woman carrying a concealed handgun reduces the murder rate for women by about three to four times more than an additional man carrying a concealed handgun reduces the murder rate for men."[15]

Through the rest of the 1990s, into the year 2000, Lott's claims won passionate attention from pro-gun organizations, which cited them, and also from pro-gun-control organizations, which challenged them. Handgun Control Inc. posted a statement entitled "John Lott's 'More Guns, Less Crime,' An Alternate Q&A," contending that Lott's measurements failed to take into account a large host of factors—apart from the passage of right-to-carry legislation—that might well contribute to a drop in crime rates from one state to the next.[16] Arguments about John Lott even spilled into amazon.com, which posted a critical review of Lott's book that had appeared in the *New England Journal of Medicine* (NEJM), and then received, and posted, a response from the author himself, challenging the NEJM critic and citing positive reviews of the book. Lott had joined the battle. In the hearings that took place before the House Judiciary Committee following the shootings at Columbine High School in 1999, Lott testified in the company of Wayne LaPierre, executive vice president of the NRA. His address to the committee was titled, "Gun Regulations Can Cost Lives."

Perhaps predictably, statistics that attract the most attention from partisans rarely seem to change anyone's opinion, since members of one advocacy group dismiss the other team's numbers. When I spoke to Diane Nicholl of SWARM, she discounted a wide range of studies conducted by "public health writers" like Dr. Arthur Kellermann and former Surgeon General, Dr. C. Everett Koop. Kellermann, a favorite source of statistics for pro-gun-control advocates, analyzed homicide data from counties in Tennessee and Washington State and published a 1993 study concluding that the mere presence of firearms in a home nearly tripled the risk for homicide in that home. He was also one of the authors of a 1986 study that analyzed data from Seattle, Washington, and concluded that a gun in the home was forty-three times more likely to be instrumental in the death of a family member (by accident, homicide, or suicide) than to kill an intruder. Both the Kellermann articles were published in the *New England Journal of Medicine*, which like the *Journal of the American Medical Association*, has run editorials supporting stricter national gun-control legislation. Physicians' organizations overwhelmingly support gun-control laws and legislation that holds gun owners legally responsible for safe storage of their firearms.[17] Anti-gun organizations rely on Kellermann as well; his articles were noted four times on the Handgun Control Inc. web page entitled "Risks of Guns in the Home," still posted in 1999.

But SWARM members weren't impressed with the credentials or reasoning of the doctors because they argued that those studies failed to take into account information that would prove that most household tragedies are actually caused by the presence of notably dangerous or vulnerable people—people with established histories of drug abuse, alcohol dependency, aggression, or depression—not by the presence of guns. (Recall Stefani Woodhams's declaration: "*The* gun *didn't do it.* He *did.*") Making this argument, Diane Nicholl referred back to her own adolescence in Texas, where "kids came to my high school with shotguns and rifles in the racks of the back windows of their pick-up trucks. These kids got into fights, they got drunk, but they didn't pull their guns out, point them at another human being, and pull the trigger. . . . You have to make a distinction between controlling a behavior and controlling an object." Along the same lines, Rebecca John related her own experiences with her ex-boyfriend in a house full of guns.

> We fought. Never once ever did it occur to either one of us, ever, to go near the gun during an argument. Because we're not criminals. . . . The people that you see grabbing a gun in the middle of an argument and shooting each other, they're already criminals. They already have a criminal record. . . . The good decent people are not the problem, and twenty states have proven that over many years, many hundreds of years collectively between these states, they've never had to repeal their law which allows decent citizens to carry guns. The people who are out there committing crimes are not the concealed-carry permit holders.

Rebecca John was passionate in her own self-defense: "I am not a bad guy, and I have never been a bad guy, and I guess the small picture is that this is life and death to me. My ability to protect my life with a tool that has the power to equalize, that's life and death to me. And my right to self-defense should not be predicated on the acts of criminals. In fact, the more criminal acts they commit, the more rights to self-defense I should get."

Pro-gun advocates are exasperated by the public health writers and gun-control groups in part because their statistics lump everybody together. These advocates contend that mayhem and tragedy generated by dysfunctional households escalate, and thus invalidate, measurements of the risks that guns pose to all households. They have long been intent on discrediting the well-publicized Kellermann studies that purport to show guns somehow cause or spawn violence. One of the most comprehensive critiques can be found in the article coauthored by five men, including two doctors, a writer who questioned Kellermann's methods in the *New England Journal of Medicine*, and Don B. Kates, a prolific pro-gun author. The article, "Bad Medicine: Doctors and Guns," quotes Gary Kleck with approval, critiques the editorial policies of public health journals for favoring essays that satisfy the anti-gun agenda of their peer reviewers, examines a number of related issues, and ends with a critical analysis of the 1993 Kellermann study, "Gun Ownership as a Risk Factor for Homicide in the Home" (called "NEJM-1993" for short). These writers argue that examination of the study shows most of Kellermann's homicide victims (between 57 and 71 percent) weren't killed by individuals cohabiting with them, and so probably weren't killed by the firearms kept in their own homes. Thus, "far from showing that the murdered victims were at higher risk because they were more likely to own guns, the comparison may only demonstrate that they owned guns because they were at higher risk than the members of the supposedly comparable control group." The authors say that "drinking and drug problems, a history of family violence, living alone, and living in a rented home were all greater individual risk factors for being murdered than gun ownership, based on the NEJM-1993 results." According to this argument, the household guns didn't in any way help *cause* tragedy; they were accouterments in households already prone to tragedy.[18]

"I am not a bad guy and I have never been a bad guy," said Rebecca John. She demanded to be recognized as a responsible citizen with a right to carry a concealed weapon.

## Former Governor Ann Richards

The November 1994 congressional elections resulted in a landslide victory for the Republican party, and certain blocs of voters—born-again Christians, gun owners, and Angry White Males—were specially credited with leverage in the upheaval. The *Washington Post* reported that 69 percent of America's gun owners were "decisively in the Republican camp in 1994."[19] Following the upset election, the new Congress seated a total of 237 members who had received an "A" or "A+" rating from the NRA, which judges legislators by their voting records. (To earn an "A" rating, a legislator must consistently vote against measures that restrict a citizen's legal rights to own and use a wide assortment of guns and vote in favor of measures that enlarge those rights.) Handgun Control Inc. called these election results "startling gains," blamed them on the NRA's lavish lobbying expenditures, and asked its supporters to send money to "effectively counter pro-gun extremists who want our elected officials to do their deadly bidding."

A number of prominent Democratic incumbents lost their seats in the upheaval. Two of the most famous were not members of Congress, but celebrated Democratic governors: Mario Cuomo and Ann Richards.

Richards had always been a straight-talking, liberal legislator who knew how to play hardball. She ran a rough campaign to defeat the inept Claytie Williams in the Texas governor's race of 1990 and fought hard, unsuccessfully, against the younger George Bush in 1994. During her tenure as governor, Richards maintained her firm support of gun control and derailed legislative efforts to pass a concealed-carry bill with a threat to veto. Her opponent, George W. Bush, promised to sign the right-to-carry bill into law if he were elected. In November 1994 he was elected, and in spring of 1995 he signed the bill. In 2000, he would become the Republican party's candidate for the presidency of the United States.

I spoke with Richards by phone in 1996. It became clear in a very short time that she was not interested in giving herself over to a rambling, meditative interview about Texas, women, gun myths, and legislation. She felt powerfully impatient with individuals who believed that carrying guns in public would enhance the safety of any Texas citizen, particularly any Texan woman. To her mind, all the arguments *for* concealed-carry rights were emotional, sentimental, and ultimately formulated by men, then swallowed by women. Sensible people committed to facts, to statistics, would recognize the obvious fact that guns endangered women much more often than they protected them.

> I think the conventional wisdom is that women cannot protect themselves without a gun, and I think that impression is fed by males, and the most ludicrous argument I heard during the time I was governor, and also the most consistent argument from males, was: "I don't want the legislation to carry a concealed weapon for myself, I want it for my wife, girlfriend, daughter, flesh," whatever other female you could name. But the reverse was true among the women who came to see me. They said: "For God's sake, do not let these men carry concealed weapons."

I mentioned the women of SWARM and tried to describe how they felt empty-handed and exposed without their pistols. Richards was not impressed. "But where are the facts? That's what I say. I don't think I'm a very valuable source for you because what you're trying to do is talk about an emotional feeling against what is statistical reality, and I don't have the statistics anymore." I mentioned that many of the women I'd interviewed felt the public health statistics did not apply to them, didn't accurately describe their lives. She responded: "Then if they are going to reject statistics, there's no answer to that. What can I say to that?"

Ann Richards herself hunts and owns guns. In her autobiography, *Straight from the Heart*, she describes her childhood growing up eight miles from Waco, Texas, in a community called Lakeview (which had no lake and no view). Her father and mother had both been raised in large, "dirt poor" Texas families—her father was born in Bugtussle, her mother in Hogjaw—and together they worked ceaselessly to support themselves and their only daughter. "They had a big garden and grew everything they ate." They raised chickens, fished for catfish with trotlines, and welcomed venison. "If we got an opportunity to go on somebody's deer lease or somebody's farm and kill a deer, that was absolutely wonderful. You could make sausage out of it; you could cure the whole thing and eat for months."[20]

As a campaigner, Richards was pictured in the news posed with a shotgun and a large dead bird. It is impossible to tell whether her childhood experiences or her experiences as a pragmatic woman running for office in Texas most influenced her stand on gun issues, but, clearly, she had carved out a compromise position that diverged from the standard arguments of both pro-gun and anti-gun advocates. The demarcation lines were self-evident to her; she called her own approach "reasonable and rational." She conceded that many citizens wish to keep guns in their homes or take guns outdoors to hunt, and she supported their right to do so. But she did not like guns infesting the streets. When asked about the theory that guns kept in a home also seriously endanger families, she reiterated: "I think that people have a right within their own home to own weapons, even given all of the possibilities for accidents that are there." Richards did not press Sarah Brady's argument that "the most effective method to protect families from firearm injury is to remove guns from the home." That approach would spell political suicide in Texas, where citizens own, on average, four guns apiece according to the Texas State Rifle Association. Richards did hold the opinion that adults who store guns unsafely in their homes should be held criminally liable for negligence in case of injury to a minor.

Ann Richards was convinced that any reasonable person could distinguish between a *decent* hunting gun and a *bad* concealed handgun carried on the streets, and that a person who equates the one with the other is either a fool or a self-interested (male Republican) politician.

> Hunting has nothing to do with whether or not you should walk around town carrying a gun, and I can't understand the confusion or the deliberate injection of that into the argument.
>
> I will tell you, I hunted as a child, I've hunted as an adult, I go bird-hunting every year when the season opens if I have an opportunity. I own a shotgun, and it's a very pretty shotgun, and I like it a lot. That does not mean that I think I nor my community is going to be safer if people are carrying arms. I think that logic and statistics are very clear, that the more people who walk around with guns, the more people who are going to be

killed, and the more children who are going to die, and the more threatened our community. . . . And any other kind of argument is GOOFY.

In her defense of decent hunting guns, Richards adopted a commonsense argument usually heard from pro-gun advocates: a gun is just a household tool. She was impatient with my own attempts to suggest that all guns—long guns, pistols—share a kind of meaning in the United States that renders them specially potent and significant. At the same time, it was clear that Richards the politician appreciated the suggestive power of guns as icons in the United States; the promotional photos showing her with shotgun in hand were aimed at Texas voters who asked to be reassured that this former homemaker was man enough for the governor's job, and even the title of Richards's autobiography suggested that she was a Texan who aimed straight.

Richards held the NRA responsible for muddy, emotional messages equating frontier self-reliance with handguns in the streets and believed that they had won adherents through a well-funded, deceptive campaign: "I think the injection of the gun issue has been a direct result of an enormously financially successful organization that has made a lot of money, and the constant feeding of fear, of anxiety, of distrust can be laid directly at the feet of the National Rifle Association." She did not accept the argument that the NRA has won members and financial contributors by representing a large slice of public opinion: "If you can load any question emotionally enough, you can tap into the feelings of the public, and you can appeal to those interests, and I think that's exactly what they've done." In her opinion, the NRA's campaign was plainly "based on a fear of taking something away."

Richards received very low grades from the NRA, of course, and according to a *Texas Monthly* cover story published immediately following the 1994 elections, "Richards' veto of a handgun referendum cost her dearly in Bubbaland. . . ."[21] The situation in Texas made her angry. Since she forfeited her place in office, the state Congress and the new Governor Bush had passed a concealed-carry bill. Grazia with her long trigger finger pointed at State Senator West had won her point.

Richards spoke confidently about the statistics that supported her position. But statistics are slippery entities. I found only one statistical source (John Lott's) that showed women who carried concealed weapons *on the street* were either safer or less safe than women who made their way bearing nothing more than wallets and checkbooks; there is a study by the Bureau of Justice Statistics that shows only one in five crime victims who defends himself/herself with a firearm suffers injury, compared with nearly half who defend themselves with other weapons or no weapons.[22] But it's also true that hard statistics in the United States reveal a horrific number of unlawful gun homicides compared with a paltry number of "justifiable" gun homicides. (A "justifiable" homicide takes place when private citizens use firearms to kill people the courts subsequently judge to have been guilty of criminal aggression.) In 1992, only 348 citizens in the United States shot and killed felons justifiably, according to FBI statistics. The number of justifiable firearms homicides committed *nationally* by *women* ranged between just 17 and 63 for the years 1978 to 1992. For example, the total number of justifiable firearms homicides committed by women in 1992 was 45; handguns were used in 26 of these cases. The total number of unlawful gun homicides that claimed female victims in 1992 was 2,479, according to FBI figures. In simple terms: "Bad people" killed by women with guns equals 45. Women killed by "bad people" with guns equals 2,479. Losers outnumber winners by approximately fifty to one.[23] Of course, if one accepts Gary Kleck's statistics, this picture changes radically, because Kleck and his supporters contend that handguns are used approximately 2.5 million times annually to defend people against attack and that many of these "Defensive Gun Uses" go unreported and uncounted because very often a person merely has to *show* her gun in order to stop a crime. Add to this Lott's contention that any woman who carries a concealed handgun—or gets a permit to carry a concealed handgun—has the statistical deterrent effect of reducing the murder rate in her state, and one concludes with a general portrait of American gun owners as a substantial, unofficial, unappreciated force for the maintenance of law and order.

Gun-control advocates consider these numbers to be absurd. From their perspective, the pro-gun claim that neighborhoods grow increasingly tranquil as more residents begin carrying concealed weapons is an incredible and a pernicious fiction.

Step up to the line. Choose your numbers. Choose your stories. Choose your allies. Choose your country.

## Notes

1. See Tom Smith and Robert J. Smith, "Changes in Firearm Ownership Among Women, 1980–1994." Paper presented to the American Society of Criminology, Miami, November 1994. Tom Smith is affiliated with the National Opinion Research Center, University of Chicago, and Robert Smith, with School of Law, Indiana University, Bloomington.

2. "43% of Homes with Kids Armed," sidebar, *Ithaca Journal*, November 14, 1998, p. B-1.

3. Stephen Power, "Gun Culture Shifts from Recreation to Protection," Gannett News Service, *Ithaca Journal*, May 8, 1999, p. B-1.

4. The quote comes from the posted biography of "Tanya K. Metaksa, NRA-ILA Executive Director." The special bio of the executive director no longer appeared on

the NRA website in late 1998, after Metaksa's apparent demotion. See http://www.nra.org.

5. For the photograph of Suzanna Grazia, see Sam Howe Verhovek, "States Seek to Let Citizens Carry Concealed Weapons," *New York Times*, March 6, 1995, p. 20.

6. Katharine Q. Seelye, "Two Sides in the Gun Debate Duel with Personal Stories," *New York Times*, April 1, 1995, p. 20. For the full texts of these personal testimonies, see U.S. House, *Guns Laws and the Need for Self-Defense: Hearing Before the Subcommittee on Crime of the Committee on the Judiciary,* 104th Cong., 1st sess., March 31, 1995. Washington, DC: U.S. Government Printing Office.

7. The biography of Metaksa, "Tanya K. Metaksa, NRA-ILA Executive Director," was no longer posted on the NRA site by 2000, nor were the "Backgrounder" articles that she authored.

8. "Year-End Report on U.S. Concealed Weapons Laws," Handgun Control Inc., http://www.handguncontrol.org/e-main.

9. "NRA-ILA Victory Report from the States, 1994–1997," NRA, http://www.nra.org/ila/victory. html. According to the NRA, states that passed right-to-carry legislation for the first time in the years 1994–97 were Alaska, Arizona, Tennessee, Wyoming, Arkansas, North Carolina, Oklahoma, Texas, Nevada, Utah, Virginia, Kentucky, Louisiana, and South Carolina.

10. Ann Jones, *Next Time She'll Be Dead: Battering and How to Stop It* (Boston: Beacon Press, 1994), pp. 50–80.

11. Gary Kleck, *Point Blank: Guns and Violence in America* (New York: Aldine de Gruyter, 1991). Gary Kleck and Mark Gertz, "Armed Resistance to Crime: The Prevalence and Nature of Self-Defense with a Gun," *Journal of Criminal Law and Criminology* 86, no. 1 (Fall 1995): 150–87. Gary Kleck, *Targeting Guns: Firearms and Their Control* (New York: Aldine de Gruyter, 1997). See also Paul H. Blackman, "Armed Citizens and Crime Control," posted by the NRA, 7/16/99, http://www.nraila.org.

12. The Violence Policy Center noted that if Kleck's statistics were true, then a person could expect that the 50 percent of Americans who lived their lives unprotected by guns should have sustained approximately 400,000 fatal injuries; yet in 1992, the United States' total homicide tally was about 24,000. See Susan Glick, *Female Persuasion: A Study of How the Firearms Industry Markets to Women and the Reality of Women and Guns* (Washington, DC: The Violence Policy Center, 1994), p. 46, note. The note discusses Brian Gluss's research, which tests Kleck's statistics by calculating data for the control group: those who don't use guns for self-defense.

13. For a report on the National Research Council's response to Kleck, see Albert J. Reiss, Jr. and Jeffrey A. Roth, eds., *Understanding and Preventing Violence* (Washington, DC: National Academy Press, 1993), pp. 264–65. See also "Guns in America: National Survey on Private Ownership and Use of Firearms," National Institute of Justice Publication no. 165476, May 1997, esp. the pages that discuss "Defensive Gun Uses" and "False Positives," http://www.ncjrs.org/pdffiles/165476.pdf.

14. John R. Lott, Jr., and David B. Mustard, "Crime, Deterrence, and Right-to-Carry Concealed Handguns," *Journal of Legal Studies* 26, no. 1 (January 1997): 1–68, http://www.law.lib.uchicago.edu.faculty/lott/guncont.

15. John R. Lott, Jr., *More Guns, Less Crime: Understanding Crime and Gun Control Laws* (Chicago: University of Chicago Press, 1998). See also: "Fables, Myths, and Other Tall Tales About Gun Laws, Crime, and Constitutional Rights," Fable VII, posted by the NRA 7/28/99, http://www.nraila.org.

16. See the Handgun Control Inc. posting, "John Lott's 'More Guns, Less Crime,' An Alternate Q&A," http://www.handguncontrol.org/lott/html.

17. See Arthur L. Kellermann et al., "Gun Ownership as a Risk Factor for Homicide in the Home," *New England Journal of Medicine* 329, no. 15 (October 7, 1993): 1084–91. See also Arthur L. Kellermann and Donald T. Reay, "Protection or Peril? An Analysis of Firearm-Related Deaths in the Home," *New England Journal of Medicine* 314, no. 24 (June 12, 1986): 1557–60. For physicians' editorials calling for stricter control of firearms, see C. Everett Koop and George D. Lundberg, "Violence in America: A Public Health Emergency," *Journal of the American Medical Association* 276, no. 22 (June 10, 1992): 3075. See also Jerome P. Kassirer, "Guns in the Household," *New England Journal of Medicine* 329, no. 15 (October 7, 1993): 1117.

In "Clinton, Guns, and the CDC [Centers for Disease Control]" (an NRA Internet posting authored by Tanya Metaksa, copyrighted in 1996 and still online through 1998, though it had disappeared by 2000), the NRA called the *New England Journal of Medicine* "a vehicle well known for its anti-gun prejudice." Writing about Kellermann in that posting: "Your taxes also fund the work of Dr. Arthur Kellermann. The CDC has provided him nearly two million taxpayer dollars in grants over the last few years. Through articles in publications such as the *New England Journal of Medicine*, a vehicle well known for its anti-gun prejudice, Kellermann argues that keeping a firearm in the home for protection against crime actually increases the risk of homicide in the home. Kellermann's findings have been widely criticized as fundamentally flawed and politically biased by criminologists and epidemiologists alike, and yet they are swallowed whole by the national media and peddled from every available platform by gun prohibitionists." http://www.nra.org/politics96/bewar.html.

18. Don B. Kates, Henry E. Schaffer, John K. Lattimer, George B. Murray, and Edwin H. Cassem, "Bad Medicine: Doctors and Guns," in *Guns: Who Should Have Them?* ed. David B. Kopel (New York: Prometheus Books, 1995), pp. 270, 271, and throughout. The article also raises questions about the sampling methods of the 1993 Kellermann study.

19. For 1994 voting statistics, see Thomas Edsall, "Will the GOP Go the Way of All Democrats?" *Washington Post National Weekly Edition*, February 27–March 5, 1995, p. 23.

20. Ann Richards, *Straight from the Heart: My Life in Politics and Other Places* (New York: Simon and Schuster, 1989), p. 41.

21. Paul Burka, "George W. Bush and the New Political Landscape: How the Republicans Beat Ann Richards and Took Over Texas," *Texas Monthly* 22 (December 1994): 128.

22. For report of the study from the Bureau of Justice Statistics, see Gordon Witkin, "Should You Own a Gun?" *US News and World Report* 117, no. 7 (August 15, 1994): 27.

23. Susan Glick, *Female Persuasion*, pp. 48–49 [see note 12].

## Postscript

In early August, as this book was in production, news reports announced that the *Journal of the American Medical Association* had published a study showing that "the federal Brady Act requiring a criminal background check of handgun buyers has had no measurable effect on gun homicide and suicide rates in the 32 states that had to strengthen their regulations to meet the 1994 law . . ." The significance of this study is now being debated. See Mike Dorning, "Study Says Brady Act Hasn't Cut Gun Deaths," *Chicago Tribune*, August 2, 2000, section 1, p. 1.

# 5

---

# Self-Defense, Part II:

## Looking for the Bad Guys

In general, handguns are meant to be aimed at humans. The women I interviewed who were worried about self-defense nearly always referred to men as their chief threat. But very few women ever actually shoot people. Again, the overwhelming majority of women in the United States do not own their own guns and more than half of them live in households without guns. Women are, in many ways, exemplary citizens. Though they make up more than 50 percent of the population, they commit only 9 percent of the murders in the United States and are arrested for spousal abuse in less than 5 percent of the cases. They are virtually never convicted or accused of rape. Thus, more than nine out of ten rapists, murderers, and batterers in this country are men. If a woman purchases a gun because she envisions protecting herself against this type of threat (e.g., she fantasizes about using a .38 to hold a rapist paralyzed and shivering on his knees), then she adopts a traditionally male tool to oppose an archetypical male enemy.

The large paper targets that get hung out on the lines in a local handgun permit course show the silhouette of a man cut off just above the knees. The black silhouette has its invisible right hand planted in its invisible pocket. There is a large bowling pin shape drawn on the torso; it includes the head, and bases itself in the lower abdomen. Shooters are advised to aim for this meaty section between the nipples, which are both marked "K5D2." This same code—K5D2—is printed between the figure's eyes, in the center of its neck, and on its navel. The "K" scores diminish if bullets hit the outer shoulder blades, outer ribs, or thighs. One earns a higher "K" score for hitting the target's right shoulder, elbow, or wrist rather than its left shoulder, elbow, or wrist. Ears and sleeves are scored at zero.

If this male silhouette were replaced with a curved female shape with breasts outlined and hands on hips, most students in the pistol course would be repulsed and embarrassed, because the shape of a woman is not conventionally used to represent a physical threat. All target practice involving real guns and imagined threats, or even metaphorical guns and imagined threats, highlights some aspect of "the enemy." Pro-gunners and anti-gunners are divided in their perception of the typical American woman's prime enemy. Inside the dark male silhouette, many conservatives envision a criminal stranger. Inside an identical male silhouette, liberals, notably liberal feminists, see a violent husband or boyfriend, an intimate who cohabits with the threatened woman and who would therefore be very difficult to surprise or subdue with a handgun. In both cases the enemy is male. But in the 1990s a key conservative assertion—one I heard many times in various forms—was that good citizens and potential criminals could be easily distinguished from one another: "*The people that you see grabbing a gun in the middle of an argument and shooting each other, they're already criminals.*" The usual liberal feminist response painted a very different picture of the world. In this world, the public face of any person—notably of any man—could not be trusted, for men who acted respectably in public very often acted badly at home, behind closed doors.

Target practice continues. An indoor firing range is a chill, athletic, nervous, and hypnotic place. Students wear stiff leather holsters on wide belts and large protective earphones, equipment that at first feels heavy and mismatched. We feed our revolvers with bullets stored in little carpenters' aprons donated by local merchants. In this context, bullets begin to feel as familiar as nails or dried soup beans. When the instructor flips on the lights behind the paper targets that have already been blasted with practice shots, constellations of bright holes appear, allowing members of the pistol permit class to compare their skills with the skills of their companions in the adjoining stalls. My target had a crescent of holes focused between the nipples. There were also a few rogue punctures, one through the top of the black paper head, one in the center of the black paper throat. When we activate the pulley system to bring our targets home, the shadow men flutter toward us like laundry. If they had legs, they would be about six feet two inches tall. Their right hands stay hidden in their pockets.

The great disparities between this paper target and a human target should be studied because they reveal something about targets and also about pistols. This paper doll lacks the power that a real attacker would have— for instance, the ability to sneak up from behind, grab the gun, and muscle the shooter to the ground. Yet the paper doll is the only kind of target that most gunowners will ever shoot. Rifles and shotguns are commonly used for the very old business of killing game; they function directly, seasonally, as fatal instruments, not toys or props, and so are more likely to earn their place as practical tools in certain households. In contrast, handguns are kept around to shoot "if" . . . if a burglar breaks in the window . . . if a rapist pushes his way inside the door. Thus, most handguns owned by essentially law-abiding citizens function largely as talismans, to puncture black silhouettes, scare away ghosts, insure the future, surprise enemies, remake the self, establish authority, and prop up fantasies of security or revenge. All this fantasy, and yet the immediate "reality" of a metal handgun is stunning: its heavy weight communicates authority and adult prerogative.

Americans who own and handle guns refer to that *weight* in a number of different contexts. To them, it identifies something actual and solid. Partly for this reason, women and men who have purchased guns for self-defense often describe themselves as having lived in a lightweight "dream world" before they finally picked up their weapons. "I was living in an ivory tower-type dream world," explained Rebecca John, president of SWARM. "I was totally ignorant . . . ignorance is bliss," said Shirley Lyon, whose family now owns nearly twenty handguns. Asked about women who refuse to purchase guns, Lyon responded: "So they're in denial. I feel we've dealt with reality."

Shirley Lyon had graduated from the Lethal Force Institute (LFI) in Concord, New Hampshire. She gave me a videotape from the institute. In the tape the LFI director, Massad Ayoob (a former policeman and firearms instructor, as well as an authority who was frequently quoted by mainstream journalists writing on gun self-defense in the 1990s) urged his students to face facts about the real world, which he contrasted with the fairy tale world that college students are taught to believe in when they take Sociology 101. According to Ayoob, the stereotypical Sociology 101 graduates are destined to join the ranks of "lightweight assholes," "lightweight yuppies" in the United States. He claims: "The world is full of assholes, people who never had to deal with a life-threatening crisis, never had the life of another person in their hands, never had the responsibility to take control of their own destiny in a moment of immediate crisis, and they can't relate, because the ones who did can relate with you."[1]

From Ayoob's perspective, only lightweight, collegiate assholes would dream of making the world peaceful through gun-control legislation and prisoner rehabilitation, and most criminals are brutal sociopaths who must be stopped with force and courage. Referring back to his own experiences as a cop on the street, Ayoob explains what he had learned about real criminals: They're like animals:

> "Sympathizing with a criminal in the prison visiting room is like sympathizing with the timber wolf caged inside its bars at the Bronx Zoo."
>
> "These predatory people don't think like you. They *aren't* people like you. They are a different breed."
>
> "Let him go into the ground and feed him to the maggots. That's where he belongs. He has become feral man and he contra-indicates his own right to survive."[2]

Ayoob's delivery was ferocious. However, students insisted that he was a wonderful teacher: conscientious, preoccupied with gun safety, well-versed in laws relevant to the use of lethal force, and according to one of his female LFI graduates, Shirley Lyon, "one of the most caring men I've ever seen, particularly concerned about women and guns." Obviously, this influential teacher invited his students to join him in a fraternity of serious people who accepted responsibility for themselves in the *real* world—a world in which criminals and "lightweight assholes" must be opposed by decent, serious, prepared citizens who accept full responsibility for their own protection and actively support the people's right to "keep and bear arms."

Again, pro-gun doctrine posits clear divisions between decent citizens and sociopathic criminals, between the good guys and the enemies. It also promises that guns in the right hands can be trusted to shoot at the appropriately evil people. Anti-gunners protest that both of these propositions are untrue and that, in fact, this dualistic picture of a world where decent citizens successfully battle identifiable criminals is too simplistic. In the real world as defined by liberals, individuals show themselves to be capable of a dizzying range of actions, some good and some evil. Widely respected men may also be batterers. Women's lives are shadowed by intimate threats and inter-family complications that no handgun can begin to solve. Any gun that a woman keeps inside her house is likely to backfire and shoot the wrong target: a beloved child or even the woman herself.

Advocates in this camp insist that the pro-gun political movement actually erodes the general safety of America's entire female population, by advertising the fantasy that American women can fight evil by taking potshots at violent street attackers and thus diverting attention away from the most serious masculine threat to women's health and safety: not the unknown criminal intruder, but the intimately known domestic batterer. Viewed by feminists, the husbands and boyfriends who parade in public as decent men, but transform into batterers once they've reached the privacy of their own homes, are at least as nasty as Ayoob's criminals. They are the enemy. Ann Jones, author of *Next Time She'll Be Dead* and an advocate for battered women, knew one such man—her own father—intimately. "What I remember most of all is my father's weepy, groping attempts at 'making up' after he'd pounded me with his belt buckle or fists. . . . He remained—as he had been all along—two people: publicly charming and delightful, privately sullen, angry, and morose." According to statistics compiled by *Ms. Magazine* in 1994, "Domestic violence is the leading cause of injury to women, causing more injuries than muggings, stranger rapes, and car accidents combined," and "in the United States, almost 4 million women are beaten by male partners every year."[3]

Writing in *Ms.*, Jones spoke against pro-gun organizations that tried to convince women that firearms would protect them. She insisted that taming dangerous men is "not a job to be done piecemeal by lone women, armed with pearl-handled pistols, picking off batterers and rapists one by one. It's a job for the collective power of women and men." This feminist approach asks for a special kind of patience and broad perspective from its adherents. It is generous and far-reaching but difficult to maintain when a person feels isolated or starkly terrified; collective action cannot help a woman during the moment she faces attack. Jones herself confessed that twice in her life, once when she received death threats through the mail and once when she was being harassed by Southern racists, she kept a .38 special close at hand to sustain herself. She argued in 1994, however, that the action was ill-judged. "It wasn't a gun I needed. It was courage."[4]

The Violence Policy Center, an anti-gun organization based in Washington, DC, works from basically the same perspective as Ann Jones and *Ms. Magazine*. It marshals pages of statistics to show that most women are threatened by acquaintances and family members, not by wild strangers in the street, which proves that advocates who advise women to buy guns to repel their enemies are selling a fantasy rather than a solution. According to a study cited by the Violence Policy Center, in 75 percent of all rape attacks, the offenders are known to the victim, and more than six out of ten rapes in this nation happen to children and adolescents under the age of eighteen. The suggestion that these endangered children might receive good advice about self-defense from the NRA would strike these advocates as grotesque. Recall Mrs. Byrl Phillips-Taylor: "*They're saying they want to arm themselves to protect themselves . . . . So do you arm seventeen-year-olds to protect themselves? Do you arm fifteen-year-olds to protect themselves? When the hell is it going to stop?*"

Liberal feminists are convinced that gun groups really don't give a damn about women's safety, and that their public attempts to demonstrate concern for women—one thinks of the NRA's "Refuse To Be a Victim" program directed by Metaksa—are outrageously hypocritical. *Ms. Magazine* commenced its 1994 study of women and guns, titled "Is This Power Feminism?" with a frontal attack against the NRA:

> Just when we thought we were beginning to turn the tide in favor of gun control, along comes the NRA with a campaign that encourages women to exercise our right to "choose to refuse to be a victim." The new focus on women comes not because this organization supports our right to be free from rape and battery, harassment and discrimination, but because these sharpshooters are trying to seduce women into becoming dues-paying, gun-toting NRA members with promises of power from the barrel of a gun.
>
> The NRA's campaign is cynically designed to sell guns by preying on women's fear of violence.[5]

In that same election-year issue, Jones noted: "During recent campaigns, in several states for legislation authorizing police to confiscate guns from men who assault women or violate restraining orders, the NRA said *nothing*. We're simply warm bodies in the great untapped female market for armaments. In short, the NRA staunchly supports the rights of wife abusers to keep their guns."[6]

Mary Zeiss Stange, author of *Woman the Hunter*, critiques this kind of "anti-gun feminism" in an essay that she contributed to a collection edited by David Kopel, *Guns: Who Should Have Them?* (See note 18 in the previous chapter.) Stange was the only female contributor to the collection. In the essay, she challenges the "majority of feminists who have tended to adhere to the conventional wisdom that to be feminist is to be antiviolence, and to be antiviolence is *ipso facto* to be anti-gun" and argues that "in a society where violence against women is so common, responsible gun use and ownership . . . among women ought to come under the purview of feminist theory as one valid option among many."[7] She identifies Kellermann's studies as characteristic of "poorly reasoned anti-gun articles in the medical literature"[8] and defends the NRA for the increasing attention it had paid to women's concerns. Dismissal of a *New England Journal of Medicine* article, coupled with defense of the NRA, certainly put her in league with the pro-gun camp, but Stange is not easy to fit into a category; she moves on to quote from a number of feminists who had asked serious questions about the efficacy of a predominantly, even exclusively, nonviolent agenda for a group of people—women—who are disadvantaged by a general perception that they wouldn't resist aggression in any case and who gain little by advocating for "niceness." She then considers the same thorny issue that Jones took up: what should women do to defend themselves against domestic violence? Not surprisingly, Stange recommends that women at least consider arming themselves, and she related an anecdote about a group of women, frightened of a serial rapist in Athens, Georgia, who enrolled in a self-defense course and conducted "consciousness-raising" sessions about handgun self-defense. Half of them eventually purchased guns; half of them did not.

> Two things stand out about this anecdote. One is that it clearly exemplifies that the choice to arm oneself may certainly arise from a commitment to feminist politics and practice: that is, from the conviction that women's lives, safety, and peace of mind matter, and that it is up to women themselves to take responsibility for their well-being. The other is that these women, in deciding either for or against gun ownership, had made an informed choice; they had not relied upon press reports or propaganda to make up their minds. As it turns out, both these facts are characteristic of women who own guns.[9]

This article's declaration in support of common sense and of women who make up their minds, independent of "propaganda," is forceful and direct. It is preceded, however, by a section where Stange joins in the effort to discredit that *bête noire* of pro-gunners, Kellermann, whose research is summarized in an earlier chapter. Stange notes a surprising comment by Kellermann quoted in a *Health* magazine interview where he said: "I don't think, in good conscience, I could advise a woman to get a handgun. Dial 911. Get an alarm instead. . . ." But then he added: "If you've got to resist, your chances of being hurt are less the more lethal your weapon. . . . If that were my wife, would I want her to have a .38 special in her hand? . . . Yeah."[10]

Based on this comment, Stange argues that "Kellermann appears to be assuming here that the only sort of violence that could possibly befall his wife is random, predatory violence," and then identifies this fear of "random, predatory violence" as characteristic of white men, rather than women, since women are statistically less likely to be victims of these kinds of attacks. Working from this interpretation of the doctor's assumptions, an interpretation based on a single interview quote, Stange asserts that ". . . most of the arguments typically employed by those who want to severely restrict or ban handgun use and ownership arise from middle-class, Caucasian, male experience," so that advocacy for restriction of handguns "smacks of middle-class elitism," "is inherently antifeminist," and ". . . ignores the everyday reality of criminal violence in poor, generally nonwhite, neighborhoods and housing projects, violence which impacts nonwhite men and especially nonwhite women in disproportionate numbers." In the midst of these assertions, Stange writes:

Robbery, mugging, and assault—random violence for the most part, and for most individuals, once-in-a-lifetime occurrences—are legitimate fears primarily for white men; thus it is only from a white male perspective that the argument that most violence occurs outside the home could make much sense as an argument against gun ownership in the home.[11]

According to Stange, it is elitist doctors like Kellermann, not pro-gunners like Ayoob or the NRA's publicists, who misrepresent and misunderstand the situation of women generally because they focus on street crime. By the time she makes this point, she has effectively expanded Kellermann's single quote into an elitist "claim that violence overwhelmingly occurs outside the home. . . ." This is despite the fact that Stange's own text and notes make it clear that Kellermann's studies—"Gun Ownership as a Risk Factor for Homicide in the Home" and "Protection or Peril? An Analysis of Firearms-Related Deaths in the Home"—rather obviously analyzed violence that takes place *in the home.* When Stange concludes that the gun-control movement is inherently elitist and "anti-feminist" because quietly motivated and directed by white men preoccupied with street attacks, I conclude that she has climbed out on a limb. Her efforts to discredit Kellermann mar a determined reevaluation of liberal feminists' uniform rejection of handguns as appropriate tools for women's self-defense.

A review of advertisements and broadsides distributed by pro-gun organizations over the last decade show that, as one might expect, they remain focused on the "criminal" and they highlight the "criminal stranger" rather than the dangerous intimate as a threat to women's security. From SWARM: "Many states' laws say that your gun may be good for nipping targets or bagging elk, but you better not have it on you when that 6-foot career criminal jumps you on a dark street!"

In similar manner, the NRA focuses on strangers, on criminals, as the chief threats to women, and when they address crime "in the home," they're talking about break-ins by thieves and rapists. The NRA has, understandably, never been deeply engaged in efforts to reduce domestic abuse against women; it's not their topic. When in March of 1999, a U.S. District Court judge in Texas ruled that a convicted wife abuser could not be legally banned from owning a gun because such restrictions compromised his Second Amendment rights (*United States v. Emerson*), the NRA applauded the decision. But by the end of the decade, the NRA had certainly become circumspect in the way it publicly addressed women's personal security issues. The web page for its "Refuse To Be a Victim" program (http://www.nrahq.org/safety/rtbav/, still online in 2000) summarizes the kinds of information women could expect to receive if they sent for the brochure "42 Strategies for Personal Safety" or enrolled in the Refuse To Be a Victim three-hour seminar. It lists "Personal Protection Devices" that women could consider using for self-defense, including "alarms, sprays, stun guns, defensive key chains, and other devices"—no overt mention of guns—and summarizes some security measures discussed in the Refuse To Be a Victim literature, including "Home Security" (plant thorny bushes under your windows because criminals don't like to hide in them), "Automobile Security" (don't give your house keys to a parking lot attendant lest he copy them), and "Phone Security." It also promises to provide women with information about "The Psychology of Criminal Predators."

Everybody's looking for the bad guy. What's more, different ideological camps are battling to define the bad guy, the true enemy, and in this way to define the situations, and outlooks, of women in the United States. But what if we imagine that there are many, different kinds of bad guys and many different ways to try and repel them? What if we imagine that these visions of the nation, and the enemies and victims who inhabit that nation, are not mutually exclusive, but mixed up together? Then everything becomes complicated . . . but also more clear.

## Battered

When contending advocates argue about which one of them best represents the true interests of women, they are driven, in part, by an ambition not only to attract, but to appear to represent, a large constituency. But what about the actual individual women, the potential constituents, who stand to the side of the ideological debates? Both the typical liberal feminist world view and the typical conservative world view exclude certain American individuals from their calculations and from their general portraits of woman, and of woman's most significant enemies. Liberal feminist doctrine makes little room for the thirty-year-old rural woman who trusts her husband, father, and brothers and thinks of herself as their close ally. And conservative doctrine makes little room for the encircled, dazed woman caught in her kitchen, once again, by her abusive partner. Such a woman requires a strong, responsive network of assistance and cooperation to help transport her into a secure life.

Ann Wexler, who helped set up a battered women's shelter in New Jersey in the late 1970s and who has advised a number of battered women through the years, remembered:

> Most of the women I interviewed were not enraged. Most of the women I interviewed were terrified, were guilty, were still wondering if they provoked it, were terrified for their kids, were devastated or confused about

what to do, were ashamed. Unfortunately, I did not see enough enraged women. I wish I had seen more. They weren't to the point of thinking about guns and revenge. They were thinking: "What did I do wrong? What will I do now? Why can't I make him change? Maybe if I try harder? What about my children? What if he comes after me?" . . . A lot of women I worked with, I would see them crumbling. Without a gun, they would crumble. With a gun, they would crumble.

Over the last two decades, researchers have chronicled the lives of battered women, including those women who eventually turned on their spouses and killed them. In approximately 80 percent of the cases where women killed their abusive partners, guns were employed as weapons. According to Ann Jones, each year in the United States approximately 750 women "kill the men who rape and batter them."[12] If the number of "justifiable homicides" committed by women annually on a national basis ranges between 17 and 63, apparently few of the incidents described by Ann Jones are ultimately defined as "justifiable homicides."

The stories that battered women relate of intimate life with abusive partners, however, really cannot be described as *gun stories,* though firearms are present in many of the households. Focusing on the gun in each case tells us virtually nothing about the grotesque, alien, imprisoned years that preceded the moment's explosion, an explosion notable because it is typically produced by a woman who for a long time tried using silent acquiescence to protect herself, and sometimes her children, against the periodic rages of a man who expected to own, control, accuse, penetrate, demean, punch, gouge, and slam her against the wall whenever a certain mood (often mixed with alcohol) inspired him. Psychologist Angela Browne's book, *When Battered Women Kill,* compiled information and reports gleaned from interviews with forty-two battered women in fifteen states who eventually killed their spouses. Browne's book included these fleeting pictures of hell: man who forgot to buy his wife a Christmas present rips down the Christmas tree, then turns to pummel wife, slams her into the wall, throws water on her, rapes her . . . woman looking in mirror comments to her new husband that they make a nice couple, he turns on her and begins pounding her with his fists, she retreats to a corner and is eventually beaten unconscious . . . man tells wife one evening: "I hate you for buying the washing machine, I hate you for turning on the light in the bathroom while I'm sleeping," throws her to the floor, pulls her up, begins hammering her head against the wall . . . man threatens wife with his .38 Colt, points it in her face, then knocks her unconscious . . . man picks up his rifle and shoots at his wife across the dinner table after she mentions one of her female friends . . . man rapes wife with a beer bottle and then drinks the beer . . . man shoots his wife's kitten and two cats with a rifle, then throws the dead animals over the fence.[13] Connecting these glimpses of depravity are large, standard patterns. The abusers' attacks occur unpredictably, but repetitively, as part of a cycle. The abusers grow outraged by even the littlest signs of independence or rebelliousness in their women, whom they jealousy guard as their possessions and try to keep isolated from potential allies: family and friends. The abusers are doggishly persistent in tracking down and hounding the partners who attempt escape. One generation of abuse typically spawns another.

In none of the stories related by Browne do women go out and buy their own guns in order to defend themselves against their partners. Instead, they use the firearms that were already in their home, weapons which had never given them any protection during the terrible years when they were confronted with walls and fists and boots and beer bottles, firearms which, in fact, had often been used to threaten them with death. The author herself noted:

> In many of the homicides involving firearms, the men were killed with the same guns they had used earlier against the women. Even when several guns were available, the weapons they had been threatened with were the ones the women reached for in their moment of panic.[14]

It is difficult to imagine anyone recommending that a woman sharing a house with an abusive man and, let's say, two of her children from an earlier marriage ought to introduce a gun into that house so that when trouble commences, she can grab it and start shooting. But what about *after* she leaves him? What if she has found a room of her own and is now being stalked by a partner who, typically, has announced that she belongs to him always, and if she makes him really, really mad, he's going to be forced to kill her?

The community expects this woman to rely on legal tools—restraining orders, warrants, complaints—to enlist the support of the police and the courts in her own defense. But even feminists who counsel against guns have pointed out that the legal system often fails to shield women from deadly attacks by their estranged partners. Having described the cases of a few women who begged for protection from legal authorities but then wound up dead, killed by lovers they had tried to quit, Jones wrote: "Every year, according to FBI statistics, roughly 3,000 men murder their current and former wives and girlfriends in circumstances like these." She herself described the death of April LaSalata who was shot twice in the head by her estranged husband, a man who had been released on bail after being charged with attempted murder following a knife attack on his wife. Jones noted that prosecutors and LaSalata appealed to the courts to increase bail and jail Anthony LaSalata, but the judge refused. Jones, who in her *Ms.* article contended that women don't need guns to protect themselves, just courage, nevertheless added a last note here: "April LaSalata was also denied a permit for a gun with which she might have protected herself."[15]

Liberal rules of the game require that we compute these victims as women "killed by an intimate" rather than "killed by a criminal stranger," which means they show up in the charts as people who would not have benefited from owning a firearm. That same doctrine suggests that women threatened by abusive partners ought to be dissuaded from considering the purchase of a gun. But are the stalkers—those jealous, childish, cold, pumping men—truly intimates or are they strangers? How well do our categories store and preserve the experiences of actual people in danger? And even more to the point, if collective social action and legal action fail to protect an individual woman against a rogue man, be he intimate or stranger, what does that mean? What should she do in that moment when she realizes she's alone with him? Are there any individual actions endangered women should learn to protect themselves when they're alone, individual actions that do not necessarily preclude or contradict participation in broader social efforts to reform the legal system and make life generally more secure for women and their children?

To answer such a question, a person must briefly steal away from the encampment of her ideological allies and listen, with attention, to the everyday conversations of her designated enemies. Forget statistics for a moment. For in order to comprehend the emotional source of an opponent's argument, one must become vulnerable to that person's stories. This can be a humiliating exercise, since adults generally rely on the strong armor of their own opinions to make them feel like citizens with stature, citizens in alliance with an army of friends. Relaxing one's opinions may leave a person feeling dwarfed and traitorous—a sour mix.

But fair thinking requires initial disarmament, even disorientation. Talk of the *real* world? It is not easy to define; *it is not easy to find.* Studies focused on firearms and women's safety usually measure events that take place *in the home,* and of course it's here, in that sanctuary so frequently containing children, that one discovers the most knotty dilemmas involving guns.

Here is a difficult story:

I spoke with Joanne Carroll* on the telephone. Her number had been provided to me via e-mail, after consultation, by Lyn Bates, a contact-person for the organization AWARE (Arming Women Against Rape and Endangerment, http://www.aware.org) and a regular contributor to *Women & Guns*

---

*Carroll will be used as last name to protect speaker.

magazine. On the day I spoke to her, Carroll was planning to purchase a handgun, a LadySmith 9 millimeter semi-automatic, which she would have modified as an "ambidextrous" gun; she wanted to be able to work the safety and shoot with either hand "because God forbid, if something happens to your right hand, you need to be able to use your left."

Before this day, Carroll had participated in a number of shooting courses. After taking a basic pistol course, a refresher course, and doing two rotations shooting with the junior Olympics, she was initially denied her right-to-carry permit by a Massachusetts police chief because "domestic violence was involved; a restraining order was involved." The chief said: "I don't like to get a handgun involved in a domestic dispute," and she replied: "Look at the evidence. He got over three years in jail. That's not just a *dispute*." The chief recommended she move herself and her young children to another city. She took the matter to court.

The judge who handled her case recommended she get more training and then reapply for the permit. While searching for the recommended courses, she met up with a representative of AWARE, who sent her a list of available classes. Carroll subsequently enrolled in a two-day course in self-protection, a "handgun retention" course, and two classes in "stress" and "lag-time" shooting. In a "lag-time" class, "they do this exercise where you stand there, and you have your gun in your fanny pack or whatever, then they have another person twenty-one feet away from you, and they show you how fast that person, running, can come up to you before you even have a chance to draw the gun and aim." Ultimately, she felt grateful to the judge who pressed her to take more classes. And she felt beholden to AWARE: "AWARE, they were so wonderful, I can't thank them enough. They took me under their wing."

Carroll's husband was incarcerated for two counts of assault and battery with a deadly weapon, one count of violating a restraining order, an additional assault and battery count in a different court, and an additional restraining order violation. He threatened her life in the courtroom, saying: "When I get out, I'm going to get you." He owned two long guns, and "he threatened to blow my brains out." According to the terms of the restraining order, he wasn't supposed to have any guns, but "they don't go and search the apartment." He was a frightening man. When I spoke to Carroll on the phone, this man was soon to be released from jail. She was steeling herself for the day.

She had been terrified and hurt by him. Once he and a friend set to banging on the front door of a condo complex where she was living with the children.

> There was really hard banging, and they started buzzing my door and trying to get in. They woke up everybody in the complex. I called the police,

but they didn't park in front, so we couldn't get a plate. They took off. They came back two nights later, and they busted the door, busted the whole complete lock on the door. My children were absolutely terrified. My oldest son put chairs and a table in front of the door, and he was crying. My younger son was totally out of control. My younger son suffered psychologically from that experience. He ended up having real bad nightmares and anxiety attacks. He was diagnosed with depression, and he had to end up on anti-depressants.

Carroll's husband had once tried to run her off Route 128 in a car. "I was in the car with my sons. He was trying to bang my car with his car and laughing the whole time." Another time he bled her brakes, and "he called the life insurance company and said: 'If something happens to my wife, make sure you have my new address and phone number.' And the insurance company told me, and we had to go to court and take the life insurance away from him." Once he attacked her in the middle of the night when she was going to her car and smashed her head down into the pavement. That was not the first time he grabbed and smashed her skull. Neurologists told her that repeated head injuries had resulted in permanent damage to her brain; she suffers from memory loss and may have temporal lobe epilepsy.

The first assault took place in Revere, Massachusetts, following an argument concerning her husband's treatment of the children one evening when he had asked to take them to Burger King (he and Joanne were separated), but instead took them to a strange neighborhood where he left them outside in a parked car. When he was confonted the next day, a fight erupted. She accused her husband of being a cocaine addict, and he mentioned her own prescription medicine. He yelled: "Did you take a bunch of those pills?" She threw her pills on the counter. Her husband called the police, who came and left. He called again. When two rookies arrived, he told them his wife had been taking pills; the policemen delivered her to the hospital. Within a short time, the staffers and an attorney whom Carroll knew from her work as a paralegal contacted the police and told them they had removed the wrong person from the house. Subsequently, her husband arrived with the children in the car to pick her up at the hospital.

I said: "Get out of the car; you are not driving these children in the car high." I said: "Stop the car." He wouldn't stop the car; he was driving real fast. I said: "Stop the car." So I was trying to put my foot on the brake, and he pushed me off him, and I was afraid, so I tried to pull the key out of the ignition, and that's when he grabbed me by the hair and smashed my face into the window. That's when I called the police, and that's when he went into phase two of his little repertoire.

Phase two. The same two rookie policemen arrived.

> My husband said to them that the reason he assaulted me was because I
> had hit my child. And he had threatened my child that he'd beat him up if
> he didn't agree with him, so when the police got there, he kept saying
> "Isn't that so, isn't that so?" My child looked up in terror and said: "Yeah.
> I was there." When the situation first started, my child wasn't even in the
> room. Here I was standing there, total black and blue, my face all black
> and blue, my eyes all black and blue!

Her husband told the police again that his wife had taken a lot of her pills.
She cried: "Go over there, go over there and look; my prescription's on the
counter; it's all there." They didn't look. "They dragged me away in the
police car, handcuffed me in front of my children."

Carroll described her husband as a smooth, convincing operator. After the
first assault against her, when he smashed her head into the car window:

> He played the game wonderfully; he had everyone totally convinced that he
> was on the road to recovery, that he was being rehabilitated, that he was going
> to change, that it was never going to happen again; he was out of control at
> that time, this, that, and the other thing, so they dropped the charges after he
> completed the probationary period, and it started all over again.

She found that the treatment she received from the justice system varied
widely depending on which policeman came to the door and which judge sat
on the bench. At a time when her husband had already been in jail for multiple counts of domestic violence, she encountered one presiding judge "who
sat up there and had the audacity to say to me: 'Well, we have to take into
account this is all to the same victim.' Like that made a difference, right?
Aren't I lucky?" At many points, Carroll's reports of her treatment by the
justice system matched up with reports of other battered women. She had
encountered responsive, reasonable policemen and judges; in her opinion,
officers who had received some training in domestic violence cases were much
more fair. But too often male policemen arriving at the scene, male judges
sitting on the bench, showed an instinctive affinity with her husband and
irritated impatience with her. "I hate to say the word, but a lot of these judges
think maybe the woman was a bitch or something and she was asking for it."

> The bottom line is, your justice depends on where you live. You live or die
> depending upon where you live. You will get some varying degree of pro-
> tection depending on where you live. You will get the perpetrator put away
> depending upon where you live and also upon the judge you have that day.

Carroll's voice did not quaver on the phone. She was matter-of-fact. At times she could be feisty. In her experience, a lot of judges on the bench were "from the old school" so that they thought of "a wife as chattel. A wife is supposed to put up with a certain amount of abuse. Or if a husband hits his wife, and it's the first time, give him a break, you know." At another point, she said: "There's a difference between whether you're a stranger being attacked by somebody, or whether you're a wife or girlfriend. It's a whole different ballgame. Your rights are nullified." Joanne felt that "there's a real backlash going on against women in society right now. Women and children. . . . It's like, okay, you wanted your rights, now you're going to have to carry the whole ball of wax."

Through support groups and political alliances, she had come to know a number of other abused wives. But not one of those women had ever told Carroll that she owned a gun or planned to buy one. "I don't think women would brag about it." She had gone through training, earned her pistol permit, tried out different pistols on the range, and chosen the gun she planned to buy that night. She wanted a gun because "I think it's an equalizer. That's the best word that I can come up with." She described to me an actual 911 tape that one of her teachers played for the self-defense class. It recorded the voice of a distraught mother at home with a child. She screamed into the phone that someone was banging on the window. She pleaded for help. The phone went dead. By the time the police arrived, the woman had been brutally beaten and raped, and the attacker was gone. In Carroll's own experience, police response time clocked in at around ten minutes from the moment a woman calls for help, and that would vary depending on the city. Ten minutes can be a very long time.

As we spoke, children's indistinguishable voices could be heard in the background, and at one point Carroll turned from the receiver to shush a child firmly. I asked her about children and house guns and safety. She said she had given serious consideration to the safety of her children. "That was my first question." Consulting with the teachers at AWARE, she decided a keypad "safe" with a four-digit combination bolted to the underside of the bed would work to hold the LadySmith where it would be accessible to her but not to the children. She had spoken to her children about the new gun she would be bringing into the house and sent for the NRA's Eddie Eagle Safety Course information. She planned to take her oldest son out on the range and possibly enroll him in a riflery course with a good instructor so he could learn about safety and discipline and understand fully that guns are not toys.

How does one appropriately tell a child that mother is buying a gun because if worst comes to worst, she may have to shoot father? Even the neatest discussion, complete with coloring books and an outing to the target range, would go ragged around the edges after a time and begin breeding night-mares. But this woman had lived with nightmares and now made a decision. She didn't choose to try alternative methods of self-defense because "I don't know of anything that can stop a bullet coming at you from afar. . . . If they're coming at you, and they have a gun, there's no way you're going to be able to stop them from shooting you if they want to shoot you, unless you have the same sort of weapon or equivalent to be able to say, 'Listen, [if] you try to shoot me, you're taking a chance of getting shot, too.' She be-lieved her husband would send a stranger to hurt her when he got out of jail. "My belief is that he's going to send somebody after me, try to kill me, and grab my six-year-old son, who he wants, while he goes out of state." To protect against getting caught in such a trap, she would need to keep her life dizzily irregular:

> I personally cannot have a regular routine schedule when he gets out of jail. Because if I do, I'll be a sitting duck with my kids. Everything in my life has to be variable. There can't be a pattern.

How would she do it?

> It's going to be really difficult. I'm going to have to be looking over my shoulder every minute. He sent people to town to follow me. He sent people to sit right in front of my house, on a main street where there's no parking. I've had contractors come over, mention there's a guy out there, twenty minutes, looking at everything I did.

She didn't yet know if she would try to alert her husband to the fact that she owned a new gun.

> That's a good question. I'm really at a toss-up as to whether or not I should tell him. The pros are that if he knows about it, it may be a deterrent for him to stay away or have other people stay away. The other side is, if he knows that I have one, he'll send somebody with a gun, thinking "then it's their problem; maybe they'll get her, maybe they won't." So it's a toss-up.

It was very clear that Joanne Carroll did not believe buying a gun would render her independent from the justice system or the social service system. She would continue to require fair treatment from policemen and judges and would probably need some assistance to manage as a single working mother who required daycare. Thus, she never thought of her efforts to ask for some protection from the justice system—courts and cops—and her efforts to get a gun as somehow mutually exclusive.

This woman was not a typical or model "battered woman." Nor could one really call her a committed advocate for handgun self-defense. During our interview, she never spoke of urging other women to decide for guns, and her political efforts had been focused on trying to introduce a referendum into Massachusetts that would require judges to undergo assessment and reelection tests periodically, and on trying to introduce bills that would mandate more consistent training for policemen and judges, and protect children from abusive fathers.

But at last, her description of the "variable" life she would have to lead once her husband got out of jail was the linchpin detail most necessary to describe and complete the mechanics of perpetual terror. Because she had lived through actual terrors, she understood that simply buying a gun and strapping it to her side would not perfectly insure her safety or the safety of her children; it would not put her on solid ground. Instead, she would be dodging and watching and worrying and varying her routine, for years, if she's lucky.

## Shooting Paper Dolls

By the conclusion of our pistol permit course, I had learned one obvious visceral lesson about handguns: they become familiar in the hand after a person has loaded, fired, unloaded, holstered, loaded, fired, unloaded, and holstered them many times. By the end of the course, I had also learned that it is impossible to glance over a room full of Americans enrolled in such a course and correctly guess what experiences or motives prompted them to sign up. The motives of the women I spoke with varied widely and were more immediately personal than political. Two of these women were relatively young mothers of young children.

The pistol permit course offered by Corning Community College was held in a utilitarian classroom usually reserved for police training sessions. There were sample paper targets, "bobbers," hung on the classroom walls and thick venetian blinds blocking our view of the back fields and parking lot. The enclosed shooting range, which had to be entered through a heavy locked door from the hall, was adjacent to the classroom; on Saturday morning, somebody was shooting a very big gun in there that struck out reports like a blacksmith's trip-hammer. Small gauge noises failed to penetrate the walls.

The pistol permit class ran through the weekend and earned students a single credit toward their degree. Thirteen men and six women (myself included) attended; over the course of the weekend, I interviewed four of the women in the hallway papered with criminal faces. Upstate New York residents cannot purchase handguns legally without first securing a pistol permit from a county judge, who will ask for explanations and personal references and may then take from three to six months before issuing. Even then, the permit itself may be literally ringed with prohibitions defining where and when, in the course of pursuing what job, the person is permitted to carry the gun; one woman recalled seeing permits issued by a judge in Cortland County with "restrictions typed all around the border line." This class didn't guarantee that anyone would be issued a permit, but it was understood that judges looked favorably on applicants who could show they'd had some training with handguns.

In Saturday's class, we received lectures on Article 35, the New York State law defining when a citizen may use "deadly force" justifiably. The subdivisions of the article come salted with the phrase "reasonably believes," as in: "A person may not use deadly physical force upon another person under circumstances specified in subdivision one unless: . . . (b) He reasonably believes that such other person is committing or attempting to commit a kidnapping, forcible rape, forcible sodomy, or robbery. . . ." We were also taught about the parts of a gun, how to clean and maintain a gun (either Hoppe's #9 or Shooter's Choice are both good solvents), gun safety, and storage. We learned about ejector rods and single-action shots. And with empty guns, in the range, we practiced slowly, step by step, repeatedly, the short dance movements used to load, holster, grip, unholster, aim, fire, reholster, and empty the pistols that would be fed with live ammunition on Sunday.

The two instructors assumed we were in class because we wanted pistols, and therefore they did not introduce arguments or statistics to dissuade anybody from purchasing a pistol. Our primary instructor was Michael Maroni, a frank, stocky, clear-faced former cop, who called women "gals" and warned his female students—all of whom arrived at class Saturday in sneakers—not to wear high-heels into the range on Sunday, who spoke to me privately with sincere concern about his wife's debilitating asthma, and who mentioned at one point that he never ventures into New York City without taking "Mary Elizabeth" (his Smith & Wesson .38 revolver, not his wife) along. Maroni informed us that keeping a house gun separate from its ammunition made the firearm useless for self-defense. "Home safety is not putting the weapons in one room and putting the ammunition in another room." He recommended keeping one loaded weapon in a place that a homeowner could reach in eight seconds from a sound sleep. In this, he contradicted recommendations published by the American Academy of Pediatrics, which advises parents who keep guns in the house to unload them and store the firearms separately from the ammunition, both in locked containers, and he also ignored the efforts of organizations like Handgun Control Inc., which supports legislation requiring child safety locks be sold with every handgun, as well as legislation that would hold householders criminally liable for accidents resulting from unsafe storage, that is, the presence of an unlocked, loaded gun in a house. Michael Maroni did not mention locks. He did say the weapon should not be kept under the mattress or in a bedside drawer because dreamy people make bad judgments. He related the ubiquitous story about the half-asleep cop (some say he lived in the Carolinas; some say he lived in New York) who fumbled for his gun and shot his stirring baby in its crib. Maroni said he always kept his own loaded revolver buried under clothes, up high in a bedroom closet. His family never had any trouble; he and his wife made sure that the kids understood the potential of that weapon and the rules governing its use.

Maroni led us into our dark range stalls on Sunday, and his voice came through the earphones: "Load with five." He paused as the class fumbled with the bullets, which are slippery, like dry beans. "Holster your weapon. Is the line clear? The line is clear. Clear to the right. Clear to the left. This is five rounds, hip-level, one shot. When I say fire, unholster and fire your weapons."

"Fire."

The first report from the line shocked me every time. I always waited for the first shot before concentrating on my sight picture and contracting my own trigger finger. When it explodes, a gun jumps. And then it's over. The weight of the gun returns to the holster, to the hip.

The women who got themselves fitted with leather holsters and revolvers, earphones and ammo aprons, who fired on command, aiming between the nipples of the paper targets, included a female army veteran, now reservist, Denise Bennett of Elmira, as well as two young mothers, 28-year-old Kim Clark and 24-year-old Jennifer Holden. Also a Corning Community College secretary in her forties, Sandy Davies, who had returned to college to earn a liberal arts degree, and one young woman who did not wish to be interviewed. All of these women had loose hairstyles that left their hair curling between their ears and shoulders. All were dressed informally. Bennett and Holden attended class with their husbands. Each woman attended class for a different reason.

Denise Bennett wanted her pistol permit because her dad was an avid hunter, and "when my Dad decides go to out in the country and I feel like I want to go, I can use one of his handguns and go out [to hunt]." She wasn't interested in carrying a handgun for self-defense because experiences in rough neighborhoods as a child taught her she could fight her way out of things. "Got jumped. But I didn't ever feel that insecure. . . . My Dad brought me up as a boy. I've been a tomboy all my life. . . . I decided I wanted to join the service because I loved the uniform."

Kim Clark was unlike Bennett, though both women had grown up in hunting families, in homes furnished with shotguns. Clark had a round, generous face and was as effortlessly well-mannered as a church girl. She wanted a pistol permit because she and her family live on a rural road, and she often takes her young children—the oldest is three years old—walking in the woods. "We've had a lot of rabies outbreaks. We had a run-in with Rottweilers, and if the kids are with me, I want to be able to protect them. We've had bears spotted up there. You just never know what you're going to run into." There were already guns at her house—she and her husband both hunt—but they were kept stored unloaded behind a wooden panel in the top of a locked closet.

Clark approved of liability laws that would punish gun owners who left their weapons where children could get hold of them. She didn't think her hunting brothers would approve of those same laws, however, because they believed "what they do in their own home is their own right." She could appreciate their point-of-view. "I think if we start regulating everybody's rules, what they can and can't do in their house, you start there, and the next thing they're saying you can't smoke in your house, you can't drink Pepsi in your house. It can get out of control." On the other hand, "my main concern is the safety and welfare of my children." Over lunch, Clark spoke about inventive crafts projects and good books for preschoolers and about diets and Pepsi. She is a good shot and plans to carry a loaded pistol in the car when driving alone at night.

Jennifer Holden, like Clark, was young, round-faced, rosy, not too tall, and married. Unlike Clark, however, she found guns physically alarming. Holden had a soft voice; the tape recorder needed to be amplified to catch her. She had enrolled in the gun class because she feared firearms. "Even just around bullets, I'd panic," and her husband suggested that this single credit course might help, "so if we ever are confronted, if we ever go and stay with our friends again, I don't have to be so paranoid." They'd both been surprised by the passion of her response to a handgun that turned up in a house that they visited during a Florida vacation with their young son. "I kind of threw a fit," Holden said. Their friends lived in a bad area, the wife had been mugged, and so the wife

> . . . had a semi-automatic weapon. She carries it with her to and from work, and at the time, it was under the couch. She took it out because we were all going up to bed, and she was taking it up with her, and I looked at her, and I said: "What is that?" And she showed it, and it just gave me a sick feeling, because I read articles constantly about little kids. I just read an article last weekend that said little boys between ages ten and fourteen are more likely to get killed in the home with guns. Like the instructor said: "if that bullet goes, you can't call it back. It's unchanging. Once you do it, that's it."

Holden thought that she might get a handgun to protect the house if she had no children, but "my son's a huge factor. He's two and a half, and he gets into everything, climbs on everything, dumps everything out. And even if you bring the kids into it and explain to them what this stuff is so they're less apt to be fascinated with it, I don't think it would work with my son. He'd want to see it; he'd want to play with it. And I'd never forgive myself if he found it. Even if he just found it unloaded, I wouldn't be able to handle it."

The voices of Clark and Holden, two young mothers, expressed love for their children the way a red tulip expresses red. Clark made a judgment about her household, based in part on her own experiences as a child raised in a hunting family, and she planned to get herself a handgun because "you can put the pistol in your fanny pack and carry it that way, and I can't carry my son and carry my shotgun too in the woods." Holden also made a judgment about her household; she is not willing to live with a gun—even an unloaded gun—hidden any place where her curious son might get his hands on it. Both these young women had picked up information about guns from magazine articles, but their experiences determined which articles, which arguments, would register with them. Clark agreed with the instructor, Michael Maroni, that young children could be educated to respect and stay away from household guns, while Holden agreed with the instructor when he said that discharged bullets can never be called back.

Of the four women interviewed, Sandy Davies, in her mid-forties, was the most interested in pondering her own motives and discussing roles of women generally. She enrolled in the course partly because she'd always been interested in crime "and why crime occurs." Her second husband, Wally, a hunter and gun club instructor, owned a number of handguns and rifles, but Davies never shot them. "We've had guns in our house as long as I've known Wally, and I've known Wally for fifteen years, and I couldn't even tell you where the guns are." Possibly because for a long time she'd been living near a cache of relatively benign, but hidden, firearms, it felt satisfying to receive and hold a real gun to fire. She said of our experience in the range: "Yesterday I found out that I really enjoy this. I like it."

She believed that women need to be able to protect themselves "because the police can't be there. We can't have one-on-one police protection." She and her husband lived at the end of a half-mile private road off a lake, and "rather than just knowing there were guns in the house and not knowing what to do with them, I'd rather be prepared."

Firearms still scared her. "I'm afraid I might do something wrong, especially when they give us live ammo here, and shoot myself or somebody else. I'm easing into this." But she was glad to penetrate one of the musty barriers that divided womanly activities—"be a wife, a teacher, a nurse, or a

secretary"—from men's activities. "When I grew up, women didn't play foot-
ball; you didn't play baseball, you didn't shoot guns; you didn't hunt; you
didn't do those things." Now, "I think it comes down to wanting a feeling of
control over my life. I find that so often, when you're a female, and when
you're a secretary, you have no control. People just kind of do with you as
they wish, and if you allow them to, then you can feel helpless." Later she
added: "I was in an abusive relationship that I got out of quickly, but some
things happened in that, and with my father when I was growing up, and I
have decided I'll just never allow this to happen again. And I know I'm not
big enough or strong enough to defend myself any other way than with a
weapon of some kind."

Davies decided for a gun. This did not mean she was necessarily gratified
to see eighteen Americans, weekend classmates, graduating into the ranks of
handgun owners. In fact, she felt uneasy watching the motley line of individuals in our class practicing on the range. One of the two doctors scared
her the most. "There are some people in this class that I hate to see have a
gun after watching them yesterday. That doctor who was sitting behind me;
he had his gun out, kind of looking at it on the range, playing with it after
they were first handed out. It scares me. He obviously wasn't listening or
paying attention. And I'd hate to see him have a gun. Be allowed to. But
what do you do about it? We all have the right."

In the plain, individual statements of just a few women, many of the key
issues raised by gun-control advocates and opponents were touched upon:
regulation, Second Amendment rights, hunting culture, safety, even women's
liberation and confidence. These women were aware of the issues, but only
mildly interested in statistics collected to show whether handguns are generally useful or dangerous in a home; their own specific histories and situations carried more weight, and predicted, for them, whether a gun would be
a good or bad risk in that context.

None of these women showed a keen desire to proselytize for gun rights.
Even though Davies's interest in guns resulted as part of a reaction to past
abuse and a feminine/feminist sense of vulnerability, she easily distinguished
between the people who had misused her and people who had not, between
one abusive partner and her current trusted husband, and she understood that
target practice wouldn't actually punish anyone who had bullied her in the
office, though the unconventional sport might generally increase her confidence and make her less amenable to bullying. The decision was private. It
had not transformed her into a gun rights advocate, however, because she
retained a healthy fear of guns. Having witnessed an instructor distributing
.38 revolvers to a classroom full of people whose names he didn't even know,
she saw what gun rights—"we all have the right"— could mean, practically.

One must imagine this disparate bunch of citizens, educated with just two days of class lectures and slow-motion paper target practice, driving out to buy handguns and bringing them home.

## Abyss

Throughout her tenure, Colorado State Senator Pat Pasco wrote and supported gun-control bills. In 1989, she sponsored a bill to ban the sale of assault weapons, "which was the first time anyone had tried any kind of gun control for ten or fifteen years in Colorado." After that, she introduced a gun-control bill every year for four years: one "Brady bill," one bill requiring safety education for gunowners, then in 1992, a juveniles bill, making it illegal for children under age eighteen to own guns. "None of them passed," she told me.

The senator also sponsored bills to require safety courses for gun owners and to make gunowners legally responsible for safe storage of their weapons. When we spoke, she was deeply frustrated by the fact that the NRA insisted that individuals with the proper training could be trusted to store and use guns safely, but then balked when a legislator attempted to establish a coherent, mandated gun education program. She attributed that response to paranoia—the conviction of many gunowners that government agencies, given an opportunity to establish regulatory controls, would inevitably expand those controls and increase their cost, ultimately restricting the right to own guns.

She believed that opposition to her many bills was "definitely created by the NRA. No doubt in my mind." She found pro-gun arguments to be "a bunch of jargon, but they believe it. They believe we need to shift attention to criminals, focus on the criminal, and they absolutely don't see the fact that the people who are committing most of the shootings and murders are not criminals until that moment." Asked about pro-gun statistics, she responded: "Oh it's a lot of phony research, most of it by the same man out of Florida," meaning Gary Kleck. Pasco had often publicly debated David Kopel, prolific pro-gun author from the Independence Institute in Golden, Colorado. She said that she'd tried to get Kopel to define how old a child should be before parents start to teach him or her about guns. "I've pushed it down to four, but I believe he'd go even younger. Not that they'd own a gun, but that he would start teaching them how to use a gun. I've never found a lower limit."

Pasco did understand why certain women would choose to own guns. "My mother had a gun, but she knew how to shoot it. She was a woman alone. She got it after I left home." But she didn't trust the impulse. "I think it leads to a false sense of security."

Her state had been visited by the patriot movement. A bill was introduced called the Colorado Sovereignty Act, which would have dictated that the state of Colorado collect all gasoline taxes due to the federal government and forward them to the federal government each month so long as the state was neither sued nor sanctioned; if provoked, Colorado would take the United States to court. In the 1990s, the word "sovereignty" was key to many far-right political manifestos. In the mid-1990s, a quick search through the Internet keyed to the word "sovereign" turned up a substantial number of home pages, like "Wepin Store" or "Sovereign's Lion Den," that warn the American people against One World Government and the United Nations and advise folks how to establish themselves as "Free Sovereign Citizens." The "Sovereign WWW Content Page," for example, promised to "cover subjects like One World Government, Militias, Patriot, AIDS, Sovereignty, Right to Keep and Bear Arms, Spirit, Awareness, Liberty, Congress, News, Rights, Solutions, and much more." The word "sovereign" in this context communicated an invitation either to defend national sovereignty against any movement toward "world government" or to defend local rights and freedoms against federal regulation. The Sovereignty Act of Colorado "would have been a bloody mess," Senator Pasco said. It didn't pass.

The senator spoke more happily of the federal government's Brady Bill, which had instituted a waiting period and background check for gun buyers (the interview took place before June 1997, when the mandatory background check provision of the Brady law was declared unconstitutional by the U.S. Supreme Court). Pasco contended that this regulation had been useful in her state. "Since we passed the Brady Bill, in Colorado about 10 percent of the people who applied for guns have been turned down, and some of them have had arrest warrants out for them. Some of these people aren't very smart."

In her work as an elected official and gun-control advocate, Pasco had met and cooperated with Tamara Mechem, a Colorado resident listed on a flyer distributed to journalists by the Center to Prevent Handgun Violence (a sister organization of Handgun Control, Inc.). Tamara Mechem became involved in the political fight for gun control after her fourteen-year-old son Patrick was accidentally killed by a handgun during a scuffle with his sister, Shanté, who was trying to take the gun from him.[16] One month later, Mechem's daughter committed suicide. Like Byrl Phillips-Taylor, another white woman whose son was killed by gunfire, Mechem addressed politicians with her story and tried to use it as a lever to influence public policy. She asked Colorado legislators to pass a law that would hold adults liable for careless storage of their firearms. Pasco helped press for that legislation. Similar safe-storage laws are in effect in fifteen states, including California, Connecticut, Florida, Hawaii, Iowa, Maryland, New Hampshire, New Jersey,

Virginia, and Wisconsin, and anti-gun organizations are at work in the courts, filing lawsuits against gun manufacturers and gun dealers they believe to be guilty of negligence for producing, marketing, and selling assault weapons, and legislating to require that child safety locks be sold with every gun. But the safe-storage bill did not pass in Colorado, and after seven years, Mechem was growing tired of the effort.

I picked Mechem's name from the CPHV literature because she lived in Colorado, like Rebecca John, and because the story of her loss, summarized on the list, was extreme. I dreaded the interview. But Mechem had allowed her name and phone number to be included on a public list, so I phoned. She was polite, and we spoke at length. The conversation profited me and did nothing for her. Talking to strangers about the deaths of her two children had not directly changed public policy or helped her recover. She was ready to go back into privacy. "I need them to be able to rest, in peace, and I need to have some peace."

"Only you can't have peace when children continue to die," she said. So she told the story one more time.

> My daughter was home from college, and a bunch of the kids were going to get together and then they decided not to and she said, "Well, we're all going to go to the drive-in." So when my children left the home, she had her fourteen-year-old brother with her, and I was under the impression the kids had left to go to the drive-in. I got a call at 12:20 and someone was saying there'd been a horrible accident, and I was saying: "Well, an automobile accident?" We lived in a fairly middle-class, affluent neighborhood at that time. I'd never been around a gun; no one in my family has ever hunted. That was never a problem. I never thought to talk to the kids. We talked about sex and drugs, but guns never. Apparently, the boy that was having this unsupervised party pulled out his Dad's gun and was showing Patrick, and Patrick got excited, ran out to the back yard . . . all the kids had been drinking also. They were drinking beer.
>
> So he took it outside and fired one shot into the air and Shanté ran over to him and said: "Let me have that gun," and they struggled over it, and the gun discharged. And it killed him.
>
> My daughter and son, from the day I brought that child home from the hospital, they were immediate friends. Patrick got shot. Patrick was kind of a clown. Everybody thought, "okay," then he said, "Oh God, it's real." My kids didn't even know this was a real gun. He ran out to the street, trying to flag down a police officer that was passing by, then he ran back up to my daughter and died at her feet.

Mechem's daughter was taken to the police department for questioning. The mother traveled with her son, who was dead on arrival at the hospital.

I remember the police officer standing there with the body because an investigation was going on to determine whether Shanté would be charged or not, and leaning against the wall and just coming down to his knees and sobbing as I was walking around the table talking to Patrick. . . . And to go up and see him lying on that table it was. . . . He was just a baby. Yet here was a child who was 5′8″ and *he was just the same.* I remember telling him: "My God, how . . . you just walked over that line so easily. Was it that easy?" And I had a friend that was in the police department, that, they taped Shanté's interview, when they led her to the police station, and him calling and saying: "Tam we couldn't even finish listening to the tape because we just started crying, to listen to the anguish in her voice." . . . And I think, I can remember my kids falling down and scraping their knees and that hurting me, and never in my life did I ever think something like this would happen, that something would happen to my child that I couldn't protect them from.

Shanté committed suicide twenty-seven days later. She pulled the family car into the garage and carbon monoxide.

Tamara Mechem recalls how everything changed.

Before my life was full, it was vibrant, I was naive. I was very proud of my children. Not many problems other than the usual arguing and fussing. Patrick was a skateboarder and that summer had been asked to tour, and they had some things coming up in California. Trying to make a determination about that. Laughter, love, phones ringing, busyness. That's the thing I remember most is all the busy activity. And then going to complete silence. My house was silence. I was a Mom for a number of years, then all of a sudden I didn't have that role anymore. My oldest son had moved out of the home. I wasn't ready for an empty nest, I wasn't ready to bury the kids, I wasn't ready for any of the movement to stop. But there wasn't anything. The music wasn't on, phones didn't ring, friends didn't come by. It all ceased. It was like I was put in a small room, and my air taken away.

After going through the second funeral, it was like people were terrified of us.

In time, she contacted a lawyer. "When I went to see an attorney about wrongful death for Patrick, I found that they could have offered me so much money *per pound* of what my child weighed. That was on the laws here in Colorado. In the last three years, that law has been revamped." Her family never heard from the man whose gun Patrick picked up at the party.

She testified publicly in favor of a safe-storage liability law. "We wanted weapons stored safely, and if not, we wanted these people to be charged. If a child accidentally got hold of a gun in the home, and it wasn't properly stored, that owner would be liable."

As a result, she received letters from members of the NRA. "The National Rifle Association, those people were horrid. I received hate mail after testifying and trying to pass gun legislation here in Colorado. I even had one of these men—Gil something, president of the NRA here in Colorado—say to me: 'Maybe if you had been a better parent, your children would be alive today' . . . Their reasoning was, had I sent my children to handgun school or safety school, that's what they called it, they would have been aware that was a deadly weapon. That the gun is nothing; it's the person holding it. . . ." She received 500 pieces of mail from NRA members, whom she describes as having shown a "total lack of compassion and understanding," and is convinced that the campaign was organized. "It didn't happen until after we had been to the legislature and tried to introduce legislation."

And yet, "one of my neighbors was a member of the NRA when the children died and had guns in the home, and after Patrick died, I remember Brad walking over and saying: 'I got rid of my gun, Tam. I cannot ever be responsible and have a gun in my home.'"

Tamara Mechem was convinced that most people distance themselves from reported tragedies. "When you read things, it happens to everyone else; it doesn't happen to you. And for some reason, you tend to justify that. There was something they did. Those people deserve this. And that's the way most of us tend to give it an okay. That's okay if it happened to them."

She herself had been tormented by questions.

> That this was 1988 and how could a child die from a handgun wound? How is that possible, that a child was even around anything like that? Or why didn't this happen down in the heart of Denver with the guns? That was expected. But this? And that my children had no right to be dead.
>
> I know after the kids died, I cut out every copy of a story of a child who had died by handgun, and I remember burning them one night and being so angry! What the hell does it take before people are going to open their eyes and say: "Gosh, this is a life! Life is so important, and how we can look at that and say, it's okay, that was just one child?"
>
> I think what I can remember most was getting to the emergency room and being taken upstairs and [being] shown his body, and having to identify his body. And to look, and that bullet hole was so small. It was like, "How did something so small kill my child?"

Pro-gun advocates speak about how their encounters with guns enable them to grasp hard reality, and they say that people who favor gun control are soft, lightweight, dreamy. In Mechem's opinion, however, people who trust guns to protect them are the dreamers. "I think their sense of reality is [as] naive as mine was before my children died."

Her political opinions resisted easy categorization. She understood why people in Colorado would want guns—"because we're seeing our law enforcement officers not being effective, our legislation not effective"—and agreed with critics that the American system for capturing and then punishing criminals has fallen into disrepair. She said: "I don't know about your state, but in my state, if you're sent to prison, you're entitled to television, you're entitled to visits from family. You can see a doctor. You can work on your degree. We need to start looking at how punitive our laws are in some ways." Asked if she would prefer laws to be more punitive, she said: "Definitely."

At the same time, she had worked with troubled teenagers as a counselor in a state correction facility for minors and as a coordinator for the Jefferson County Health Department's drug and alcohol program. And when she called to mind the casualties claimed by gang-related violence in downtown Denver, she imagined the dead as children: "Here in Colorado we have so many children that die by gunfire. Most of that is gang-related."

She did not think private individuals in Colorado should be legally permitted to carry concealed handguns in public. "If it comes clear to the bone, I don't think people need to be carrying guns." But, "I don't have any answers." Like many citizens, she could recall a time when the streets were safer, the neighbors were more attentive, and children could explore their neighborhoods without fear late into the evening. "And we don't have that sense of community or family any longer. I don't know. But guns won't do it. They are not the answer."

The legislation she would like passed in Colorado would make individuals liable for accidents that resulted from negligent storage of their firearms.

I described Tamara Mechem's story and proposal to SWARM cofounder, Diane Nicholl. She asked about the teenager's party and whether alcohol was present. She listed the range of irresponsible actions that led up to the tragedy, as she understood it from my report, and she asked whether legislation of any kind could be expected to eliminate risk in such a situation: "Where do you draw the line where you legislate how people behave?" She said that the children she knew who had been trained to respect guns would have acted differently: "I know so many kids who are in our juniors program who would look at this and say: 'These kids are too immature, and they don't respect firearms enough to be allowed to touch them.'" She agreed it was "irresponsible of the owner of that firearm to leave it in such a way that a child could get hold of it," but did not support legislation that would punish the owner for his negligence unless the legislation "was equally applied to every other potentially dangerous object and substance in everyone's household. Screwdrivers, prescription drugs, anti-freeze. Toilets. How many kids drown in bath tubs and toilets and swimming pools and five-gallon buckets?"

I then described Diane Nicholl's argument to Senator Pat Pasco. She responded: "That's a phony bologna argument. We had a cover story in the *Rocky Mountain Journal* saying people could be killed with frying pans. Well, of course, they could, but it's a whole lot harder, and you're much more likely to survive. A gun is an extremely dangerous weapon."

Both of these women had been involved for a long time in public legislative contests and had faced and returned their opponents' standard volleys repeatedly; they each had an arsenal of forehand and backhand swings ready and were quick around the court. This is how contemporary gun debates tend to work. Advocates select and deploy national statistics and personal stories as evidence to portray a nation that would be well served by their favorite prescriptions. Thus, an individual, personal story becomes valuable insofar as it can be analyzed and publicized to achieve results, to drive home a point, to help win the game. A tragic personal story becomes important for its "talking points," its bounce, its scoring potential.

I find this process disheartening, but at the same time realize that it would be a mistake to denigrate the results achieved by political combat in a democracy. The outcomes of these debates have very real consequences. They shape real life. They can save real lives. Good legislation can sustain and direct a country, while bad legislation opens the way to inequity, civil dissolution, and economic miseries. This country was born through an act of written eloquence; political and legal rhetoric outlined its original skeleton. No legislative body comes to decision without debate. We must debate.

But the debates should not overwhelm our instinctive, and intellectual, understanding of what it means to be private, to be alone. We must remember that individuals and their situations are usually too complex to be fully framed by ideological categories or made safe by partisan advice. Tragedies spill and spread beyond words, beyond frames and boundaries of all sorts. A "talking point" can be endlessly repeated and resurrected. A person cannot be.

A woman who chooses to buy a handgun for self-defense has imagined herself alone somewhere without help, probably facing a dangerous man. She calls out: "I have a gun." He is the one who gets the surprise. On the other hand, a woman who chooses to keep guns out of her house and prays to keep guns forever out of her life has imagined a different, equally lonesome moment with as much clarity. She is at home. A sound shoots out from a door in the house. She is the one who gets the surprise. And though we adopt preventative measures, none of us is immune to terrible surprise, no matter what decisions we make. That's real life.

Guns are dream-makers in this country. Too often, they promise to identify and shoot "bad guys." Target practice is fun because it concentrates our energies and funnels our vision. But *it's not real enough*. Target games teach us very little about human terror or about the patient work involved in mobilizing a community to heed and assist its threatened citizens. The horrible lonesome moment and the strong communal years coexist in real life. Any woman who wonders about handguns should certainly read up on the literature generated to calculate how often guns act badly in this country and how often they act well and explore different options for self-defense.[17] But then she must close the books and look around at the physical world to remember how it acts. Forget liberals, conservatives, even legislation, forget enemies, heroes, and eloquence. A modern handgun is a lethal weapon that fires projectiles at great speed in response to the force exerted by a single finger. That is a gun in real life.

## Notes

1. Massad Ayoob, "Post-Shooting Trauma" videotape, available from Police Bookshelf, P.O. Box 122, Concord, NH, 1990.
2. First two quotes from Massad Ayoob, *In the Gravest Extreme: The Role of the Firearm in Personal Protection* (Concord, NH: Ayoob & Ayoob, 1980). Third quote from Massad Ayoob, "Post-Shooting Trauma" videotape [see note 1].
3. Editors, "Domestic Violence," *Ms. Magazine* (September/October 1994), pp. 37, 48, sidebars.
4. Ann Jones, "Living with Guns, Playing with Fire," *Ms. Magazine* (May/June 1994), pp. 43, 44.
5. "Is This Power Feminism?" *Ms. Magazine* (May/June 1994), pp. 36–37.
6. Ann Jones, "Living with Guns, Playing with Fire," p. 41 [see note 4].
7. Mary Zeiss Stange, "Arms and the Woman: A Feminist Reappraisal," in *Guns: Who Should Have Them?* ed. David B. Kopel (Amherst, NY: Prometheus Books, 1995), pp. 15–52.
8. Ibid., note 19, p. 44.
9. Ibid., p. 39.
10. Ann Japenga, "Would I Be Safer With a Gun?" *Health*, March/April 1994, p. 57.
11. Mary Zeiss Stange, "Arms and the Woman: A Feminist Reappraisal," p. 37 [see note 7].
12. Ann Jones, *Next Time She'll Be Dead: Battering and How to Stop It* (Boston: Beacon Press, 1994), p. 101.
13. Angela Browne, *When Battered Women Kill* (New York: Free Press, 1987), pp. 40, 48, 60, 67, 98, 105, 154.
14. Ibid., p. 140.
15. Ann Jones, *Next Time She'll Be Dead*, pp. 41–42 [see note 12].
16. I did not confirm with Tamara Mechem the spelling of her daughter's name. By the end of the interview, it seemed too painful a question to ask.
17. There are nonlethal self-defense weapons available to women. Nonlethal weapons recommended by Massad Ayoob include a long police flashlight swung against the hands or arms of an attacker, a can of pepper spray with a 5 percent concentration (illegal in some states), and a Kubotan, a martial arts stick that a trained individual

can use to incapacitate an assailant. Other alternatives: Model Mugging courses are offered to women in many states. These "padded assailant courses" teach students to repel attackers from a prone position using the strength in their legs. Contact Bay Area Model Mugging for information about chapters across the country. BAMM/ Impact Self-Defense, 629 Blair Island Road, Suite 104, Redwood City, CA 94063. For national referral, (800) 345–KICK, http://www.bamm.org. The Center to Prevent Handgun Violence had recommended a book by Judith Fein, entitled *Exploding the Myth of Self-Defense: A Survival Guide for Every Woman* (Duncan Mills, CA: Torrance Publishing, 1993). Fein advises women to train themselves to resist attackers with aggressive fury and tear gas. According to Fein, the three best ways to attack an assailant would be to smash the Adam's apple; break the knee cap with a swift, pendulum swing of the lower leg "to bring the ball of your foot through the assailant's knee cap"; or spray the assailant in the face with tear gas. For a discussion of lethal weapons for self-defense (firearms) and their use, see Tanya K. Metaksa, *Safe, Not Sorry: Keeping Yourself and Your Family Safe in a Violent Age* (New York: Regan Books, 1997), or Paxton Quigley, *Armed and Female* (New York: E. P. Dutton, 1989). To contact organizations that advise women in the use of both nonlethal and "lethal" (guns) methods of self-defense, contact the National Rifle Association, "Refuse To Be a Victim" program, http://www.nrahq.org/safety/rtbav, phone: 1-800-861-1166; or AWARE (Arming Women Against Rape and Endangerment), P.O. Box 242, Bedford, MA 01730-0242, http://www.aware.org, phone: 781-893-0550 or 877-672-9273.

# 6

## Gun Games and Homegrown Rebellion

### The Practical Shooters Invitational

The United States has a reputation as a country where dreams become reality. It began by inventing itself in 1791, when the last section of the Constitution—the Bill of Rights—was adopted, and went on from there, busily generating mountains of improbable blueprints that were subsequently translated into steel.

In the center of this vast mythic and legalistic land, there stands a single figure: an independent man with a long gun who represents authority and rebels against authority at the same time. We are taught that the spirit of this rebellious father lives on, not only in story, but also in the body of the citizenry. Americans don't seem to be content to enshrine champions under glass. We expect democratically to reincarnate them or, at very least, to replay them.

Such expectations often lead to frustration. They also generate monumental role-playing games. Carrying real guns, citizens dodge through pressboard constructions surrounded by targets representing bad guys. Others more ideologically committed gather on weekends to run through military drills, preparing themselves to take on the U.S. federal government. Are these games potentially threatening? Do they serve as vents or magnifiers for aggression? Are they good or bad or just fascinating theater? Are they *games* at all? These are questions that should be asked.

It might be said that a game is a dream of conquest that allows one's body to take part in the action. Certain criteria distinguish games from life or from war. Violence, place, and time are circumscribed in a game, as in theater; set boundaries prevent a competition from getting too rough, ranging too far, or going on too long. What's more, the outcome of a game is not supposed to affect the actual lives of people who play or watch the action. Ideally, the results of a sporting contest evaporate the moment the final whistle blows. All the statistics and passions resulting from games should remain inside their own insular dimension. A true game must never result in death, even obliquely, for modern Western civilizations ask for a strict division between sport and bloodshed. By our lights, once players begin using any game to prepare for a physical battle where death may result, the atmosphere changes and the "play" becomes something else. It becomes a military drill.

In the United States today, women and men engage in a wide range of combative exercises with real guns. They take part in outdoor theatrical assemblies that allow them to engage their fantasies physically. Hunters who march into the woods, hoping in part to retrace the footsteps of their fathers and grandfathers, engage in a sort of theatrical ritual as well. We call hunters "sportsmen," but we hesitate to call hunting a "game," since it concludes (when successful) with actual death. The games, the theatrical drills, to be considered in this chapter involve not real hunts for animals, but imagined fights against bad guys; depending on the group, the bad guys may be bank robbers, burglars, or federal agents.

Some players of gun games in America are more purposeful than others, for they have convinced themselves that the approaching battle looms near, and therefore they must begin to prepare, to train, for potential war. Civilian militia members would bristle to hear their activities described as games, just as religious believers object to hearing their faith described as make-believe. Their firearms attach them to the past, to the rebellious Founding Fathers, and also direct them to the future, where they perceive the darkening outlines of a great war between the forces of tyranny and scrappy, American resisters. It is not difficult to understand how such a clarion alarm would rouse sympathetic religious vibrations. The militia member whom I interviewed had her gaze fixed on Armageddon.

But not all of these exercises are equally serious or purposeful, even though real bullets do zing into the dirt. This is the point I find most difficult to explain: that a number of people I met who enjoyed playing gun games did not impress me as being contaminated, titillated, or even empowered by *violence*, though certainly they were excited by the realities of their pistols, which distinguished their sport from a child's pastime. None would have driven four hours to a shooting contest that had them dashing about with squirt guns.

Plenty of gun games are carnival events, and people who attend them have arrived for fun and an adrenaline rush. In the sun, in the noise, they focus on the contests, the instructions, the sequence of targets, the sight pictures, and the PING of struck steel. The hazy aggressions that one can occasionally discern rising off a crowd of players in these games do not direct themselves against the cardboard targets or steel poppers at the end of the field; they're more likely to settle over absent anti-gunners, invisible killjoys who would like to close down the amusement park. I spoke to a number of practical pistol contestants resting at a picnic bench, and it was talk of new gun-control legislation in Canada that made their temperatures rise. Yet I did not judge that the emotions generated in this situation were measurably more threatening than the emotions generated at most carnivals, even though the picnickers had to yell to be heard over a firecracker background din of pistol shots.

Players will join the games for a variety of reasons and bring with them a variety of predilections. In Fulton, New York, at the United States Practical Shooters Association (USPSA) Smith & Wesson Invitational, a visiting Canadian told me at the picnic table that he thought private citizens should have the right to buy machine guns "to play with." At the same event, however, I also met a woman, a former gym teacher, now a physician and grandmother, who said she started going to practical shooting competitions because they relaxed her after stressful weeks as a doctor. Doreen Planck had driven up from West Virginia to play the game. Outfitted in light khaki jeans and a thick leather holster belt hung with spare ten-round magazines, she walked honestly, her feet striking straight into the ground, her gray ponytail disarrayed and swinging. Planck had grown up on a farm in New York, in a family that sometimes relaxed in the evenings by shooting target. Her father hunted, her son hunted, and she used to hunt, though she had not in about ten years, possibly because of her experiences as a physician. She couldn't find the right words to explain why she'd stopped hunting or why she liked guns.

"I can't get to the bottom of it." She attested that none of the people she'd met in three years of USPSA competition seemed violent and that she'd never felt self-conscious as a woman among them. They were "conservative Republican-type people," but "there's not hostility here; there's no practicing for violence. This is just fun."

Individual women who take part in the theatrical gun games organized on various fields and ranges throughout the United States contradict stereotypes with their comfortable voices and collective physical presence. Yet it feels wrong to surrender all attempts to try and analyze, then judge, the hidden messages at work inside these shooting games just because a number of individuals who participate in them happen to be articulate, personable men and

women. A writer scrambles vainly for surgical instruments keen enough to separate the dancers from their noisy dance. Thus, fantastical American gun games
have attracted critical attention. In his book *Warrior Dreams: Violence and
Manhood in Post-Vietnam America*, the writer William Gibson analyzed a bris-
tling array of paramilitary magazines, novels, movies, and sports introduced
into the United States since the 1980s. He theorized that they appeal to American men who require war fantasies to reaffirm their masculinity in the wake of
the nation's military defeat and liberal social revolutions.[1]

Gibson witnessed a serious game of paintball involving grown men, including a retired Minnesota Viking; paintball games are essentially field tag
contests played between two teams outfitted with guns that shoot paint cap-
sules. He also attended a week of combat pistol training at Gunsite Ranch,
Jeff Cooper's school in Arizona.[2] After blasting his way through the ranch's
rigged Fun House and Play House, Gibson looked back to discover that he
had been physically seduced by the thrill of shooting the "bad guy" targets
that Gunsite had arranged in the closets, hallways, and ceilings of their fright
houses. Gibson recalled that as he prepared to maneuver through the final
course, "It felt like the energy roared down my arms until it formed a tunnel
that extended out to wherever I aimed my weapon."

The powerful seductions and effective indoctrination at Gunsite convinced
this writer, again, that America's growing paramilitary culture rouses pernicious instincts in groups of men. Along similar lines, news that Dylan Klebold
and Eric Harris, the two students who killed twelve of their classmates in
Littleton, Colorado, were fans of the interactive target video game, Doom,
raised questions about popular American target games and their effects on
young men. A military psychologist, David Grossman, with a coauthor, subsequently wrote about the "desensitization" that results from hours of playing sophisticated target video games. He noted that during World War II,
only 20 percent of America's soldiers found themselves capable of aiming at
and shooting the enemy, but that percentage increased markedly after the
military switched from using old-fashioned bull's eye targets and began using human-figure targets in practice sessions. During the Vietnam War, 90
percent of American soldiers had lost their inhibitions and found themselves
able to shoot at other people. The military now uses interactive video games
in training. According to Grossman, "With the advent of interactive point
and shoot arcade and video games, there is a significant concern that society
is aping military conditioning but without the vital safeguard of discipline."[3]
Journalists noted that Klebold used video game techniques in shooting his
classmates. He went for head shots and moved his gun efficiently from one
target to the next, rather than shooting repeatedly at each new target, as inexperienced gunmen tend to do.

This story is so horrible it is difficult to step around it and consider any other side of the question, but that is what I want to do. For, in fact, Gibson's Angry White Male theories and even the actions of Klebold don't reveal all there is to know about these target games, something you realize when talking to women who shoot. The gun fantasies Gibson explores are elementally offensive—not defensive—and phallic. Women who attract his critical attention are the statuesque bitches and holstered nudes that frolic through paramilitary pornography. In the gun world as Gibson interprets it, women are always victims or targets, not participants.

He is right to critique this macho strand in our culture. It generates violence . . . often violence against women. At the same time, machismo is not the only force that comes packaged with a handgun, and frustrated masculine aggression not the only impulse that persuades an individual to pick up a gun. Women say they like to shoot because it's exciting and, surprisingly, some find it relaxing. Clearly, they also enjoy running through theatrical sets that allow them to face make-believe dangers with hearts pounding, and to blast away at those dangers. This thrill is defensive as well as offensive. It is part of a fantasy effort, and I find it impossible to advise what measures should be imposed—if measures should be imposed?—to suppress or redirect popular fantasies.

The USPSA's Smith & Wesson Invitational was held at Pathfinder Fish and Game Club, just south of Fulton, a town where the rich scents from a local Nestle's factory haunt the roads and enter car windows unexpectedly. In mid-August, the streets of the town were still decorated with Fulton Chocolate Festival banners, but only one sign announced the Invitational, and that was at the Quality Inn where most of the contestants were registered. The clerk at the local newspaper office hadn't heard of the Smith & Wesson Invitational, which I would learn later had attracted 340 competitors, 26 of them women. The USPSA sponsors about ten regional/national competitions of this size annually, and though gun magazines feature them as significant events, the one I attended was much humbler than a county fair and smaller than a chocolate festival.

It was a hot day. It had been a hot summer. The river was low and clogged, and the road to the Pathfinder Club was dusty. The club owns a sweep of dry valley land extending along the base of hills that have been bulldozed to serve as backstops. The huge arena resembles a quarry, with bare and weed-covered slopes topped by a continuous wall of trees, many of them old pines. Often the gunshots echo back from the hills (and from the clubhouse and parked automobiles and flagpoles), giving the impression that invisible soldiers are hidden behind the curtain of pines. The noise at the Invitational was constant. Participants didn't mind the noise. Everyone nearing the range was required to wear ear protection. When orange foam plugs are worked into the ears, a person hears her own loud breath. On a dry day, in a summer so hot that the dust on the ground is soft as ash, this ear plug effect can be suffocating.

Under a tent near the clubhouse at Pathfinder's, gunsmiths and industry reps and advocates had set up their tables and spread their wares. To get from these tables past the red frame clubhouse to the actual competition "stages," one crossed through a plot of salvaged woods and passed behind the club's rifle range, a field deep as a golfer's driving range. Distant targets had been set up against the slope for contestants interested in testing their "practical" skills with long guns. I watched a man carrying a high-powered, well-accoutered rifle shimmy up a detached little roof and shoot from there, then run and fall on his belly behind a wooden wall with a hole in it and shoot from there. To discover how well he'd done, the shooter and an official buzzed off toward the targets in a golf cart. Before they headed out, the Range Officer ordered all guns emptied, holstered, and cleared from the range.

But the main action was down the road, inside a series of open-air dirt bunkers where a crew of sportsmen had built nine "stages," rude outdoor theatrical sets, variously named "Aussey's Wall," "Port Barrel Polka," "Invasion from Mars," "Prison Bus Blues," "Three's a Crowd," "Base-a-Ball," "Bath Night" and "Rosa's Demise." Like neighborhood festival booths, the stage props were constructed from pressboard, nailed together in haste and then coated in single coats of aqua, red, yellow, or black paint. Targets had been anchored in various places inside the sets, many of them cardboard, others steel "pepper poppers" shaped like ghosts and pock-marked with bullet dings. A number of the targets were marked with white crosses: these were the "no-shoots." Occasionally, a fallen target would trigger the release of other targets on a pulley or spring. If a competitor hit the central steel Martian in "Invasion from Mars," three green cardboard shapes suddenly appeared floating on pulley wheels down a wire strung behind two spaceships. The spaceships were pressboard triangles outfitted with red blinking lights.

The idea was to run around the course as directed and shoot the targets, avoiding hits on "no-shoots" (hostages) that were scattered between the representative escaped prisoners, burglars, and green pressboard aliens.

Separated from the action by lines of yellow sheriff's tape, a few spectators watched from under tents. Inside those small plots of shade were card tables, yellow Igloo water coolers, designated officials with clipboards, and a few women on folding chairs. Men and women in blue jeans, with holstered guns covered in big protective sleeves, passed under the booths aimlessly.

No one wore camouflage gear or military gear. There was just one t-shirt that looked threatening: "Co-Ed Naked Law Enforcement: Up Against the Wall and Spread 'Em."

Competitors who stood inside the protective ring of sheriff's tape, ready to begin a round, came in all shapes and sizes. When called to start, however, they took their places with a uniform, lively nervousness, like people advancing to be baptized in a cold river. Each one would speak a few words to the range officer, then freeze in position as the officer lifted the timer near his or her ear. BUZZ. The action that followed was motley, middle-aged, and obscured by plywood trees and walls, but it must have felt wonderful to the ones who were in the game. Many contestants told me that they never heard the booms from their own guns once the buzzer sounded.

The many detailed rules of practical shooting competitions have been codified by the USPSA. A competitor in a squad must follow the directions set for each stage, directions which may require him to start off lying face-up on a cot, or standing inside a bus made of green netting with hands on the prop steering wheel, or sitting at a picnic table gripping a rubber hotdog, or crouching like a hostage in a plywood bank lobby or, as it happened in "Bath Time," standing inside a transplanted outhouse with the lid up. When the range officer's timer sounds, a contestant will variously leap out of bed, throw down the hotdog, or slam the outhouse toilet lid before grabbing his or her gun and dashing to shoot as many targets from the designated positions as accurately and quickly as possible.

Scoring a USPSA round is complex, for not only speed and accuracy, but also the class of a competitor's weapon is taken into account. There are stock guns and souped up "race" guns. In the game itself, stages may be designated as "Virginia" rounds, where competitors are limited in the number of bullets they can shoot, or "Comstock" rounds, with unlimited shots on goal. A "Mozambique" round requires something like two shots to the head and three to the chest. Generally, a hit to the target's head or chest earns five points.

But participants are strongly discouraged from calling the target's head "a head," just as they're discouraged from calling the no-shoot targets "hostages." The head of a target is officially described as the "upper AB zone."

I had attended another practical pistol competition, a small local one put on by the Cortland County Pistol Club, and I had read descriptions of others. The magazine *Women & Guns* reported on an Invitational held in the Pine Barrens of Long Island, organized by the group AWARE (Arming Women Against Rape and Endangerment).[4] The two organizers listed were men. Of the 220 armed competitors gathered to compete in an event sponsored by an organization that proposes to arm women against rape and endangerment, 208 were men. Lyn Bates, the reporter for *Women & Guns*—also the president of AWARE and an instructor at Massad Ayoob's Lethal Force Institute—did not remark on the ironies of the situation. Names for the different stages at the AWARE Invitational brought to mind board games and television movies; they ranged from Bank Job, Drop the Cash, Zig Zag II, and Don't Spill the Paint, to House Beautiful, Nothing Is Clear to Me, Too Many Civilians, and AWARE Campsite Horrors.

I was told many times that this sport does not simulate the actual shooting of people. The head of a target is not a head; it's a zone. A Cortland County club member with his hearing protectors temporarily slung around his neck acknowledged that some participants did hope the competition would sharpen their gun skills under pressure, and those skills might be useful in a self-defense situation. But none of the individuals that he met at competitions thought about practicing to shoot *people*.

The women whom I interviewed all said that they never imagined shooting people on the course. Barbara Seamans was freckled, ponytailed, tan and at ease; she looked like a growth-up version of a very pretty high school student. I met her at the Cortland County pistol shoot, where she told me that I ought to go to the big Smith & Wesson Invitational; her husband, Jerry, had a table under the tent at Fulton where he sold specialized competition equipment that he manufactured at home. Seamans began attending practical pistol competitions because she and her husband enjoyed doing things together. She spoke of the adrenaline rush that they both experienced, and how after a day of shooting, "the ride home is just quiet time." The whole family— Barbara, Jerry, their daughter, and their son—travels to the Smith & Wesson Invitational each August and stays at the motel; it's their summer vacation. Recently, her son tried out paintball. She drove a Bronco full of boys way up into the hills, to the rugged paintball course, and paid a fee per head, as she would for miniature golf or go-karts. Each boy received a paintgun. The paint that shoots out of the game guns is bright yellow and washable; $CO_2$–powered paintguns were originally developed for foresters and ranchers to brand trees and cattle. The boys had a great time. "On the way home, these kids had paint all over them, and they were bruised up." Her son got a bloody nose, but he emerged happy and thoughtful. He'd been "wounded" in the thigh early and told his mother that if this were a real war with real ammunition, he would have been shipped home on one of the first planes.

Since the day I talked to Seamans, both of my own sons have tried paintball. They each said it was fun, but they never pressed to go again because the action was a little rough; both suffered a few bruises and scratches from throwing themselves on the ground.

A real war involves human attackers, human targets, and dangerous ammunition. Games introduce substitutes for at least one of these elements.

Paintball substitutes harmless ammunition for bullets, but keeps the humans. USPSA events keep the bullets, but replace human targets with cardboard and steel silhouettes. Barbara Seamans said that when she competes in USPSA events, she doesn't think about shooting people; she thinks about scoring. Other women described their experiences the same way. In fact, there was really only one competitor I encountered who acknowledged frankly that he expected his practical shooting drills to prepare him for action in an emergency. Robert Hohberg—director for the Blue Mountain Shooter's Club; member of the Northern Westchester Rifle Association; biologist and chemist; specialist in water analysis; water monitoring consultant for the town of Mamaroneck; lector, Eucharistic minister, and acolyte at St. Augustine's Roman Catholic Church in Westchester—took part in the rifle competition at Fulton. His wife, Ruth Merson, was commissioner for the Conservation Advisory Commission in Westchester, a former social worker and teacher, and also an artist. Merson doesn't compete in USPSA events. She and her husband hunt together, and when Hohberg took a break from the action at Fulton, they wandered off to shoot target.

Both Hohberg and Merson had known real war. He was an infantry member in the Korean War. She was Jewish and in western Poland, where she was taken into custody at the age of four as a political prisoner along with the rest of her family and transported to Siberia; for the next seven years, her family would be transported from place to place, from Siberia into Central Asia, to Uzbekistan. She remembers that animals were slaughtered in the open at Uzbekistan, a slippery business that still makes her uneasy around red meat.

Hohberg told me that the USPSA's motto is "Diligencia, Vis, Celeritas," which is Latin, he said, for "accuracy, power, speed." He explained: "What we do is, we practice defensive skills in a sporting atmosphere, so that it becomes a very practical and useful thing in case you ever are in trouble." He believes that skills are acquired in three levels. The highest level is "unconscious skilled." "When you get the unconscious skilled part, that's the part where you can literally rely on your training to save your life. If you've been in the service like I have, the infantry does this all the time. That's the training they give you. Thank God. I *do not* want to be a victim." Hohberg was forthright and comfortable, rather pink-skinned in the heat. He described his own experience as a sporting rifleman acutely: "You are in such control of the instrument that you hear the report, there's a little span of time, and then way out there somewhere, a steel disk falls to the ground. And you're like Zeus; you point and the thunderbolt comes out."

However, I found Merson's presence at the Invitational most interesting and disorienting. She stood under the long pavilion roof just behind the rifle range. She was small-boned and spoke the endings of her words precisely, as people do with a second language, and to protect herself from the sun, she wore a round straw hat with a thin elastic band that passed under her chin. For most of her life she had disliked guns. When her children were little, they were not allowed toy guns, not even water pistols. "Nothing with explosiveness. I think that was because of my feelings about the war I had gone through, having watched someone pick up a grenade and lose their hand, maybe it had something to do with that, maybe again, maybe not. . . . The whole BANG BANG BANG feeling, I'm still uncomfortable with it." On the audiotape as Merson speaks, BANG BANG BANG noises ring out in the background like hammer strikes on aluminum walls.

In her middle-age, six years after her first husband, the father of her children, had died, Ruth Merson met Robert Hohberg, and after a span of time during which they became acquainted, he told her he wanted to show her something. She remembers that they were in his living room, and he brought out a pistol. "And I was absolutely in shock, and I searched myself very rapidly: 'Do I get up and leave or do I get the new impression and find out how I feel about it?'" She stayed. They were married nine years later.

Her opinion of "gun people" had altered substantially since that time. "I thought they were just people who shoot other people by accident in the woods, who drink when they shoot, who use foul language all the time. And I'm finding that, yes, that's part of the population in the world, but that's not what *they* are as a group or as a class." Attending practical shooters competitions: "I have met people here who are artists, attorneys, machinists, dentists, doctors of every kind, from orthopedists to gynecologists." And her husband. "I have known this man for thirteen years, and I have never lost my respect for him."

Merson was licensed as a gun owner. She recalled attending a meeting of Hidden Children—a group of people who survived the Nazi onslaught in hiding when they were young—where members began to discuss what they would do if another holocaust appeared to be looming on the horizon. She announced to the group that "this time I would defend myself, first of all because I am an adult, but attitudinally, I would not volunteer to be herded like it was before." When she mentioned that she had a license to own a gun, people were shocked: "The membership around the room said: 'Ah are you carrying a gun now. Do you have a gun on your person now!?'" She refused to answer the question until she had explained her point of view. "And they all pushed back in their chairs and said: 'AHHH, are we safe here with you?' At the end, I told them no, I was not armed at this time, but it was a very personal question, and it was not relevant to my behavior."

Merson said that she was agitated by the sound of gunshots if she heard them at home. But they didn't worry her in the valley at Fulton. Competition shooting didn't remind her of war. "No, not at all, because the entire atmosphere—if you watch those men walking off the field, you'll see there is a calm about them; there is a settled, emotional serenity that I trust." I remarked that many people would look at that same group of men, one of whom was carrying a well-equipped rifle, and never think of serenity. She spoke of the safety precautions her husband and other competitors followed at all times. She said the shooters that she'd met held themselves to a high standard and were markedly gentle men.

A member of the Cortland County Pistol Club let me stand behind the pressboard barricade and shoot her competition pistol. All I had to do was look through the electronic sight and place the weightless red dot on the target. Pull the trigger. One steel popper hovered, struck, then dropped backward. Holes appeared in the cardboard. I did not see the faces of people in the targets and did not imagine killing rapists. Taking the cowgirl stance was a pleasure. Knocking down the popper was fun. Both my sons love "action" video games.

## What and Where Is a Militia?

### Oklahoma City

On April 19, 1995, a rental truck loaded with chemical fertilizer exploded outside the Alfred P. Murrah Federal Building in Oklahoma City, Oklahoma. The multileveled public building was filled with people, many of whom had entered to take care of transactions involving registration, paperwork, or money. The Ryder truck ignited with force and accuracy.

The news media provided readers with a jumble of perspectives on the devastation. In *Newsweek*, computer-generated charts and maps alternated with photographic long shots and close-ups of rescue dogs, burnt cars, a shirtless man covered with blood sitting on a street curb, the Nichols's white farm house, Timothy McVeigh groomed for a high school yearbook shot, and the smiling Michigan Militia Corps, in camo gear, with rifles, kneeling for a snapshot.[5]

In many reports, the pictured face of Timothy McVeigh (since convicted and sentenced to death), looking scrubbed and carved, was juxtaposed against pictures of children matted with gore and gray insulation material. Editors understood that their readers wanted to imagine the suspect, McVeigh, confronted by the full force of his action, the weight of actual walls his experiment uprooted and the grief of the people mourning the individuals he'd killed. Editors also understood that their readers would want to see the enemy identified quickly, very quickly. Therefore reports about civilian militia organizations appeared. McVeigh had been peripherally associated with various militias, unofficial, grassroots field teams organized by men and women determined to practice what they interpret as their Second Amendment right to "keep and bear Arms" as a defense against potential federal tyranny. In *Newsweek*, the members of the Michigan citizens' militia kneeling with their polished guns in a stubble field look well-padded and jovial.

Almost immediately after McVeigh was arrested as a suspect in the bombing, and information about his politics was broadcast, writers unsympathetic to the nation's "paramilitary gun culture" began analyzing the tragedy, assigning blame and broadcasting warnings. Many of the news reports were careless in their assignment of responsibility for the horror. In a gargantuan, technological nation inhabited by local individuals, it is difficult to know how to map not only the aftereffects of a violent explosion radiating outward, but also, the preparatory effects of instigating forces that once rippled inward, preparing a particular individual to fantasize about and then effect an attack.

Gun rights advocacy groups were quick to respond when they felt themselves maligned by writers who wished to assign them partial responsibility for the horror. They accused their political opponents of opportunism, reasserted the distinction between law-abiding gun owners and terrorists, and often proceeded from that point to reiterate their critiques of the U.S. federal government, critiques which liberals charged were dangerously provocative. David Kopel, an influential pro-gun author, testified before the House Judiciary Committee in November 1995:

> "Government is the great teacher," Justice Brandeis told us. Without the unjustifiable, illegal, militaristic, deadly federal violence at Ruby Ridge and at Waco, there would be no militia movement. The federal government should set a better example. If Ruby Ridge had led to a real investigation and corrective measures—instead of years of cover-up by both the Bush and Clinton administrations—then we would not be in the current situation.
>
> Ruby Ridge and the Waco tragedies were not the fault of a few bad officials, but the inevitable result of a culture of lawlessness, militarization, and violence that has permeated far too much of the federal law enforcement establishment.[6]

Distrust of the federal government is shared by a wide range of Second Amendment advocates, from those on the far right to the near right. Timothy McVeigh was reportedly enraged by the sieges at Randy Weaver's cabin in Ruby Ridge, Idaho, and the Branch Davidian compound in Waco, Texas, both of which concluded in assaults by U.S. federal agents that left civilians dead. The Republican Congress called for another hearing on Waco to be held a few months after the Oklahoma bomb exploded, as if the tragedy and subsequent media reports alerted them to an issue whose force they hadn't fully appreciated. The NRA appears to have been more prescient; it broadcast scathing critiques of the Bureau of Alcohol, Tobacco and Firearms (BATF) approximately one month before the bombing, and it distributed a fund-raising letter by Wayne LaPierre calling federal agents "jack-booted government thugs" who threaten to "break in our doors, seize our guns, destroy our property, and even injure or kill us."[7] Soon after April 19, 1995, Tanya Metaksa angrily denied that the antigovernment rhetoric her organization published was in any way responsible for the terrorist payback. In a public letter dated May 5, 1995, sent to the NRA's Board of Directors and broadcast on the Internet, she began by referring to herself as a grieved, speechless "mother and grandmother of small children," who was shocked, but not surprised, to discover that the liberal press and politicians were trying to pin some of the blame for the Oklahoma bomb on the NRA. She reaffirmed her organization's commitment to legal, political action—not terrorism. Metaksa moved on from there, however, to reassert her own accusations against federal agents by describing two BATF raids into the private homes of gun owners. According to Metaksa:

> This past summer, 15–20 armed men (IRS and BATF agents) burst into the rural Pennsylvania home of Mr. and Mrs. Harry Lamplugh. The family cooperated . . . but cooperation did not cool the intruders' wrath. One held a machine gun in their faces. Another uttered a racial slur. One emptied vial after vial of cancer medicine, crushed it on the bathroom floor, and confiscated cancer treatment records. Another stomped a pet cat to death. The Lamplughs are gun show promoters. BATF's purpose here seems clear: reduce or eliminate lawful commerce in a lawful product through intimidation and brutish intrusion. I maintain it is the right role for NRA to speak forcefully when federal agents rough-up cancer patients. . . .

Metaksa's references to "intruders" and "intrusions" clarify something about the perspective of Second Amendment advocates generally. Living in a nation protected by two oceans where very few citizens have experienced the horror of a real military invasion since the 1860s, many Americans in the 1990s nevertheless seemed haunted by the sense that they had been invaded or were being threatened by invasion, especially invasion of their homes and property. To escape the invaders and bureaucrats, they dreamed of living in a freer place where they could do what they wanted. In this process, physical freedom and civic freedom collapsed to become a single concept: American independence. In his testimony before the House Judiciary Committee, David Kopel quoted from an article that described this attitude:

> [U]nderlying the gun control struggle is a fundamental division in our nation. The intensity of passion on this issue suggests to me that we are experiencing a sort of low-grade war going on between two alternative views of what America is and ought to be. On the one side are those who take bourgeois Europe as a model of a civilized society: a society just, equitable, and democratic; but well ordered, with the lines of authority clearly drawn, and with decisions made rationally and correctly by intelligent men for the entire nation. To such people, hunting is atavistic, personal violence is shameful, and uncontrolled gun ownership is a blot upon civilization.
>
> On the other side is a group of people who do not tend to be especially articulate or literate, and whose world view is rarely expressed in print. Their model is that of the independent frontiersman who takes care of himself and his family with no interference from the state. They are "conservative" in the sense that they cling to America's unique pre-modern tradition—a non-feudal society with a sort of medieval liberty at large for everyman. To these people, "sociological" is an epithet. Life is tough and competitive. Manhood means responsibility and caring for your own.[8]

It is interesting to note that even as Kopel read this quote, it was already outdated for, in fact, the "conservatives" described were no longer so romantically hobbled by backwoods illiteracy and poor communication skills. Increasingly, far-right, pro-independence, pro-"sovereignty" conservatives were expressing themselves in print, communicating with friends and potential allies via the Internet, and testing their political clout. And many liberal citizens feared them.

Following the destruction of the Oklahoma federal building, liberals argued that the "antigovernment" movement was truly dangerous. They found their most compelling evidence in western states like Idaho, Montana, Nevada, Oregon, and Washington, where antigovernment activists, many of them associated with citizens' militias and property rights groups (e.g., Wise Use, the Counties Movement) had threatened judges and government employees attempting to police national parklands, uphold environmental laws, or even collect income taxes. Martha A. Bethel, a city judge in Montana, testified in 1995, in Washington, DC, that she had been terrorized by a citizens' group that called itself the "Freemen" after she ruled in cases involving a few of their members. The members told her she held no jurisdiction over them and threatened to attack her house, kidnap her and try her in a "common law" court for her "treasonous" actions. Ellen Gray, an organizer for the Pilchuck Audubon Society in Everett, Washington, was accosted by members of the Snohomish County Property Rights Alliance after she testified in favor of an ordinance to protect streams and wetlands. The leader of the alliance threatened her with a noose. A short time later, she was stopped by another man who told her: "We have a militia of 10,000, and if we can't beat you at the ballot box, we'll beat you with a bullet." In Nevada, a county commissioner, backed by his armed posse, faced down two Forest Service rangers who attempted to stop him from bulldozing an illegal road through the Toiyabe National Forest. "All it would have taken was for [a ranger] to draw a weapon, and fifty people with sidearms would have drilled him," said the proud County Commissioner Dick Carver.[9]

Equipped with stories of this kind, leftist critics characterized right-wing militia members as violent gangs and incipient Nazi thugs. They also portrayed them as low-class and stupid. Adam Gopnik, writing in the *New Yorker*, implicated media stars of the Left and Right as gamesters who unwittingly legitimized violence by treating it as an expressive, dramatic form of speech, but he reserved most of his sarcasm for the Right's favorite public speakers and their audience:

> The point, of course, isn't that Limbaugh or Pat Robertson or G. Gordon Liddy caused the killing. It is that they seemed never to have given a moment's thought, as they addressed their audiences, to the consequences of stuffing so much flammable resentment into such tiny bottles.

He added that the Left always "liked the thrill of seeing its musty intellectual beliefs acted out as dashing cultural theater," but the bombs that Leftists concocted were generally less efficient, proving "the difference between the kids who paid attention in social studies and the ones who paid attention in shop."[10]

Writing for the *Nation* in 1995, Marc Cooper described militiamen sympathetically as frustrated, dispossessed workers whose jobs in the Montana timber towns, the Arizona mining towns, the Michigan mill towns, and the California aerospace towns had dried up over the last decades. But he also said: "One hesitates to use the words Brain Center when describing a movement that is fueled much more by visceral fear and ignorance than by rational ideology. . . ." His reaction was understandable; he had just finished interviewing Randy Trochmann, cofounder of the Militia of Montana (M.O.M.), who told him that if Timothy McVeigh did prove to be guilty of planting the bomb, then reporters would have to "look seriously at his claim that the government experimented on him, that they put a microchip in him or something like that."[11]

Confronted by an arch-conservative portrait of the world teeming with evil foreign faces, federal agents who stomped pet cats to death, and parasitic microchips, liberal writers found it virtually impossible to resist irony.

Ironic critiques of paranoid conservatives invariably assert the writer's own superiority and blur recognition of the nightmares that leftist anti-Establishment and rightist anti-BATF critics share in common—the Orwellian nightmare featuring omnipotent, omnipresent Government.

### *"The People I Know Are Average People"*

When I spoke to her, Sherry* was a member of the Chemung County Militia in central New York. On the evening we talked, she wore an American Heart Association t-shirt—she worked as a laboratory technician—and glasses with transparent frames. On her feet were new, thick-soled, fawn-colored hiking boots; she was an experienced Adirondacks backpacker, and said she thought of herself as more a "survivalist" than a gun lover. Her hair was close-cropped and turned auburn red as the sun went down behind the porch. She would have looked at home in an adult's scouting uniform, with a kerchief tied around her neck, except for the fact that she liked to sit with a lit cigarette. At one point, she named a few American habits that used to be considered "normal" but were now, in the 1990s, considered "fanatical." "People who smoked used to be considered normal. People who had guns used to be considered normal. People who went to church used to be considered normal." Her father was a World War II veteran, and a hunter, and part Indian. "He grows this wonderful garden, and he hunts and he fishes and basically takes care of himself." After the war, he brought back a collection of guns from Germany. "He had a machine gun and all these beautiful German hunting rifles with silver inlay." In her experience guns were normal. "A gun was a natural part of things. My dad wasn't a violent person; [he] never went out and shot up the neighborhood. To me, my dad was a normal person and having a gun was part of what a normal person had." Her mother also hunted.

Sherry and her husband, Bob*, met me at the house of their friend, Sue*, because Bob was going to help her fix a problem she was having with her above-ground pool. Sue and Bob also belonged to the Chemung County Militia, which was founded by a man named Jerry Loper in late 1994. Sue worked as a rural mail carrier and owned a small house in a tightly packed country subdivision; the unique situation of the house gave her a long, misted backyard. At one point, Bob had to climb into the pool. It was not a warm evening. We heard the splash and an exclamation from where we were sitting on the front porch, alongside a trellis, beside the old painted coffee table that held an ashtray for Sherry and a Diet Pepsi for me.

As she spoke, the physical integrity of Sherry's face and life asserted them-

---

*Last names omitted for privacy.

selves. She was the mother of a teenage daughter who advocated for anarchy: "She says anarchy rocks." Sherry described trying to explain to her daughter that government is necessary for some things, for example, maintaining and repairing roads, contracting trade agreements with other nations, defending borders. At the same time, she made it clear that she didn't think the current U.S. government was doing a very good job. She believed anarchy and "aberrations" were increasing in the United States largely because government, of many sorts, was not functioning properly. This meant that this rebellious daughter couldn't enjoy the same physical freedoms Sherry herself had enjoyed when she was young—freedoms like riding a bicycle fifteen miles to Corning, New York, on a lark, when "the only thing Mother worried about was if we would get hit by a car. She didn't worry about child molesters and she didn't worry about kidnappers." Sherry concluded: "It seems as if the more the government has tried to regulate people's lives, the more out of control everything has become."

Sue had joined us briefly. Sherry and Sue began to speak about bicycle helmets and the law requiring all bicycling children under fifteen to wear protective helmets. Both felt that this kind of law trespassed on their rights as parents to make judgments for themselves and for their own children. "They're not the government's children, they're our children and God's children. They don't belong to the federal government or the state government." In the same context, Sherry referred to a law that was intended to allow "a mature teenager to be able to leave home if there was an abusive situation," because it made parents legally and financially responsible for minors of a certain age who chose to live on their own. She was made aware of the law when her older daughter, then sixteen years old, pressed to move out of the house. "She had a car, she had a job, she went to school, she got good grades, life was fine," but, "she didn't feel she had enough freedom and she wanted more privileges." Sherry spoke with a few people who worked in Social Services who didn't care for the legislation either. But there it was. "The end result of that law was that any teenager could leave any home situation if they didn't like what time their curfew was set at." The way Sherry saw it, too often the government's laws "fail to recognize the sanctity of the family unit. There is a higher law, and that is the law of God and the law that comes within a family. In my mind, a lot of the problems we have with young people these days are because that sanctity has been violated."

When speaking about their children, notably Sherry's daughters, these women swung back and forth, sometimes expressing concern that their kids would grow up in a restrictive, conformists' world—"I could see my children aren't going to live as free a life as I lived. They're going to be under control, they're going to be little puppets walking around," said Sue—while at other times asserting their parental rights to exert more control over these same kids. The message was contradictory, but it made sense if one accepted the premise that old-fashioned methods of child-rearing are best; in an ideal rural setting, children roam freely in the physical woods, but they are prevented from crossing certain ethical or sexual boundaries by strict parental discipline and moral training.

Sherry and Sue spoke about the North American Free Trade Agreement (NAFTA): they didn't like it. They spoke about Newt Gingrich: you have to keep your eye on him. Sherry said she would support Bob Barr, Republican from Georgia, and Helen Chenoweth, a Republican congresswoman from Idaho famous at the time for defending the authority of her state's county sheriffs over the authority of federal agents, as presidential and vice-presidential candidates, respectively. I said that I found it difficult to follow the links between these wide-ranging issues—bicycle helmets, NAFTA, guns. Sue immediately responded: "The guns are the main issue. If they take away our rights to keep and bear arms, then we lose all the other rights in the Bill of Rights." Sherry agreed. "The Second Amendment is the backbone of all the amendments that guard civil liberties."

> If the government becomes repressive to the point where people can't tolerate it anymore, constitutionally we have the right to overthrow a government that has ceased to operate under the Constitution. Nobody's planning on overthrowing the government, so let me clarify that. Let's say the voting process stops because something happens in this country where martial law is declared. Castro came into Cuba and the first thing he said was, "Give us your guns, we're here to take care of you." Stalin: "Give us your guns, we're going to take care of you." Hitler: "Give us your guns, you don't need them anymore, we'll take care of you." When a government tries to disarm its citizens, that implies a distrust of those citizens. A government that wants to disarm people like me, like you, like Sue, like Bob, is a government that's suspect.

We started to talk about Sherry's militia group. Sue had left us to go see about the swimming pool. The sun was sinking. The Chemung unit of the Chemung County Militia typically scheduled a public meeting once a month. Sherry's commander held other meetings on Saturdays and Sundays at his house. The Sunday group usually consisted of ten people or less—sometimes just five or six—but Sherry said that there were many units in her militia. It wasn't easy to keep track of them because they weren't regimented, and since the Oklahoma bombing, membership in the Chemung County militia had risen from 250 to 1,000. She added that her sources estimated national membership in citizens' militias at 4 or 5 million (most newspapers and magazines topped their estimates at 100,000), and she asserted that the Oklahoma bombing and subsequent publicity had sparked an increase in militia membership across the country.

On Sundays, Sherry's unit usually gathered to talk, she said. "Ninety percent of the time what we do is talk. We talk politics. And we have people who just gather information constantly from all over the country, and we sit down and try to read through these things and talk about them, assess the situation, see what we feel like's going on. See if we need to write some letters, if we need to make some phone calls to elected representatives, whatever. . . . It's 'here, I got this on the fax machine,' or 'here, I downloaded this from the computer.'" Members dressed in everyday clothes. They wore hiking boots and brought their guns only if they were headed outdoors into the target field. Some members didn't shoot target at all. They just talked. Nobody in Sherry's unit went through military drills. A few might wear camo gear, though the popularity of that outfit has diminished since the Oklahoma bombing. "The kind of training we do is survival-type training. Learning to read a compass. Learning to use a map to orient yourself to an area."

Sherry had never been made frightened or uneasy by any of her fellow militia members. "People are screened." She echoed the assertion I had heard from so many other gun rights advocates, that the government spent too much effort restricting the good guys and not enough effort going after the criminals. "I obey the law. I don't rob anybody. I don't kill anybody. I'm not the one who's the problem. . . . They're after the guns; they're not after the criminals; they're after the guns." She dismissed the public perception that books and tapes disseminated by active militias in Montana and Michigan stirred up hatred in the United States and were potentially dangerous. "I never saw so much hate talk in my life as I saw after Oklahoma City, and I heard most of it from the Artful Dodger himself: Bill Clinton."

She described how her own perceptions of the Waco siege altered after she "started getting downloads, started seeing information on the [Internet] bulletin boards and even the general news." At first, she and her husband thought David Koresh's band of religious zealots were crazies; on the news, Waco looked like another Jonestown. But then:

> We stopped and we started really thinking about it, and we said: "What are these people really doing? Are they really doing anything other than defying the federal government, saying: "We're going to live the way we want to live?"

Sherry would not dismiss stories she'd heard that survivors of Waco claimed federal law enforcement agents were "grabbing people who were trying to escape out of the back of that compound, shooting them, and dragging them back inside. It seems to be pretty uniform, what they have to say. And maybe they're crazy, but maybe they're not." As for Timothy McVeigh, she pointed out that he was stationed at Fort Riley and "they've had a couple people go berserk out there." So the question should be "not what is going on with the militias. What's going on at Fort Riley?" She believes the federal government did plan to raid the flagship Montana militia at the end of March, but intervention by sympathetic politicians prompted them to cancel it. Rumor of this proposed action circulated on the Internet. The government reportedly intended to uncover evidence through the raid that would then allow it to pass a law banning militias. Sherry had a friend in Florida who e-mailed her a message in late March warning her that the government might well be planning "to do something very senseless and extremely violent" on April 18 or 19, since the nineteenth was the anniversary of the battles at Lexington and Concord, of the Warsaw ghetto's burning, of Waco, and of the gunfight between Randy Weaver's family and federal agents at Ruby Ridge. Sherry did not claim that the federal government bombed the Alfred P. Murrah federal building, but she thought federal agents knew more than they were revealing: "There's a lot of speculation that there were some foreign nationals involved."

When I told her that I thought many people hoped the Oklahoma bombing would dissuade people from joining militias because it demonstrated what happened when gun talk escalated, gun games turned real, and local people died as a consequence, Sherry replied that she didn't think many militia members entertained illusions about war and guns. "The majority of people who are in the militias are men. A lot of them are veterans. I think a lot of them are veterans of Vietnam. We have a couple of World War II's. Korean veterans. These people already saw what war is about, up close and personal." And she insisted that her fellow members were *not* part of the lunatic fringe. McVeigh was lunatic fringe. Not Sherry and Bob and Sue:

> The people I know are average people. They're like me. They go to work every day, they own houses, they support their families, they have a pool in the backyard or whatever. You know, Sue's a member of a militia. There's the house. There's the pool. There's the truck and Jeep and the dog and the cat and the kids and the whole works. These aren't crazy people. These aren't people who are bombs waiting to go off. These are people who feel that the government is pushing so hard that they don't want to be pushed anymore. So they're saying: "Look, this is the line; this is the Constitution; live by it. We intend to."
>
> It doesn't mean we're going to pick up our guns and go shoot people if

they vote in laws we don't like. That's not what it's about. But it does mean that if the government insists on passing laws that make us criminals, if the state of New York passes a law that says if I'm in possession of a semi-automatic weapon that is capable of holding a magazine with more than ten rounds, then I'm a Class D felon, then they, with a legislative swipe, have made me a criminal, made me a felon. Well, the day before they signed it into law, I'm not a felon; I'm a law-abiding citizen. The day after they sign it, I'm a felon, and I can go to jail for ten years. Who's right and who's wrong? I say when you push people who obey the law, people who are the backbone of this country . . . like *It's a Wonderful Life*; did you ever watch that movie? The people who do the living and dying, the people who go to work every day and pay their taxes and mow their lawns and buy the cars and buy the refrigerators and buy the school clothes for the kids and keep the economy going and keep money in the hands of the government so they can do all the wasteful things they like to do with it, when you start pushing those people into a position where there's nothing left to do but be defensive, then the government has gone too far; the government's become too intrusive. All we want to do is live. We don't want to do anything except go to work and get our paycheck, get a swimming pool, go on vacation, have birthday parties, take the kids to Darien Lake, do all this stuff we've always done.

The porch was darker by this time, and occasional electric lights shone in the neighborhood. It was not yet the season for crickets, but we could hear the sound of cars swiping at great speed down the nearby two-lane highway and see dark summer hills. Bob had changed out of his wet clothes, and I was offered coffee from the lit kitchen by Sue. I declined, Sherry got more cigarettes, then we were left alone on the porch again. We had been speaking for more than an hour by this time. I had tried to explain my doubts about her vision. My skepticism didn't surprise her and, of course, I expressed many of my own doubts obliquely by attributing them to "some people," as in "some people think. . . ." I said that her vision of militia members as plain, everyday people didn't seem to fit with all the talk of international conspiracy theories. Prompted, she shifted from speaking about birthday parties and swimming pools to Bosnia and the United Nations; did I know there were United Nations documents that proposed global disarmament? Then, easily, she mentioned Armageddon. "There are a lot of Armageddon theories out there. I know you've heard that too. If you're a Christian and you believe what Revelations says, you believe there will be an Armageddon and a one-world government will be part of that."

Sherry did not attend church often, but she had read books about Revelations and noted evidence from her local school, from Florida, and from Sweden, that proved sinister forces were massing to identify individuals by number and allow only those individuals who would have been properly numbered to participate in the life of the state. At her local school, students were issued ID cards and prevented from buying lunch unless they had their cards. She'd heard the Clinton administration was proposing a national ID. Someday people were going to be implanted with ID's. She asked me if I knew what an "implantable transponder" was and then explained:

> It's a little electronic device, about the size of a grain of rice, that you can put under someone's skin so that you can find them if you want them. They're unique identifiers. Well, in Florida, as an experiment, they're using implantable transponders and implanting them in these children who are at risk of parental abduction. . . . At the same time in, I believe in Sweden, they're doing it to people as a sort of credit card, identification system, and you run your hand under this scanner in the grocery store, and it can pick up your ID, and then it just debits your account for your groceries and stuff. In the context of the Christian religion, that's a pretty alarming thought."

I said it sounded like an Orwell novel, but why would implantable transponders be anti-Christian? She answered that "this is considered by some to be the mark of the beast. This little thing, that without it you will not be able to buy groceries and you will not be able to acquire housing and you will not be able to go to work. Without it, you're going to be denied access to everything that society as we know it has to offer."

I noticed that Sherry was probably using my own method: attributing her opinions to "some people." Pressed to explain her own convictions, she said she did believe that Armageddon "is going to happen," though she doesn't know when, and she felt that there was "a lot of darkness in this society." Asked about the source of the darkness, she spoke of controlled chaos.

Controlled chaos theory says: "The government will create situations that will then require the government to step in and provide solutions to the problems." (This is not a nonsensical theory; Suharto's New Order government in Indonesia frequently made it a practice first to provoke riots and then "restore" order in Jakarta.) The national increase in violence was "due to a failure in the legal justice system that's planned," said Sherry. Crime makes big money for lawyers. "Lawyers grow up to be politicians." No one was proud to be an American anymore. "I think we're editing out a lot of pride in being an American." Getting away from nationalism, getting into globalism, and "the increase in aberrations of behavior is due to the snowball effect of inevitable doom." Rapists, criminals, "these are all signs of the tribulation. The decay of the family was preceded by laws meant to protect children, but those laws led to the loss of authority in the parents and to the loss of morals."

According to Sherry, at the time of the Second Coming of Christ, He would immediately save all those men and women who lived totally righteous lives. These saints would disappear off the face of the earth, but everyone else—the majority of humankind—would remain and continue going about their business. Those left on earth would be given a choice: either to take on the "mark of the beast" and accept their implantable transponders in order to be able to "work and eat and live," or to refuse the mark of the beast and "somehow find a way to survive, in spite of not having a job and not being able to buy a house and not being able to go to the grocery store."

"That you will be self-sufficient enough to survive in order to have a chance to become a righteous enough person."

We didn't talk much longer. I said it didn't seem to me the New Testament was much concerned with self-sufficiency, and I couldn't understand how a Christian would equate survivalism and physical independence with righteousness. She tried to explain; I didn't understand her explanation, though later I would think variously of the poor widow and her mite, Christ's revolutionary Beatitudes, Jonathan Edwards's Puritanism, Thoreau, and Gary Cooper. Certainly, I'd heard in her talk the old American message that virtue must be achieved in a difficult, lonesome encounter with the wilderness, and that the plain people are the backbone of the nation. Sherry's vision was distinctly American in its changing focus on local detail, purification through ordeal, firearms, and God. It borrowed something from the two Coopers (James Fenimore and Gary) as well as from *Invasion of the Body Snatchers*, Orwell's *1984* and Huxley's *Brave New World*, John Birch Society dogma, and the upsurge in alien abduction tales.

Sherry dreamed of walking an actual, recognizable road that took her from the edge of the porch to glory. And she had the map; she had inherited a map showing swimming pools and driveways to be located at a measurable distance from hellish beasts and heavenly sanctuaries. Guided by the map, her imagination moved effortlessly between local actualities, governmental conspiracies, and the clouds; our Puritan forebears were adepts at this same extraordinary allegorical vaulting exercise. If one asked her why she and her friends didn't jettison their houses, cars, dogs, and computers *immediately* and advance into the solitary woods to prove their Christian dedication, she would say it wasn't time yet. Her unwillingness to acknowledge the inconsistencies in her rigid theories and her refusal to perceive the dangers involved in building a self-appointed force of dissatisfied armed citizens were irresponsible, in my opinion. But I found her desire to get hold of a map of the world understandable, especially given the fact that she had two teenage daughters who apparently shared their mother's characteristic American love of rebellion. Saying this, I don't mean to imply that Sherry's commitment to her cause is frivolous or feminine, for it may ultimately be rooted in a desire to establish firm control over her own family's life, safety, and habits. Family is serious and not "just feminine." The twentieth-century morality tale that warns us Big Brother will initiate his depersonalization program by separating mother from child and husband from wife and then outfitting kids in uniforms and training them to denounce their own parents has been adapted by storytellers of the far left and far right. In the twentieth century, it has not always been a fiction.

In August of 1995, just a few months after I spoke with Sherry and Sue, their militia mobilized to protect the property rights of a man named James Dacey, who had been ordered to vacate and remove the trailer in which he was living off his own 5.5 acre plot in order to comply with a local ordinance. Dacey resided hours away from Chemung, in the town of Perry, in Wyoming County, east of Buffalo, New York, but after the Supreme Court ruled against him, he began contacting local and national militia groups for help. Word of his predicament reached Jerry Loper, founder of the Chemung militia, and he traveled to the property followed by a few other members and a straggling tail of journalists. Dacey also attracted the attention of Norman Olson, leader of the Michigan Militia Corps, who subsequently arrived at the site. A large close-up photograph of Olson, in heavy camouflage gear, with his name COMMANDER OLSON stitched in black above the front pocket, appeared in *Newsweek* after the Oklahoma bombing because the suspects were known to have attended meetings of the Michigan Militia. Interviewed by journalists at Perry, Olson said: "I'm afraid there could be a confrontation" and suggested that conflicts of this kind might trigger the civil war that he believes will occur.

Jerry Loper did not agree with Commander Olson that this action could trigger a civil war. "I can't foresee anything like that. It would be wrong if Jim gets hurt or if he hurts someone else in the process."

No one was hurt. By late August, weeks past the August 9 deadline designated by the New York Supreme Court, the story had faded.

I spoke with J. Michael Mucci, captain of the Criminal Division of the Chemung County Sheriff's Department, in mid-August. The Chemung County Militia founded by Jerry Loper and joined by Sherry and Sue meets inside his jurisdiction. Captain Mucci did not sound alarmed. He said that when he heard the militia was forming, he acted to get in touch with the leader. No deputies attended the militia meetings, because they didn't want the members to think they were trying to infiltrate. But they had initiated communication before Oklahoma and maintained communications after. In the captain's opinion, it's unfair to smear all militia members with guilt for the Oklahoma bombing. "It's like one bad cop shouldn't affect the reputation of all police officers." He remained "cautiously optimistic that the militia will remain very organized and cooperative and very civil." It was clear that Mucci has dealt with other residents of Chemung County whom he considered more threatening than Jerry Loper and his followers. Asked if stories of the Internet-ready militia movement filled him with dread, he replied: "No, not this one locally, and that's my concern." He trusted that he got straight talk from the self-appointed commanders of the Chemung County militia. "When we ask them a question and we get an answer, I feel comfortable that it's right on line." His judgment was based on experience—he'd never caught the group in a lie.

I phoned Allen Capwell, sheriff of Wyoming County, in late August to find out what had happened with James Dacey and his property dispute. Like Captain Mucci, he proved to be a practical man of few words. Asked what had happened with the James Dacey situation, he said, "Nothing." Did Dacey move? "No." What was happening now? "The deadline gave him thirty days to move it, and he has not done that, so now there's a civil penalty being assessed at fifty dollars a day, and at this point the clock's ticking; each day is another fifty bucks." Has Norman Olson left? "I have no idea." Would he be willing to say what he thought of Olson's appearance on the scene? "No." Would he be willing to say what he thought of the involvement of the out-of-town militias? "Well, it has no bearing as far as I'm concerned." Sheriff Capwell explained that a sheriff is a constitutional law enforcement officer. To fulfill his constitutional duties, he does what the court tells him, and in this case, the court hadn't told him to do anything. "They're having a party up there." Did he see guns in evidence? I asked. He didn't even go up there, he said. No one from his office went up there. He left James Dacey and his guests alone. "They're not doing anything wrong that I'm aware of." So the only people who went up to the Dacey mobile home were journalists? "Oh, there were plenty of them," said the sheriff.

## We the People . . . and Others

Local faces, local games: Annette Rupe, daughter-in-law of Joan Rupe, the woman who first told me about practical shooting competitions, kindly brought her USPSA booklets to the Ithaca Paper Cutter, where she worked as manager, and left them in an envelope for me to pick up. National games, national legislation: Republicans and Democrats both press for legislation to fit their general pictures of the country's citizenry.

It is tempting to assume that plain local faces are always more real than these general, ideological, and statistical portraits of *the people* concocted to justify national legislation, but this assumption runs into two problems. First, history proves that bad national legislation is *real*, since when it fails, certain groups of people become vulnerable to injustices. What's more, individuals —*locals*—participate in national networks of fantasy and argument and have both their voices and their perceptions markedly altered by shared rhetoric. Virtually nobody's purely local anymore.

It is possible for a civil, generous person to adopt uncivil, ungenerous political theories which eventually do harm in places that the individual can't reach or even imagine. The twentieth century has proven this dilemma repeatedly. Ideologues of both the right and the left have been implicated in the mess; it would be difficult to calculate whether Hitler on the right or Mao, Stalin, and Pol Pot on the left erased more human lives. There seem to be certain obvious characteristics that join killers from both ends of the political spectrum. First, they establish strict party boundary lines to separate the politically "good citizen" from the bad, and they are merciless in condemning those who've been identified as bad or ideologically "incorrect." Second, they have no love for local faces. They effortlessly forget the people's faces. And third, they are masters of manipulating national fantasies. The patriotic tales that they maneuver to incite proper action are really streamlined tools, powered by self-righteous intolerance, camouflaged under snapshots of humble national heroes. A democracy can't afford these deadly simplifications.

The most radical pro-gun advocates in the United States have mixed together a doctrine that feels secure to them because it very clearly identifies the un-American enemy. New World Order theories circulating through the movement predict that U.S. citizens will awaken one morning to discover that the country has been roped and harnessed by an evil, international cabal. Given an American penchant for paradoxical doctrines that promise both idealized rebellion and idealized homogeneity (we will live free as the Indian once the Indian has been exterminated), it is not surprising that even a quick analysis of this most radical conservative dogma shows it to be perforated with contradiction. For instance, committed militia members often speak of their loyalty to an American heritage predicated on physical self-reliance and rural fortitude, yet in their literature references to reloading and downloading share equal time. It is a dizzying exercise to try and understand how such a contradictory message (go, reclaim frontier virtue, then report back via modem . . . ) can function as a postulate for a doctrine that believers obviously find so consistent.

The good hero of the new American Christian/survivalist myth struggles toward Jesus with a canteen of fresh water in one hand and a semi-automatic in the other. Now, the basic outline of this virtuous, lonesome, armed Daniel climbing to the mountain peak is nothing new. He has been with us since the end of the eighteenth century and deserves our attention whenever he reappears, because the longevity of his heroic image proves that he has penetrated deeply into our collective imagination. He is patron, *pater*, father, explorer, revolutionary, Founding Father. Players who pick up rifles like baseball bats and adopt his fighting stance trust that they keep his spirit alive in the United States.

In some ways they do. The spirit of this country has always been martial, rebellious, contestatory, and physical. But in other ways they do not, because the Founding Fathers were actual people, not poster boys, and they lived as we do, in the midst of contradictions and perplexities. They fought in a revolutionary war whose conclusion could not be foretold at the time; if they had lost the contest, they would figure in history books now as malcontent rabble rousers, rather than as national heroes. What's more, their eighteenth-century attitudes toward guns, fighting, and women were the attitudes of the time, more forthrightly masculine than many liberals prefer to remember and more genteel and exclusive than many conservatives like to admit. The actual Founding Fathers were not uniformly rebellious explorers but, in fact, spent much of their lives as wigged, studious, landowning, slaveowning men who had little sympathy for localized rebellions and no interest in granting rabble—here one must include women—the right to participate as full members of the state. George Washington's forceful suppression of the Whiskey Rebellion of 1794, a citizens' armed protest against a federal excise tax on homemade whiskey, tells us something about the Founding Fathers' attitudes toward duty and liberty, civic responsibilities and civic rights, which in their minds were always linked. After crushing the Pennsylvania rebellion with a force of 15,000 armed militiamen mustered by the federal government, Washington addressed Congress and spoke against all "self-created societies" that prompted small groups of citizens to resist the authority of the federal government. He repeated the sentiment in his farewell address:

> This Government, the offspring of your own choice uninfluenced and unawed . . . has a just claim to your confidence and your support. Respect for its authority, compliance with its laws, acquiescence in its measures, are duties enjoined by the fundamental maxims of true liberty. . . . Towards the preservation of your Government . . . it is requisite, not only that you steadily discountenance irregular oppositions to its acknowledged authority, but also that you resist with care the spirit of innovation upon its principles however specious the pretexts. (George Washington, Farewell Address, 1796)

In this speech, Washington made firm distinctions between America's justified revolution against Britain and recent "irregular" oppositions, between true Soldiers of Liberty and malcontent troublemakers. The fact that he would need to spell out this distinction points up a difficulty that any nation born from rebellion must encounter: how to establish the authority of a government conceived through resistance to authority. The Founding Fathers accomplished this task in many ways, through philosophy, by force, and also by limiting the electorate of the new nation. The majority of people living in the United States today would not have been considered People by the authors of our Constitution, for to them "We the People" meant propertied men—essentially propertied white men.

The situation of certain American minorities and American women as inheritors of traditions and laws composed by men who plainly did not perceive slaves, Indians, or women as citizens and who thought of *effeminacy* as a threat to the state is uncomfortable, but it is also illuminating. It highlights the slippery relationship of any citizen to aging traditions and laws that demand to be interpreted in contradictory ways: interpreted according to the author's intent and audience's understanding at the moment when they were composed, and also interpreted by what they continue to say as human or legal declarations surviving through time. The critical tensions resulting from contradictions between a text's original meanings and its accumulated interpretations challenge legal scholars and everyday readers; religious men and women whose faiths are text-based encounter similar dilemmas. The Declaration of Independence and the Constitution of the United States have acquired through time a golden, religious familiarity. Many citizens feel that they still speak to us and for us. However, to judge our heritage accurately, we should stay aware that the genteel men who composed these documents would have been shocked and dismayed by the sight of many of us, combative feminists and belligerently t-shirted guys ("God, Guns and Guts Made This Country Great!") included.

Today we declare that all men are created equal and breathe a postscript: and everybody else, too. But few of us *fully* believe this maxim, because democratic sentiments tend to conflict with personal judgments. The impulse to full democracy is always opposed by persistent reliance on ideological allegiances that split the nation into teams, and also on hierarchies —economic, educational, gender-based, or racial hierarchies—that enable individuals to feel themselves quietly superior to some other group or class. The designated rabble will always be with us.

One must visit this nation's cities to find the populations of people implicitly used to represent the "outlaws," the "bad guys," "the criminals" in contemporary American political dialogues. They can be generally identified by their poverty, and even more easily by their race.

# Notes

1. James William Gibson, *Warrior Dreams: Violence and Manhood in Post-Vietnam America* (New York: Farrar, Straus & Giroux, 1994), p. 187 and throughout.

2. The Colorado pro-concealed-carry organization, SWARM (Safety for Women and Responsible Motherhood) lists Colonel and Mrs. Jeff Cooper as advisors.

3. David Grossman and P. Siddle, "Combat," in *The Encyclopedia of Violence, Peace, and Conflict*, ed. Lester R. Kurtz and Jennifer E. Turpin (San Diego: Academic Press, 1999).

4. Lyn Bates, "AWARE Action: Two Stages Too Many?" *Women & Guns* (August 1995), pp. 26–28.

5. See "This Doesn't Happen Here," "The View from the Far Right," and "Get Me Out of Here!" *Newsweek* (May 1, 1995), pp. 22–47.

6. See testimony of David Kopel in U.S. House, *The Nature and Threat of Violent Anti-Government Groups in America: Hearing Before the Subcommittee on Crime of the Committee on the Judiciary,* 104th Cong., 1st sess., November 2, 1995. Washington, DC: U.S. Government Printing Office. To read the testimony of militia members, including John Trochmann (the Militia of Montana) and Norman Olson, see U.S. Senate, *The Militia Movement in the United States: Hearing Before the Subcommittee on Terrorism, Technology, and Government Information of the Committee on the Judiciary,* 104th Cong., 1st sess. June 15, 1995. Washington, DC: U.S. Government Printing Office.

7. The full text of the NRA fund-raising letter was read into the *Congressional Record* by Democratic Senator Christopher Dodd, Connecticut, and is in the public domain. See "Letter from the NRA," *Congressional Record,* 104th Cong., 1st sess., 1995, vol. 141, no. 69.

8. Again, see testimony of David Kopel in U.S. House hearing, November 2, 1995 [see note 6].

9. For the story of Martha Bethel, see the *Washington Post*, July 12, 1995. For stories of Ellen Gray and the Nevada county commissioner, see David Helvarg, "Property Rights and Militias: The Anti-Enviro Connection," the *Nation* (May 22, 1995), pp. 722–24.

10. Adam Gopnik, "Violence as Style," *New Yorker* (May 8, 1995), pp. 7, 8.

11. Marc Cooper, "A Visit with MOM: Montana's Mother of All Militias," the *Nation* (May 22, 1995), p. 714.

# 7

---

# In the Cities, on the Edge

In the national gun debates of the 1990s, the figure of the not-law-abiding citizen, the not-responsible gun owner, has been called on to play a significant role. Often this discourse is racially charged, influenced by unspoken assumptions about the general appearance and identity of the typical criminal. This happens because our country is still bedeviled with racism, but also because young black males in the United States shoot guns, are shot by guns, and are incarcerated for crimes in disproportionate numbers. A study published by the Bureau of Justice Statistics (BJS) found that "blacks were six times more likely than whites to be murdered in 1998," and "blacks were seven times more likely than whites to commit homicide in 1998" (in 1995, the homicide victimization rates for black males aged 18–24 was 148.8 per 100,000, compared to 17.3 per 100,000 for white males of the same age). Other studies by the BJS found that "Dramatic increases in both homicide victimization and offending rates were experienced by young males, particularly young black males, in the late 1980s and early 1990s," although "During the past few years [prior to 1998], homicide victimization rates have dropped for all groups," and "Homicides are most often committed with guns, especially handguns."[1] The BJS also noted that the overwhelming majority of these homicides were intraracial—black on black, or white on white—crimes (94 percent of black homicide victims were killed by blacks), a statistic that challenges us to remember that the homicide perpetrators and victims who generated these numbers were, and are, *local* people.

Deborah Prothrow-Stith, former Massachusetts commissioner of public health, who would become assistant dean of the Harvard School of Public Health, herself an African-American physician, wife, and mother, computed the white and black, male and female "lifetime risk" for homicide in the United States, using figures compiled by the Centers for Disease Control, and concluded that if the risk a white female incurs is set at 1, then the risk for white males would measure 2.4 (more than twice as likely to be murdered), black females 4.2 (more than four times as likely to be murdered), and black males 18.4.[2] According to Dr. Prothrow-Stith, individuals at highest risk to die as homicide victims in the United States are "young males growing up in severely impoverished 'inner city' neighborhoods" and "young men of color," meaning African-Americans and Hispanic-Americans. She described the dilemmas of fatherless young men looking for stable male role models, and the "free-floating anger" of these same young men when they discover that they live "so far outside the economic and social mainstream that they can never find a place inside."[3] And she describes the psychological toll exacted from children who live shadowed by threat and uncertainty. She knows a Chicago physician, director of Chicago's Community Mental Health Council, whose surveys of children attending schools in a high crime section of Chicago's South Side revealed that:

> By the age of eleven, four out of five of the children in the survey had seen someone beaten up either at home or in the street. One out of three had seen a shooting or stabbing. One quarter had seen a killing. . . . Extrapolating from Carl Bell's figures, we can begin to sense the dimension of the problem. All across the nation hundreds of thousands—perhaps millions—of inner city youngsters are daily exposed to what can only be called toxic levels of violence. Harm—great harm—is being done. This is tragically obvious.[4]

The situations in communities described by Prothrow-Stith are so extreme that they become difficult for outsiders to imagine. Martin Weaver, an African-American physician who specializes in pediatric rehabilitation in Camden, New Jersey, described kids he knew who planned their funerals in detail when they were in elementary school. "They know they're going to die," he told me.

> It's not even a question, because they've basically given in, and it's easy for them to understand that even if they live to be over twenty-one, in their environment, they're going to be the guy they see on the corner who's addicted to something, alcohol, drugs, whatever, or the other guy who is basically homeless. They don't have anything to look forward to. There's no model they can look at and say: "That's a possibility." But then they see

this guy, he may only be twenty-one, but as they put it, he's *living large*. So, if I'm going to live, I want to live fast and live large, because at least I can see that. And if you're asking me to go beyond that, what I see in my neighborhood are excuses for a man, or excuses for a person, and if that's what I have to look forward to, I'd rather die. Just be a bigshot between twelve and twenty-one.

I visited Camden, New Jersey, to interview women there and came away with the impression that the African-American women I met who worked or lived in public housing in Camden seemed to understand very well the reality of living on the edge of a *frontier*. Women whose sons had been wounded by bullets talked fatalistically about the dangers in their neighborhoods: ". . . if the Lord's going to take me away from here, I'm going to go one way or another, whether it's shooting, stabbing or just dropping dead." Their fatalism was intermixed with an abiding sense of attachment, not only to their children, but also to their neighborhoods, where they had lived for many years, refusing to flee despite an accumulation of terrible events, including the maiming, by gunfire, of their sons' arms, legs, and chests. To my mind, this mix of fatalism and attachment characterizes a prototypical frontier voice.

The nineteenth-century frontierswomen quoted in the early part of this book were in many ways "conservative"; the enormous challenges they faced left them more interested in digging down and holding on to their property than in planning egalitarian reforms for the future. The urban black women with whom I spoke often surprised me with statements that might also be classified as "conservative." They often expressed a desire to reclaim, to conserve, habits and values from yesterday that seemed to be threatened by the chaos of today. A number of the women communicated a wish to return to the recent past, to an era predating the 1960s. They wanted to go back to a time when neighbors looked out for other people's children, and more families attended church, and prayer was allowed in school, when girls preferred nice young men, and fathers mowed the lawns, when Martin Luther King was still alive, and their friends had never seen a gun up close and had never heard pistol shots at night outside their windows.

It should be added, however, that these women did not adopt other markedly conservative articles of faith. For instance, none of them expressed interest in legislation that would make it easier for citizens to acquire concealed-carry permits. None of them, in short, showed faith in the proposition that putting guns in the hands of law-abiding neighborhood residents would intimidate criminals and ultimately reduce neighborhood violence. This does not mean that they all avoided guns. At a particular juncture in their lives, two of the women did ask family members to get them guns for self-defense. As it happened, however, both of these women discarded their guns after a little while because ultimately they didn't feel much safer or better protected living with a firearm tucked in a book bag or bedroom. The small, explosive tool didn't do anything remarkable for them.

Led by considerations like these and inclined by my own age and situation, I found that the stories of African-American women that caught my attention were usually stories of maternal concern or grief, so that at last the general portrait of women in this chapter is surprisingly old-fashioned, even Victorian. It is a portrait of mothers who pray, preach, mourn, and fight, and of young men who carry weapons, young men lured away from home by the attractions of life "on the edge"—similar to frontier life. Significantly, only when a person looks behind the powerful dramas that play out between black mothers and their sons to the less well documented dramas involving young black women do the most contemporary ironies and tragedies emerge.

**Patricia Murray and Mary Ann Wilmer**

I met Patricia Murray and her sister, Mary Ann Wilmer, at an anti-gun conference in Washington, DC. We sat down and spoke in a vacant piano bar located inside the Sheraton, near the hotel's gift shop. Mary Wilmer, an experienced elementary school teacher who had become an employee of the Department of Education, lived in Washington, DC. Patricia Murray, a politically active Democratic committeewoman, had lived most of her life in Camden, New Jersey. In Camden in 1968 her husband was shot and killed. Years later, her youngest son, Jerrell, would be shot two different times and convicted on drug charges in Camden. She was at the conference to learn ways to save not only her son, but all the other boys who might otherwise be predestined to stop bullets with their bodies.

The three of us spoke for a long time. Listening to one another, these two grown sisters recalled people they'd known over the years and puzzled over the way so many things had changed since 1968. Mary Wilmer had never married, but she certainly knew kids and, quite plainly, had loved many of them and wished them success. She related stories about young men and women she'd watched growing up in Washington, DC. One "bright young man" named Jonathan went off to college in Pennsylvania on a scholarship, came home for a brief visit, and was shot and killed by an acquaintance who owed him money. One young woman, "lovely young woman," decided against attending her senior prom because she was afraid of being shot. And Wilmer had watched a boy spinning like a wild little top on the street after he'd witnessed a shooting. "He SPUN. This was a third-grader. He spun around and he spun around and he SPUN around. I sat there and I looked at him. I said: 'Come here sweetheart.' And I started talking to him. 'Yeah Miss Wilmer,' he told me, and so on and so on, all about what he saw. It's just heart-breaking." Once she saw a teenage girl try to drag a corpse back into life.

> They don't understand. The first young man that I knew who was shot was a member of my church, an excellent student, very much involved with the church. I think he too lived on the edge. I don't think he was very much involved, but he just kind of lived on the edge and enjoyed that side of life. I went to the viewing at the church because I knew his parents and I knew him, and I couldn't believe it. And I heard this rumbling at the viewing, and I didn't know what it was, I did not know if it was a gang come to retaliate or something, and I had to move back to the corner, and when I looked, there was this girl, she was trying to pull him up, pull him out of the casket, you see, because they don't see it as final.

Wilmer felt that her neighborhood was unfairly targeted as a crime center by police, even though the web of commercial drug transactions stretched far beyond the city limit. As a member of the Metro Orange Hat Coalition, she had stood on corners in Washington, DC, trying to intercept drug traffic. She said: "You'd be surprised the number of cars with Maryland and Virginia tags that are coming into the city to do their drug business. You'd be surprised the number of people in those cars who have white faces." At the same time, she felt that the drug transactions taking place in her neighborhood were somehow part and parcel of a ruinous erosion begun in the mid-1960s. She had not approved when prayer was banned in the schools. "I firmly believe that Madalyn Murray O'Hair, since she was successful in getting prayer out of the schools, there's been a change. Some of these young people have no value systems." She wanted a return to values. In her opinion, black families traditionally did not keep guns in the house—"that is antithetical to how black families are." Both she and her sister pinpoint the birth of gun violence in the country somewhere in the 1960s, that decade of assassinations. They named the deaths of John and Robert Kennedy and Medgar Evers. Patricia Murray's own husband was killed in 1968, the same year as Robert Kennedy. And both women spoke of the death of Martin Luther King as a bleak turning point. Wilmer said: "Here you had a person who had promoted nonviolence, and he had violence inflicted on him and died. And I think that this was internalized by people. You know, 'What you talking about, nonviolent? Look what happened to him.'"

Murray added: "That opened the door."

This identification of the 1960s as a lawless, liberal decade that separated folk from old values, specifically church values, is typically right-of-center, and I was interested to hear how Mary Wilmer and Patricia Murray were able to borrow planks on the one hand from a typically rightist platform, and then, on the other hand, from a typically leftist platform, in order to hammer together a foundation on which they could stand. Their attitudes toward young black women were complicated and, to my ear, even old-fashioned. Wilmer and Murray never failed to refer to female students and young mothers they had known as "young ladies," and they wished that these young ladies would assert a firmer moral influence over their young men. My questions about "women and guns" undoubtedly prompted these meditations, but both women were interested in the question. Wilmer told me: "Our focus is on the male, and what you're doing is interesting, because we have forgotten the important part the female plays." She said that when violence erupted in the Washington, DC, schools, "invariably it's been because of something that developed because of relationships with the young woman." She said that she wished that the young ladies she knew would pay more attention to books and less to their outfits. "I made the observation when I was on the train once, and the Asian kids, they were loaded down with books in their book bags, and the young black girls were carrying the Chanel bags and the Gucci bags. . . . I think the girls are strong motivators behind the activities."

Murray agreed with her sister's assessment of the interactions between young drug dealers and their girlfriends. Her youngest son, Jerrell, was about to start serving time for a drug conviction; thanks to her own Democratic political connections, she had managed to get him into a program that would allow him to serve just eighteen months, rather than three years. Her son was in his mid-twenties and had already been shot twice:

> He was shot in the side and the bullet went just through the fleshy part, in and out. You'd think he'd know better and he'd come out of the situation, but he lives on the edge. . . . And then this last time he was intervening for a friend, and he was shot in the leg, and it shattered his leg and his leg had to be rebuilt. And I look at him now from a distance, I see him walking with a limp, but I still believe it was a blessing for me.

Murray described speaking to her son in the courtroom. When she asked what he did with the money he made dealing, he answered: "Buy my girlfriend things."

> And I said to him: "Okay, what'd she do, your slimmie?" He calls them slimmies. I said to him: "Okay now, your slimmie, if you're incarcerated, she'll find another drug dealer who's driving the Jeep, the Mercedes. . . ."
> And I said to him: "You know when I was coming up, if I had to choose between a young man that was out working and the roughneck that these

young ladies now want to identify with, we didn't identify with the rough-neck because my parents would tell me: 'Don't bring him home.'" But these parents of today, these young ladies' parents, I can't understand it. If that young lady, someone he was interested in, was to say to my son: "As long as you're involved in that, you can't talk to me," he would have changed his ways. It's not happening.

According to Murray, who got the information from her son, a young female would often carry the gun for a dealer, because police were wary of frisking women for fear of being accused of sexual harassment. "So the young lady, she's like the mule, that's what they call her." At the same time, a few of the women were capable entrepreneurs themselves. "In this development I worked in, we've got the females driving around in their point-eights. These are little cars, they're like Toyotas, and they take and soup them up and drop them down to the ground and put speakers in, big speakers, and they call them point-eights. That's a drug car."

Sitting at a round table near the hotel gift shop, speaking passionately under the blare of hotel music, Murray described how her own son broke down and cried one day in her office. He had just spotted someone he'd known in school now climbing into his car to drive to a job:

> And he and I were just having a little quiet time together and then he broke down crying, and I said: "What are you crying for?" and he said: "Look at my life. I don't even have a job, Mom. I don't have to get up to go any-where. I was just existing. That guy, I always looked at him like he was a geek, but he has a car. He's going to work. He's doing something with his life. I had a lot of money but I don't have anything to show for it now. And now I'm going to have to go and do some time." And I said to him: "This is going to be the beginning, not the end. This is going to be the beginning of the rest of your life. It's like you're going to be reborn."

At the time of our interview, Patricia Murray's son was still alive, despite having been shot twice. As mentioned previously, her husband was killed in 1968 by a gunman. I listened to her tell her story in the empty piano bar of the Sheraton–Washington Hotel, and I would listen to her again, after driving to Camden, New Jersey, in thick fog nearly a year later.

Patricia Murray worked in the Chelton Terrace housing authority office on Chelton Avenue in Camden, and she could look out the window of that office to the house on the corner where her parents used to live, the house where she grew up. In 1968 she was in her own home, preparing to visit her mother, when she heard the shot that killed her husband. Before that day, in Camden, she had never heard a gunshot. "I was in the house, in the kitchen, and the reason why I know . . . it was 11:00—I could only remember up to that time—I heard the shot, and it was so uncanny, I had this feeling, and I knew it was my husband. I had this wrenching feeling, this stabbing feeling inside of me. When I heard it, it was like a crack. I'd never heard a gunshot before. I screamed, I was on the phone to my mother, and I screamed: 'They shot Tony!' Wasn't out front, didn't know. Then my brother-in-law ran in, wanted the phone, and I had to hang up. At that point, I went to the door, and all I could see was the people, in the middle of the street, around a person. But I knew in my spirit that it was my husband. I was seven-months pregnant, and all I remember was running out of the house and just running, running in the complete opposite direction, and people running after me to catch up with me, to stop me. And after that, I can't remember any longer. When they finally caught me and were bringing me down the street, and I watch enough TV to know when someone has passed, and I saw them drawing the lines in the street, I knew that he had died, was killed. So for twenty-six years I walked around and made a lot of bad moves in my life." Her voice shook. "Looking and searching and not knowing what was wrong, until . . . I'm claustrophobic and I was caught in an elevator in September, first of September, and I think that when I walked on that elevator the first of September I was one person, and when I came off, I was a totally different human being. I had panic attacks, and as a result I had to go to a counselor, and the counselor and I started talking, and things started coming out of me that I didn't know was there. From those counseling sessions, I had realized that I had built things—I had a little room that I just put it in and left it there and closed the door. I couldn't open the door because the pain, there was so much pain, and I didn't want to deal with it."

Just two days before the counseling session that jolted her awake, she had lived through an experience that prepared her to read her own tragedies inside a larger context.

> I'm involved in politics in the Camden City area, and a young man was shot after I'd just left a meeting, and I was sitting at a friend's club, I was there waiting for some people, and they came in and said: "A kid just was shot around the corner." I was sitting there with mixed emotions. One was because I didn't want it to be my son, and he hung around in that area. So I sat there, and I was almost in a panic state, sitting, waiting to get a report of who it was. They asked me did I want to go and see, and I said: "No, I'll just sit here." And when they came back, I heard reports that it was a young boy fifteen-years-old, shot in the head. He had his hair corn-rowed, and his clothing . . . and I could feel myself start to relax because I knew it wasn't my son. But then I said to myself: "But he still was my child. Even though he wasn't Jerrell, he was my child and something has to be done." And I

had this visual picture of this young man, this baby laying on this street and his life just oozing out on this concrete, this blood, and I made up in my mind at that moment that, if no one else spoke out about this in this city, it was incumbent on me to do something.

## Camden, New Jersey

When I met up with Patricia Murray in her home city, more than a year after our first interview in Washington, DC, she could not report any dramatic anti-gun successes. I had already looked on segments of Camden City as I drove to her office in Chelton Terrace, where we had arranged to meet. The landscape surrounding the Econo Lodge where I had a room struck me as bereft and uncivil. Plots of land had been transformed into shopping centers surrounded by huge parking lots, and the small businesses that had kept their place along the highway were just remnants. The road itself, Route 38, was four fast lanes tightly barricaded down the middle . . . apparently it had been a country road that became a city road and then finally devolved into a speedy, blind shunt from here to there. Trying to make motel reservations in Camden, I'd learned that the nearest Super 8 Motel had closed in the previous year, and I expected this lodge would surrender soon. Visitors to this general area now made their reservations to the east . . . a little farther away from Camden.

It was a foggy Thursday in late winter. Navigating by instructions I'd received over the phone, I turned at the Dunkin' Donuts and found Ferry Avenue. As usually happens when one enters an American neighborhood that has undergone a particular sort of American transformation, after I drove across an unmarked boundary, people walking on the sidewalks changed from white to brown. This was a mundane, unhurried phenomenon, familiar to me since I'd grown up in St. Louis, Missouri. Tokens of defensiveness began to appear. The Ferry Avenue United Methodist Church had its rear parking lot guarded by a chain-link fence topped with big curls of razor wire.

I had imagined that the "housing project" Murray named would be constituted of huge towers, similar to Chicago's. But it turned out that Chelton Terrace is a settlement of two-story, dark brick townhouses, and in fact I had been driving around and through it for a while unaware. I parked outside the Levi Combs Community Center, a cinderblock building with its exterior painted bright green. Around me were rows of townhouses, the strips of ground between them bare, lacking shrubs and bushes, though not unkempt. To the west of where I stood, a high earthen dike, foundation for elevated train tracks, shut off any further view. A long row of similar townhouses built along the base of that slope were boarded shut.

Murray's stories in Washington, DC, had alerted me to the fact that the interior door to the Chelton Terrace administrative offices would be locked for security purposes—she'd described squeezing her own hand through an opening in the plexiglass reception window to grasp the hand of a sobbing young mother, a resident and a dealer of cocaine, whose boyfriend was about to get out of jail—and now I entered the community center and stood at that same window as if to buy a ticket for a performance and bent down near the opening to ask for "Patricia." There was a moment of incomprehension. I would discover that my own informality was not in style here, where women referred to one another and their friends as "Ms. Pat," "Ms. Blackshear," "Ms. Keyes," and "Ms. Roundtree." The habitual, respectful "Ms." as they said it was not the feminist title—instead it came off as a friendly verbal shortcut for either "Miss" or "Mrs."

Murray unlocked the door and brought me into the back office, saying, "There you are. You made it." She was busy. A practiced political woman, she had been trying to keep up with her own office work and make appointments for me. She had tried to find out the name of the doctor at Cooper Hospital who worked with young gunshot victims, the one who'd attended the anti-gun conference in Washington, DC, so I could interview him. She had talked to Brenda Roundtree, whose son Gregg was killed in 1992 on the same street as Patricia Murray's husband twenty-four years earlier. . . . I should phone to set up an interview after she got off work. . . . And there was the grandmother whose grandson was shot and killed following an argument about a puppy, but Murray hadn't been able to get in touch with her yet. As I stood in the office, Murray dialed one more friend and found out the name of the doctor: Dr. Martin Weaver. But then she had to get back to her own work. I said I wanted to visit the Camden Library and Cooper Hospital and would return later.

Reading newspapers at the library, then driving up and down Broadway, provided me with the kinds of details I had expected to find. In the mid-1990s, Camden, New Jersey, had been recently designated the fifth poorest city in the nation, and it usually claims a spot on lists of the most violent cities in the nation. The city can raise only a quarter of its own budget; in the late 1990s, approximately 50 percent of its funds came directly from state aid. New Jersey state troopers were invited into Camden to help keep order, and in 1996 the city proposed to introduce uniformed policemen into the high schools, where according to the *Camden Courier-Post:* "School officials describe an out-of-control atmosphere, where fistfights erupt almost daily, students threaten teachers and then vandalize the cars of those who stand up to the intimidation." A senior at Woodrow Wilson High School was quoted in the same article saying: "Some students are very ignorant. They have no respect, no motivation. We call them hall scum."[5] In 1995, homicides "attributed to random acts of violence" in Camden, a city of approximately 87,000 people, numbered sixty. The homicide rate for the beginning of the 1996 was running lower—only two people were shot in the month of January, rather than fourteen—and a few community leaders were quoted speaking optimistically in the *Courier-Post*. None of the women I would talk to, however, believed that significant changes had been made.

On Broadway in Camden, many of the buildings were distinguished by the color of plywood used to board up the windows and doors. A massive stone church in the city center had its stained glass windows boarded over with plywood cut into gothic shapes. On the side streets, blinded, charred properties alternated with houses where people lived. There were plenty of Chinese restaurants and storefront churches—United House of Prayer for All People—and currency exchanges and drugstores. Many telephone booths. More razor wire. All the clean buildings appeared to be government administrative buildings, constructed of fresh new brick with few windows.

Over the next two days, I would hear stories of the Camden that used to be, when the big churches had windows, and the barbed wire was on the farms. Women I spoke to who had lived in the city for decades all said it was lovely in the 1960s. Broadway had movie theaters—there were now no theaters left. Young people could attend dances on King Avenue and at the school on Eighth Street. And Chelton Terrace—located in an area that used to be called Centerville—was a pretty place to live. The Centerville townhouses were constructed in 1943 to house workers for the Shipyards, which have since closed. According to Murray, Centerville was a predominantly black, working-class settlement, where the townhouses were government-owned, but not subsidized. "They were all homes. Homeowners. Picket fences. Cherry trees. People had stables where they had horses. They rode horses. It was just a lovely, lovely area." She remembers this lost home place as green and flowered and trimmed:

> It was a grass walkway as far as your eye could see, with rose bushes and well-manicured lawns. And if the neighbor next door wasn't home and you were going to mow your lawn, you did the neighbor's lawn. The manager that was here, if you didn't mow your lawn, you got a letter in your mailbox. And they were hand-pushing lawnmowers at that time.

Things changed. By the 1970s, a steady exodus of white homeowners and businesses had begun, as Camden lost population to suburbs like Cherry Hill, which were built east and north of the city, on available acres of New Jersey farmland. The Jewish neighborhood used to be Parkside; the Jews left for the suburbs. The Polish neighborhood used to be Whitman Park; the

Poles fled to the suburbs. Where the Italians moved out, Latinos moved in. Low-income black residents moved into many of the houses. Murray reeled off a classic, thumbnail history of a ghetto's creation. At one time, Camden residents could work for the New York Shipyards, Monsanto Chemical, Knox Gelatin, RCA, or Campbell Soup, the company famous in the city for its landmark: a towering red soup can. But then one by one, the businesses left, even though Camden appears to be ideally located for business, as it sits directly across from Philadelphia on the Delaware River and connects to New York City by the New Jersey Turnpike. But the jobs were gone. Tax income was gone. And now, according to Murray: "If you drive through this city, you will see telephone booths like you've never seen before" because so many residents "can't afford a hundred dollars to get a telephone in their home, and they have to go and use a public telephone, which puts their lives in jeopardy, because while they're on the telephone, somebody could just come up behind them with a pistol."

That afternoon I moved around with my tape recorder, guided by Murray's advice and instructions. I did manage to tape Martin Weaver at Cooper Hospital and also Kathryn Blackshear and Deborah Keyes, then president and vice-president of the Chelton Terrace Resident Management Corporation, back in the Chelton Terrace community room. Dr. Weaver spoke about young black males and his own efforts to study and reduce the number of gun tragedies afflicting that population. Blackshear and Keyes talked about guns and drugs and kids: "If you want a gun, you can get a gun." "Guns are a part of our daily existence. We live in public housing and we're constantly bombarded with gunfire. Our first instinct is to drop to our floors, and maybe look later after the gunfire has ceased." "Camden is under siege." "You have some kids out here don't have no remorse for nobody. I mean, fifteen years old and they tell YOU what to do. Some of the parents are scared of them. They know they carry a gun." Deborah Keyes's son had been shot twice, the first time running after someone who took his car, the second time for a reason she didn't understand. "This boy was running up the street and started chasing him. I don't know what happened before then, but he said he was coming from the store, he had some potato chips and pretzels in a bag which he left on the ground." The problem was kids wanted the "fast life," which had to be fueled by a combination of drugs, money, and girlfriends. Guns were part of it all. Keyes described the summer ritual she and Blackshear go through outside their doorsteps:

> Where we live, we don't want the drugs on the corner, so we walk up to the ones that are selling and we say: "I'm not trying to stop you from doing what you're doing, all I'm asking you is please leave here. What can we do

to get you off these corners?" They said: "Get us a job making money." We say: "We're trying to do everything we can to get you kids some jobs, but until we can, we just asking you not to be on the corner selling drugs." But you know, they'll leave that corner, go to another corner. Summer probably be coming soon, we going to have to go out and do the same thing again, 'cause it's a new group of kids now, and they're young—twelve and thirteen years old.

I had phoned Brenda Roundtree's house earlier. It was determined through intermediaries that she would drive to my motel room for an interview after she got off work. None of the women wanted me driving around town, looking for an address in the dark. I accepted this favor without protest.

When I dialed Roundtree's number that evening, her daughter answered and put her mother on the line. She told me she'd been waiting for the call. She hadn't yet taken off her work clothes; she worked as a manager at Kentucky Fried Chicken. She said she'd be over in a little while, after she contacted her son.

Roundtree arrived at my room with her grown son, Raymond. She was dressed in a clean white polyester shirt and a navy blue nylon winter jacket, and she carried two framed pictures and a small scrapbook. Raymond wore a Phillies cap. They came in. She and I sat down at the little round table against the window curtains. He sat on the edge of the bed near the wall.

Brenda Roundtree is a substantial woman who grew up in North Carolina on a farm—"I don't know if you know anything about tobacco, cotton, corn, stuff you grow that you have to work. My brother and I—I was the oldest—we had work to do before we went to school; we had work to do when we came home from school." Her oldest son, Raymond, was a solid, polite man, and the father of five children. They talked about Gregg.

## Gregg's Mother

Gregg Roundtree was shot in 1992 at the age of twenty. Thanks to a multitude of legal delays, by February 1996, at the time of our interview, his alleged killers remained in custody—they'd been picked up in 1993—but had not yet been brought to trial. Neither his mother nor his brother understood why Gregg Roundtree had been killed. He had been at home, then he went for a walk, and forty-five minutes later a friend knocked on the door and said that he had been shot. People reported seeing a car with four young men in it, two of whom had guns. Roundtree was visiting a friend's, and the gunmen entered the house, as if for a robbery. "My son took a shot in the chest, and what I hear is his friend grabbed him, and when he turned around, he got shot three times in his buttocks and different parts of his body." But at the hospital, Brenda Roundtree found money in the pocket of her son's discarded clothes, so the robbery never took place. A retired police detective had promised he would tell her what he knew someday, but added that he couldn't so long as the trial was in progress.

Roundtree didn't know his killers. "One boy they do have, that's been charged, admitted that he didn't even know my son. He just bragged about . . . when they got him from North Jersey, he was in a jail up there, and they brought him back to Camden, he came into the jailhouse there bragging about how he shot this kid, but he admitted to the police he didn't know who my son was. . . . I want to say, 'Why, why, if you didn't know him and you did rob somebody, [but] you didn't rob him, why did you shoot him?' I haven't been able to find that out. And I'm sure the police have some information they're not going to give me." Roundtree was revived at the hospital. He was shot on May 6, 1992. He died on May 18.

Gregg Roundtree was quiet and liked sports. His mother had sent him to a vocational school; she didn't want him going to the schools in the city "because he's too good of a boy to be out here and get with the wrong crowd." After graduation, he hoped to go to a junior college, and the family had been involved in trying to figure out how to get him accepted and funded. He was an enthusiastic Chicago Bulls fan, a basketball player himself. When he died, the school team retired his jersey and gave the family a frame with the jersey inside it.

But even the memorial rituals were haunted by threat and chaos. The family required police protection at the funeral and the cemetery because Raymond, Ms. Roundtree's older son, had tangled with a street kid who was rumored to be his brother's killer. He had reached in and grabbed the keys from the boy's car, and when the boy, nicknamed KK, scrambled out of the car, he had a gun in his hand. His sister, Jackie Roundtree, tried to throw herself between them. He told me that she was in the way, "so I threw her on the ground, so if he did do something, he wouldn't hit my sister. But I wasn't really thinking about what would happen to me."

Having lost one son, Brenda Roundtree now saw her eldest boy poised on the edge:

> I stood there, myself and his father and my mother and my family, and watched this boy wave this gun on him, telling him: "If you don't give me the keys back, I'm going to shoot you." His father begged him so hard, 'til he finally took those keys, and he threw them over in the neighbor's yard, and the boy still held the gun on him. Anyway, when . . . the boy, he kept the gun on him, he walked over and got the keys and got back in the car,

and he pulled off, but he stopped in front of my house and said: "I'll be back, and I'm going to spray some more bullets." So he made himself look like he was guilty, but he was not the one. But he had this gun in his hand, and all of a sudden he was a big man.

Following that incident, KK's allies threatened the family. This was the one time Brenda Roundtree considered buying herself a gun, but finally she decided against it. "I don't really think I'm strong enough to have one because of what I'm going through emotionally. I'm an even-tempered person, but sometimes having that can change you." Instead, she began to work to discover who killed Gregg. She was implacable, and she had connections. "When you're locked up in the county [jail], there's a lot of people in there. . . . Lots of people who knew my son. Lots of friends of the family." She heard from her friends.

> The word would get back to me when something happened to him [KK] when he was locked up. Every time something happened to that boy, I knew. Then I would call up the detective bureau and say: "Is he ready to talk now? I just heard he was in another ruckus." And they wanted to know how I knew that. I said: "That's all right how I know. I want to know when are you going to try to talk to him. Maybe he's ready to talk now." And finally he did talk. He was the one that got them on the right track, because he was catching so much stuff in jail.

She took to the street. When she discovered KK was not the killer, she learned the name of another neighborhood suspect and started to follow him. She frankly hoped to entrap him. "I used to be in cabs riding. I tried to get this boy set up, just to get him caught, maybe if they could catch him with something, maybe they could sweat him and get some information out of him." She would call the police and tell them things. "They were wondering where I was getting my information. I said: "Because I'm out here." They said: "But you're putting yourself in danger." "Things ain't moving fast enough for me," I said. "I want to find out what happened to my son."

At last it was KK, in jail, who named the men ultimately accused of shooting Gregg Roundtree. And so the slow legal process began. Brenda Roundtree was in the courtroom one day—she organized her work schedule around regular visits to the courtroom where she hoped the trial would someday begin—when the suspects were brought in for the first time.

She said:

> They had to restrain me. I tried to climb over after them. They restrained me, but there wasn't a lot of physical force because these people have seen

me up in the courtroom so much, they know what I'm up there for, and they was just trying to calm me down. All I was trying to do was to get to one of them.

They [the suspects] know me because they won't even look me in the face now. I sat close enough up there and stared at them boys just to get them to look, so you could see—this is the mother, this is the mother. I want you to see my eyes.

There was a time that evening when we looked over the photographs and scrapbook Brenda Roundtree had brought from home. One frame enclosed a collage of high school yearbook photos. In the scrapbook, there was Gregg Roundtree at the Hershey Park basketball booth; he sank so many baskets that the roustabout asked him to call it quits. And there he was as an alert, fat-cheeked baby in a ring of children surrounding a minuscule, wizened woman, his great-great grandmother. "He was her heart. But all of them was her heart," Brenda Roundtree said. The scrapbook contained funeral documents, newspaper articles, and family photos. One professional portrait of Raymond, Jackie, and Gregg showed the family as it had been: a threesome of clean-cut, brown-skinned siblings, all fine-boned, with matching smiles.

Brenda Roundtree understood she couldn't get her son back.

I try to keep busy. I have my times when I get into. . . . I try to be strong for the most part because I gotta go on. I have my children, my grandchildren, but sometime I slump back into it. Like this court thing, and that gets to me 'cause I'll be strong for a while, and then I'm getting my hopes built up in court, and I say maybe we can start to try to piece our lives together, this is not going to bring him back, but at least if we could see something done, there would be some kind of peace. If we can try to get on with something getting done, some justice getting done, for taking my son.

And she would not let him go. She said:

Where I'm working now is next door to where he's buried, and in the beginning it was kind of an adjustment, but now I look at it, and I'm close to him.

Some times I can go visit his grave and I'm okay, and other times I go there and it tears me up. One time I said I was going to move out of the city, 'cause this area, you know, this is getting so bad, but I can't go because I'd be too far away from him. I can't let him go. To me, he's dead but I haven't let go. To me, it's still like he's living. And I know he's not, and there's times, you know, I used to wake up in the middle of the night and listen for him to come in, and it took a long time to get past that. Sometimes I'll wake up, I'll dream about him. Sometime I'll go, and I'll look out the window where he used to park his car. And I'll just have to try to get past it and all the time it's not easy, it's not easy, it's not easy at all, because my arms are still wanting to put my arms around him. It's hard. It's hard. I have forgiven God now. I couldn't forgive Him. But I have.

There isn't a day goes by I still don't think about him, dream about him, sit and wonder what he would be doing now.

Brenda Roundtree and her son, Raymond, wanted Gregg's killers to be punished strictly. Twenty years incarceration was not enough. Roundtree favored national laws restricting guns, and she would have liked to see a return to "family values": "These families need to get together and raise their children. These drugs are rampant and a lot of these kids are raising themselves—don't know where the parents are—or trying to raise each other; you know, if they got little brothers and sisters, they stick together. You got one will go out of the house and do whatever he has to do to take care of the rest, and that's not right."

Raymond Roundtree did not keep any guns in his house. "I don't tolerate guns. I don't like guns. Not just because of what happened to my brother, I just don't like guns period. I wouldn't want a gun in my house around my kids. Kids are curious and they tend to find things."

Brenda Roundtree once attempted to organize people and stir them to action in Camden. But like Patricia Murray, she met with frustration. "At times when I was out trying to talk to different people, a lot of people just didn't want to talk. I communicated with some different women I met through other people. One woman—we were keeping contact because she moved out of the city—she lost her only child here. I really wanted to do something, but you know, I went around knocking on some people's doors in '92, and a lot of people, I guess they wanted to do their grieving, they just didn't want to get involved."

Like the other mothers I spoke with in Camden, she wished there were more things for the children TO DO—gospel singing in the high school, art classes, sports, movies, dances, ice skating. "Gotta be something, gotta be a change. I'm hoping, for my grandchildren 'cause they're good kids. They need things to do, and to see that this life out here on the street, that's nothing but show and tell." And like the other mothers in Camden, she remembered a time when there were more things for children and teenagers to do. She had moved to the city in 1967, when her oldest child was a six-month-old baby. And he didn't want to move away from his mother. When I asked Raymond Roundtree if he wished to locate his children in a safer place, he said: "Nowhere's safe." At the same time, he hopes to keep his children out of the Camden high schools.

When I put my hands on the framed pictures of Gregg Roundtree, I felt physically slight and artificial. Interviews are not satisfying rituals; they skip around and stop and start. But Brenda Roundtree did show me that this young man, Gregg, had been her son, was still her son, and I felt her ceaseless maternal desire for him to return to her. That is it, one of the oldest American stories about women and guns.

Patricia Murray related to me how she'd told her son, Jerrell, who was arrested and convicted on drug charges: "You're running down a one-way street, and at the end of that street there's only two things—either death or incarceration. You're throwing bricks at the penitentiary. *What is wrong with you?*" In the mid-1990s, for every one black man who attended college, there were ten who attended prison. According to a 1996 study by the Sentencing Project, a research group based in Washington, DC, approximately one-third of all African-American men between the ages of twenty and twenty-nine were being superintended by the criminal justice system at that time; they were either imprisoned, on probation, or on parole. This percentage had increased dramatically even since 1990, when a quarter, not a third, of the nation's young black Americans were under the system's control, and it had not fallen in the late 1990s. The prison population is growing. In 1999, sociologists from Princeton and Indiana University published a study showing that the incarceration of low-skilled men in the United States was so enormous that it makes our unemployment statistics look better than they really are because low-skilled laborers kept in prison are not counted as "unemployed"; these researchers argue that our statistics would look much worse compared to Europe's if our incarceration rate were as low as Europe's.[6] Also, critics have noted that this trend in incarceration permanently weakens the African-American and Hispanic electorate, since in a number of states convicted felons lose their right to vote. According to another Sentencing Project report, "Losing the Vote," in the late 1990s 3.9 million Americans were being denied the right to vote because of a felony conviction, of whom nearly 1.4 million were African-American men.[7]

Independent journalists and the Sentencing Project attributed the increase in the number and proportion of imprisoned African-American men to strict new federal sentencing guidelines for drug offenses, especially crimes involving crack cocaine, the marker drug for high-risk urban neighborhoods. Between 1983 and 1993, the number of drug offenders sentenced and incarcerated increased fivefold.

> For the most part, these offenders are low-level, nonviolent sellers (many of them users) who have been scooped up in the continual drug raids fa-

vored by the police and who have been sentenced under the harsh penalties on the books in every state. The draconian federal penalties for selling crack—a mandatory minimum of five years for five grams—have helped fill the nation's pens with petty drug violators. (The penalties for selling cocaine powder, which is preferred by middle-class users, are much less severe.) [8]

In the article quoted here, Michael Massing outlined his own conclusions about the situations of young black and Hispanic drug dealers. He noted that recent reports of decreasing crime rates in many of the nation's large cities—particularly New York City—had reinforced a generally conservative conviction that the best way to combat crime was with tough law enforcement, not job programs or educational reforms. He quoted from two inherently contradictory editorials published in the *New York Times* in 1996, when newspaper reports of the nation's falling urban crime rates were beginning to appear. One of the stories criticized the sentencing policies that resulted in the incarceration or legal superintendence of a third of the nation's young black men, while the other congratulated the city's police department for reducing crime throughout the city by cracking down on drug dealers, upping arrests, and winning more convictions. Massing concluded: "We can't have it both ways." Yet the policies were working and continued to function. A front-page story in the *New York Times* just a day before Christmas, 1998, announced that the total number of metropolitan homicides for 1998 was the lowest recorded since 1964. "The huge drop in crime means that if the pace continues, the city will log less than a third of the number of homicides this year than it did in 1990." According to the article, the reasons for the decline were: ". . . the stronger economy, a drop in the number of people in their late teens and early twenties, the waning of the crack epidemic, and an increase in the number of people behind bars. But a growing number of criminologists now also give credit to police strategies."[9]

Where the drugs circulate, the guns circulate. Some of the newly strict policing strategies in big cities were meant to net those guns. Both Massing and the *New York Times* described the "frisking" strategy in New York: "By more thoroughly frisking the people they stop on the street, the police have picked up many young men carrying concealed guns."[10] According to the *Times*: "The increase in friskings of low-level offenders has been sharply criticized by some civil libertarians and is one reason for a two-year jump in abuse complaints, but it apparently has discouraged people from carrying unregistered guns on the street."[11] The inherent dangers of these get-tough strategies were becoming apparent by the late 1990s, however, when news reports appeared that suggested some newly empowered police officers were misusing their authority. The 1997 sodomy-torture of a young male Haitian immigrant, Abner Louima, by a group of New York City policemen, coupled with the 1999 killing of an unarmed immigrant in the Bronx—plainclothes police shot at Amadou Diallo forty-one times, hitting him with nineteen bullets, and were subsequently acquitted of wrongdoing—and another killing of an unarmed black man by plainclothes New York City police in March 2000 stirred up angry protests in New York City against Republican mayor Rudolph Giuliani and his police force and thus attracted national attention. Also in 1999, New Jersey's governor, Christine Whitman, acknowledged that New Jersey police had unofficially, but consistently, used "racial profiling" to determine which "suspects" they would stop, question, and search. Not surprisingly, the New Jersey troopers frisked black citizens in greater proportion because the black men looked like potential drug dealers. In response to widespread reports of discriminatory "racial profiling" practices by law enforcement officials, in April 1999 Attorney General Janet Reno called for police departments to begin collecting hard data that would document the gender and race of people they stopped to interrogate.

The African-American women I spoke with generally supported gun-control legislation and enforcement, but had little faith that a new piece of *control legislation* would solve the central problems in their home neighborhoods. Already so many of the people they knew were imprisoned, and it was clear prison didn't help rebuild anything. What's more, they had found that law enforcement commitment to their neighborhoods was spotty at best, that federal monies designated for preventative programs soaked deep into the pockets of bureaucrats before trickling out to the people, and that the underground economy built on guns and drugs was so well established that it could maintain itself. "All you got to do is say: 'I want a gun,' put the word out, somebody'll approach you and say: 'I heard you want a gun,'" Kathryn Blackshear of Chelton Terrace told me.

Dr. Martin Weaver, specialist in pediatric rehabilitation at Cooper Memorial Hospital in Camden, knows what guns can and cannot do. He had worked for years trying to repair kids who'd been shot. Like so many other residents of Camden, Dr. Weaver approved of gun-control laws but was convinced that significantly broader, positive efforts would be needed before his city—and the country—would see a real change in the homicide and incarceration rates of young black males. He described gun-control legislation as:

> Just a Band-Aid on a gooshing wound. It appears to be helping, it appears to be an attempt, but no one's trying to find out what's causing the bleeding. They can put gun-control laws in. They can wipe out guns tomorrow. Something else will happen because they haven't solved the problem, the problem that people don't value their lives.

Weaver remained committed to working with young urban men and women. He was trying to encourage researchers, specifically medical researchers, to study the full sequence of interacting factors, "vectors," that infect a neighborhood or nation with gun violence, vectors that prepare an individual to pick up a gun and shoot someone else. These questions pressed on him not only because as a specialist in rehabilitation he has met and treated so many gunshot victims, but also because he was the father of a young son.

He knew about street life; he'd been there. He knew what it meant to be physically afraid to walk to school. "I understand what these kids are going through when they say: 'You can talk to me all you want, doctor, but if I want to go to school tomorrow, I'm either going to have a gun, or I'm going to walk to school with Joe, who I know has a gun that I've paid 50 percent of.'" And he knew how a young man must hold himself if a loaded handgun is pointed straight at his forehead. "I've had guns to my forehead."

> It feels like a leap of faith. It feels like you have to hold on to every ounce of faith that you have. This minute that isn't meant to happen is happening, but the outcome that you want, you can still hold onto that. You can make that outcome happen. So you face it. You can't run away from it, because if you turn your back and try to run, you're going to get shot. But you don't want to be too much of a tough guy. You don't want to do what we call "fade" him; you don't want to embarrass this person holding the trigger because that would force him to pull it. But you have to stand there with enough confidence . . . and believe me, I can't describe it, but I'll look the person in the eye, and the only way . . . when I talk to my friends, I say: "I let them know that I'm just as crazy as they are." You have to let them realize that my life is just as meaningless to me as yours [is] to you. So, same thing, you let them know: "If you're going to kill me, go ahead kill me." Then they see beyond it. You're standing there looking at the person. And then it makes him realize: "Is it worth it?" It's really . . . it's faith. Then you have to let it go. When you walk away from it, you have to do it in a way that says there's no anger. You both walk away.
>
> The bottom line is respect. When you grow up in that type of environment, all you have is your name. All you have is your self-respect. You can't wear the right clothing, you can't have the right amount of money, you can't have the right career, but you're a person, and you want respect. So that's the thing. *Don't fade me; don't disrespect me; don't diss me.* If you go through the language, the bottom line through all of it is respect. When I grew up, people were killed or beat up for stepping on someone's shoe or talking about someone's mother. Now it's different; it's over drugs or something like that, but the bottom line is still respect.

Weaver told me he delivers many lectures about gun violence. He shows people slides of children in the morgue and slides of children "coming into acute trauma with a bullet injury in the head." If his audience is predominantly white, Dr. Martin Weaver would begin with pictures of dead white children—"my first slides are usually of young white males"—to catch their attention "before I start showing all the numbers about the urban community." For a young black audience, Weaver will arrive without his white coat. He is a taut man of average height, dark skinned, with his hair sheared flat across the top. He wore a small gold loop in his ear for the same reason he sometimes shows up at lectures in a baseball cap. "When the kids see me, they see this guy walking around, and they're still looking for Dr. Weaver. And then when I get up there, it's like, yeah—I am Dr. Weaver."

He wants to lead people away from guns. He is convinced that a good, focused leader can accomplish something—"every gangbanger in the country would follow one good person, one leader"—but so far "no one has the agenda, the true agenda, pure and simple, of ending gun violence in the inner city."

> I don't follow Mr. Farrakhan, but the power you saw in that Million Man March . . . If there were an acceptable leader for something like that . . . If that man were someone who did not have that garbage trailing behind him, if he were to say to that group of people: "Don't pick up a gun; that's the worst dope in the world. No matter who's coming, we're not claiming enemies here, we're saying: that's dope. You're killing yourself, and you're killing others, too. Let's not pick it up. Everybody promise you're not going to touch a gun."

And Weaver thought young women could change things.

> If the word on the street was that any man who shot . . . let's make it more specific, if the word on the street was that any black male under sixteen that shot a weapon was a punk, not one kid would shoot a weapon. That's how powerful that sexual component is. Everything a young man does is geared toward that, either towards their mother or the female counterpart in that community. And therefore there's this wealth of power in women.

## Young Ladies, Slimmies, Mules

### A Wealth of Power in Women

There is a wealth of power in women. There is also a wealth of powerlessness. These statements are both true of female hunters and anti-hunters, gunners and anti-gunners, eastern and western, and white and black women.

Meeting the women from Camden, I found myself asking the hackneyed question: Why can't these individuals who speak with such strong voices guide and save their endangered sons? The answer that came to light was mundane: I simply imagined trying to plant my own slippery teenage sons on an eroding slope where the forecast for tomorrow was rain and then more rain and rain and rain.

Contemporary speculations about women's *powers* have guided this entire book. Is a woman with a gun more or less powerful than the woman who works for legislation to outlaw guns? Is a woman who allies herself with her father and his culture more or less powerful than a woman who resists the patriarchy and a constellation of American macho traditions? What about a woman who buys a gun to protect herself against an abusive husband . . . would one describe her as powerful?

The African-American women with whom I spoke had personal power. Again, relying on a commonplace explanation, I judged that their individual strengths had developed in adversity, just as frontier courage and faith are said to develop in response to hard winds and disappointments. These women lacked, however, certain kinds of economic and civil power that many Americans inherit without much effort. For three years, Brenda Roundtree had been waiting helplessly for the trial of her son's alleged killers to begin. Camden's women lived in a city so empty of job opportunities that the landscape had become surreal. And they lived divided from the men one would expect to husband and help them over time (just as their men lived divided from the job opportunities that would allow them to function as conventional husbands). In a way, this meant that they lived inside an exaggerated version of an old American dream that directs the men out into the wilderness with their guns and instructs the women to stay home with the children.

Patricia Murray's husband was killed and she did not remarry. Mary Wilmer never married. Brenda Roundtree told me that her older son, Raymond, acted as father to Gregg, because Gregg's father was not available. Kathryn Blackshear told me of her "children's father" and did not call him husband. Deborah Keyes, Blackshear's close friend, described the general situation of single mothers in Chelton Terrace:

> We don't have many men to come out and fight with us. Most of the people out here, heads of households, are women, single women. If they do have a man, they don't have him, because if you do have a man he has to be under cover 'cause they going to take his income and your income, and your rent's going to be too high to even live here. So people don't bring their men out, don't let their men come out, 'cause they're afraid the housing authority's going to jeopardize their way of living. And it's rough.

The women I met in Chelton Terrace were all "single," but not alone. Each one had accepted a good measure of responsibility for her community and its children. Kathryn Blackshear and Deborah Keyes, president and vice-president of the Chelton Terrace Resident Management Association, spoke with me in the community room down the hall from the Chelton Terrace administrative offices. It was Thursday afternoon and the room was noisy with children, about six young boys and a few teenaged girls, who watched our proceedings with various degrees of frankness and interest, depending on their age. Four of the boys were settled on folding chairs at a long folding table around the checkers game. The cinderblock room, with its walls and a few exposed pipes painted over, had no windows or cushioned furniture. Pictures of cartoon characters—Minnie and Mickey and Donald, a Ninja Turtle, Ernie and Bert and Big Bird, and Tweetie—brightened one wall, though it seemed these characters had been there a long time and no longer won much attention. Elsewhere around the room, small unframed posters of African-American notables were displayed. I learned from the interviews that women in the center had staged protests to get more money for the kids. "The only thing Chelton Terrace citizens has here is one Monopoly Game, one checker game, a Kwaanza candlestick holder without the candle, crayons and crepe paper, and that's it," Blackshear told me. "We want opportunities for our children like everybody else, but I don't see it happening."

When our interviews were done, Blackshear and Keyes let me out the strong back door—by this time, the front entrance of the center was locked. These two friends stood together near the sidewalk as I got into my car. Kathryn Blackshear, a broad-shouldered woman, was studying to earn her bachelor's degree in social work at Rutger's University, Camden: "I thank God that I was able to get myself together, go to school, and now I have excellent self-esteem. I'll talk to anybody. I'll tell anybody off!" According to the way she interpreted her own history, there was a time in her life when she had been afraid, but then education and religion had strengthened her. "I found Christ. I started going to church and I just turned it over to God and the fear left."

It was during her earlier, fearful years that she had bought a gun because:

> When you have a son, they get in altercations, and you feel as though you got to be the man and the woman. So, therefore, I needed a gun in case somebody came after my kids, that I was going to have something to protect my kids and do that job. Plain and simple.
>
> It was a hot gun. When you have sons . . . I had a son, he said he wasn't into drugs but I knew he hung with people who were participating in such activities, and how I got the gun was, my children's father. My son told

him, said: "Mommy's looking for a gun," so my children's father called me up and said: "You're looking for a gun, I'll give you a gun."

But at last, Blackshear never used it. After a few years, she literally threw it out.

What I did was, I prayed about it and I put trust and faith in God that he was going to protect me, and I started feeling more comfortable in my community, 'cause I learned that I had to take control of my own life. How I got rid of the gun was, I put it in my trash where we put other trash, and I just prayed to God that when the trash people came, nobody found it, and nobody else would use the gun. I wiped it clean of my hand prints, and then the trashman came and I haven't seen the gun, and I pray to God the gun never turns up to hurt anybody.

It is difficult to categorize the signs of power in Blackshear's history. Pressed to act as the father of her children, she bought a gun. In retrospect, however, she does not remember that doubly "male" action as commanding, but as somehow helpless: an act instigated by fear. She hopes she has conquered the fear. But the future, as she saw it, was uncertain; her own new convictions, even her faith, didn't promise to control tomorrow. She would have liked to move out of Camden, but says: "Who knows, when I go to that other environment, fear might take over 'cause I don't know it and I might have to purchase another gun, because I feel as though I'm not in my comfort zone, whereas now I'm used to my community, I know the people, I can deal with it. But you know change is hard for people. So I don't know."

Deborah Keyes was smaller than her friend, and so quietly unassuming that I felt like a hunter catching her for the interview. She hated and feared firearms. Her son has been shot twice, and like Patricia Murray's son, he walked with a limp. Keyes spoke about her fears for her son and, because she had acted as a mentor for a number of teenage girls, she also spoke about the girls she'd known.

Earlier, Kathryn Blackshear had informed me that young women in her community didn't usually fight with guns, but with fists and knives: "Women in Camden, it's either fistfight or cut." Female gunshot victims were usually victims of domestic violence: "Men shoot one another. And if a woman is shot, it's due to domestic violence—the husband threatens her and he shoots to kill her." Weaver had said essentially the same. Only about one in eight of the gunshot victims he treated was female, but he added that girls who chose to be initiated into gangs were often pressured to take part in a "drive-by" shooting. It was his general impression that "For some reason, the girls can come back to their senses very quickly, a lot quicker than the males."

Deborah Keyes reported on young women along the same lines. "At one time it was a big problem with the girls and gangs out here, but that seems to have curtailed." Girls didn't do guns. "They had knives and sticks. But they would fight with the hands." At the same time, many of the young women she knew were very much involved in the consumer culture nourished by drugs and guns:

> These young girls today, if the guy is selling drugs and he's strapped—he's got a gun—they think that's big time. You're somebody. He's got money and he's strapped with a gun. You think you're with somebody, and you're important. But these girls are naive, because you're not important. . . .
>
> It's hard for them not to have a guy that's selling drugs, because the guys take care of them, they give them money, buy them clothes, and this and that. So to say you're gonna get a nice young man that got a little part-time job and going to school—uh uh. That ain't no money for them. He got just enough money to take care of his own personal needs, not hers. They're looking for somebody that's got thousands of dollars in their pocket and can whip out two or three hundred at a time for them to go to the mall and buy a pair of jeans and a pair of shoes for three hundred dollars. . . .
>
> It is so many young girls out here, and they get hurt on these drug dealers, because once they start giving you money, and these young girls they're still in school, you get to be a possession to them, and if you don't do what they say, they beat 'em up. Then they leave her hanging; she's probably pregnant because she wants a baby by him because he's this big drug dealer that carries a gun. And then look, her life is ruined.

Mary Wilmer, an experienced educator; Patricia Murray, a politically active mother of a grown son who'd dealt drugs; Martin Weaver, a physician experienced in rehabilitating gunshot victims, and Deborah Keyes, a tenant organizer in a Camden City housing project, had all told me, in so many words, that girls were an important part of the action. Interpreted plainly, this statement is not surprising. Where young men risk their lives to make illegal money, young women must be near. It interested me, however, to hear how meditations on these young women shifted between describing them as irresponsible consumers of Gucci bags and expensive blue jeans—"slimmies"—and, on the other hand, as entrapped victims—"mules." Both Patricia Murray and Dr. Weaver had entertained the notion that young women, "young ladies," might change everything by using their sexual powers to reassert their moral authority, rejecting young men, the "roughnecks," who carried guns. Patricia Murray had imagined: "If that young lady, someone he was interested in, was to say to my son: 'As long as you're involved in that, you can't talk to me,' he would have changed his ways," and she regretted that no such young lady had appeared.

To designate young women as the guardians of young men's good behavior is nothing new. One can easily imagine the feminist response to this proposition: tell the young men to govern themselves . . . teenage black females have plenty enough to worry about without accepting responsibility for ending urban gun violence . . . get some other mule to do this labor . . . maybe a couple of white guys in Washington? A feminist would be justified in firing back this response. Yet she might miss something, too, in the midst of her justified outrage, and that would be paradox. Judging from first-hand reports, a young black woman (or any woman or any man of any race in any place) can be a slimmie and a mule, an active player and a victim. She is a full member of her neighborhood in its sickness and its health. I do think she must be granted room to save herself before anyone requires her to save her brothers. And she must also be credited with irresponsibilities and appetites. She's probably no angel. But even if she were an angel, her virtues would be insufficient to lure companies such as Campbell Soup and Knox Gelatin back to Camden. Their absence is part of the context.

## "I Just Walk Down the Street"

Back in central New York, I interviewed a young African-American woman, a college sophomore, who grew up in Harlem. Cana* had chosen to be neither slimmie nor mule. Her comments about the young men she'd known were plain. Many of the boys had died. She knew she couldn't have saved them.

She lived on 122nd Street in New York City. She had known so many gunshot victims that "I can't count them." "I remember my friend Marlin getting shot over a girl. He was either seventeen or eighteen. From what I was told, he was sitting on a bench with a girl and a couple of guys came over and shot him, kept shooting him." Marlin died. When Cana was fifteen, her boyfriend shot himself. "I don't know why. He stuck the gun in his mouth." She lived through it. "Not too much I could do. I took it like anybody else would. It could change some people, but for me . . . I knew it was going to come sooner or later, but I didn't think he would do it to himself. I knew sooner or later he would be shot, because of the people that he hangs with."

None of Cana's girlfriends had been shot, but she was acquainted with girls who carried guns. Still, in her experience young women didn't usually fight with guns. They fought with insults and stuff picked off the street:

> I used to get jumped a lot by a couple of girls who live two blocks away from me. . . . The first time they didn't really get violent, but I was coming

---

*This is a pseudonym.

home from the train station, I was walking home, and one girl that I *never* laid eyes on her before in my life—I still don't know who she is—she went: "Oh yeah, that's the girl that rolled her eyes at me." Then all of a sudden I got twelve girls surrounding me, saying: "Why'd you roll your eyes at our friend?" I was like: "That's real stupid. If you want to jump me, jump me because I spit on your mother or something, you know what I'm saying? Jump me because I just kicked your little sister in the back. Don't jump me because I rolled my eyes at somebody." . . . Every time after that, they would try to find a reason to get me. One girl was like: "If you walk past my block again, I'm going to jump you." And I walked past the block an hour later. I got jumped.

There were about seven girls and they all wanted to fight me at the same time. So while they were trying to fight me, I was concentrating on this one girl. I was like: "It may be seven girls on me, but I'm going to kick somebody's ass." So I beat her really bad and once I got finished with her, I found another person to beat up.

That was when I didn't own a gun. So the first girl, I banged her head on the car window a couple of times and threw her down and stomped on her. The second girl, I don't know what I did to her, but I beat her up real bad. Her sister ran to the garbage and got a pipe out of the garbage and then she came and started hitting me with the pipe, so after I kicked her sister, I grabbed her and started fighting with her and the pipe dropped and I got it and I started now with it. So after that, I had the pipe, so nobody wanted to fight me anymore.

Cana distinguished between real "gangs" and a bunch of girls, because a gang would stick together, but with girls: "It's just a group of friends that always want to cause trouble. . . . After two weeks, one girl is going to be mad at another girl within the group, and whoever the groups like better, they're going to join sides with that person." Asked why the men carried guns more often than the women, she answered: "It's more expected of them." Asked if she ever found a man who wished he could get loose from those expectations, she said: "Never asked." Relationships between young women and young men were edgy because so many young men rode the edge: "It's kind of hard because if you fall in love with somebody that's in danger of being shot or anything, and you want to be with this person, then you know right there that you're also putting yourself in danger. Because if they can't get to him, they want to get to the closest thing, and that's going to be you."

She did not think that removing all the guns from her neighborhood would improve the situation. "Nope, because people would resort to the next best thing, which would be a knife, and then we'd be talking about knife violence instead of gun violence." Churches, social workers, police hadn't helped, in her opinion. "There's a police station across the street from me. They know about the problem, they don't do nothing. There's a church across the street from me. They know about the problem, and they might attempt to do something but it never gets through. People have to *want* to give it up, and most people don't want to." Schools weren't the answer. "People in this lifestyle don't like school. They don't like the fact of people telling them what to do." She did not believe women could get together and change things: "It's not impossible, but it's just a matter of this: Who's going to listen?"

When she was younger, Cana once found herself running inside a spray of bullets. She understands that such things happen and real bullets are invisible:

> Sometimes you know. Sometimes you can sense it. Because if it's twelve o'clock in the afternoon and it's seventy degrees outside, and somebody's walking in a big black coat with a hood on it, you know. If you were sitting on a stoop outside and all of a sudden a black car rolls by with dark tinted windows and all of a sudden a window rolls down, you know. But at this moment, we were talking, minding our own business, and one person noticed a group of people approaching us, and they recognized that those were the people they had a beef with. So somebody said something and everybody reacted real quick. I don't know if I jumped or was pushed out of the way. It's brownstone buildings, with steps up like this. I was sitting on the steps, and in between the steps are the railings, and I was pushed down into the basement part.
>
> At the moment, you're just like . . . all I can remember saying is: "If I get out of this, I'll never do anything wrong again." You don't see anything, or I didn't. All you hear is the gunshots, the gunshots. You don't know where the bullets are going, which way. I was frozen. I heard bullets but I didn't know where they were, so I didn't know which way to duck or if I should crawl this way or crawl that way. I just froze.

For protection, Cana carried a gun in her bookbag for a while, a little .22 she got from a family friend, and she recalled that it "boosted my self-esteem because I knew that if anybody was to mess with me, I was going to shoot them." But she never had to use the gun and soon gave it up. "When I got it, I didn't really need it. And then when I gave it up, I felt like nothing happened to me when I had it, so how much more could happen to me when I didn't have it?" She had seen that a gun could act as a magnet, not a shield: "If another person knows you have a gun, and they know that you don't like them, they don't know that you're not going to shoot them, so they're going to shoot you before you can get to that person."

Pressed to generalize about her experiences for my benefit, Cana resisted. "I don't choose to make generalizations." Because they're no use, I asked?

"Not to me." She said yes, Ithaca, New York, was calmer than Harlem, New York. "As far as being here, I am a little more relieved than I would be if I were at home, just 'cause I can walk down the street without worrying about bullets flying. It's calm. It's much more calm." That didn't mean she lived in a constant state of fear at home. "When I go home, I don't necessarily walk down the street thinking, 'What am I going to do to be safe?' I just walk down the street. I *lived* around here all my life, so it never occurs to me that I'm in danger just walking down my own block, even though that's in the back of my mind. But that's not what I think about when I walk." And she was not convinced that other girls had it better. "There could be just as much violence in a white suburban area as there is in Harlem." She herself might choose to live in another place after college. Or she might turn around and go back home. "I can get away from Harlem and go anywhere, but anywhere I go, there's going to be something. It may not be guns. It may be something else. . . . The right direction for me can be headed right back towards Harlem, and that would just be the direction I follow." Cana was majoring in recreation and hoped to work with the elderly.

Because my interview with Cana focused on guns, it left me with a skewed picture of her life and her neighborhood. I don't know why she was interested in working with the elderly or what thoughts occupied her as she walked down the street to her house. "I just walk down the street." She sat in front of me like a practiced, skeptical student, dressed informally, but armored. Speaking to her, I felt like a teacher, but not quite, and also like a member of an audience. Her descriptions of bullets and battles on the street were cinematic, and my own situation akin to a spectator's. But Cana told me plainly that she didn't live in a movie or in the Metro Section of the *New York Times*. She lived at home.

Dead young men lie in the street. This scene is familiar. Recall Luzana Wilson's description of a western mining camp in 1849:

> Men plunged wildly into every mode of dissipation to drown the homesickness so often gnawing at their hearts. . . . They were possessed of the demon of recklessness, which always haunted the early mining camps. Blood was often shed, for a continual war raged between the miners and gamblers. Nearly every man carried in his belt either knife or pistol, and one or the other flashed out on small provocation to do its deadly work.

The word "homesick" resonates. According to our stories, the American rebel leaves his mother and ventures out past the edge of civilization into the wilderness because he has not been satisfied, because he hasn't found in his home place either sufficient money to fill his pocket or sufficient challenges to slake his spirit. Yet all the time, according to Luzana Wilson, this violent exile is homesick—*sick with longing for home*, for a place that had receded into the past.

Certainly Americans don't hold exclusive rights to nostalgia, but it seems that our mobile, repeatedly uprooted populace, so often described as forward-looking and adaptable, suffers from a pervasive backward-yearning nostalgia that has grown very strong in the 1990s. After the April 1999 shootings in Littleton, Colorado, *Newsweek* featured reports on "The Secret Life of Teens," with articles entitled "Searching for Answers," "Follow the Firearms," "How Well Do You Know Your Kid?," "When Teens Fall Apart," "Their Dark Romance with Risk," and "The Truth About High School."[12] One of the articles noted that half of the teenagers in the United States had lived through their parents' divorce, 63 percent lived in households where both parents worked, and that a University of Chicago study had found teenagers spent, on average, three and one-half hours alone every day.[13] In short, a high proportion of teenagers in the United States lived lonesome, unstable lives, and the situation was worsening. The underlying theme was familiar: Life in *fin de siècle* America is disorderly and toxic.

American is becoming an increasingly *homesick* nation.

The women of Camden remembered the years before the 1960s as more stable, neighborly, and literally rosy. Journalists, columnists, psychologists, and sociologists have taken up similar themes. The compassionate Cornell psychologist, James Garbarino, who wrote the book *Lost Boys: Why Our Sons Turn Violent and How We Can Save Them,* cites numerous psychological and sociological studies to show that American culture is becoming increasingly "toxic" for the young. He names the gun culture, violent video games and movies, a Southern code of honor, parental neglect and abuse, alcohol abuse, and materialism, among other factors, as desensitizing influences that incline young American males to commit violence. In *Lost Boys*, he writes both about the young male criminals, most of them African-American and Hispanic, whom he's counseled in an upstate New York juvenile facility, and also about the misfit schoolyard gun men (gun boys?) like Michael Carneal of West Paducah, Kentucky, Luke Woodham of Pearl, Mississippi, Mitchell Johnson of Jonesboro, Arkansas, and Kipland Kinkel of Springfield, Oregon, white "boys of the American heartland." It is Garbarino's opinion that the psychological similarities between these two "groups" of violent boys—their depressions, shames, lack of empathy and resilience, confused ideas about justice, longings for justice and power—are significant and deserve study. Like many anti-gun advocates, he speaks of violence in terms of "epidemics," arguing that we are now in Stage 2 of an epidemic of youth violence that began in the inner-cities and has since moved into the "suburbs and small towns," and that the "social environment for children and parents has continued to deteriorate." He writes: "By getting to know the circumstances under which the epidemic of youth violence first took hold among low-income minority youth in inner-city areas, we can begin to gain some insight into the lives of the boys in places like Jonesboro, Paducah, and Springfield."[14] Dr. Garbarino, like the women of Camden, recalls a time, a few decades past, when America was a finer, more stable place, and he wishes we could reclaim the benefits of that healthier era.

> Looking back on my childhood and adolescence with the benefit and bias of hindsight, I realize that adults shielded me and my peers from some of life's nasty realities. We had a social contract. Children knew their place in the scheme of things, which was to experience childhood—to play, to learn, to do what they were told, to stay within the rules. And adults were in charge. Their job was to take care of kids—to teach them, to play with them, to guide them, to protect them, and to support them. . . . One sign of how much things have changed was the release of sexually explicit material about President Clinton in September 1998.[15]

Cultural diagnoses and prescriptions of this kind are powerful strains in our national discourse, and they can lead to enormously useful reforms. At the same time, I think we should beware of prescriptions grounded in the assumption that America used to be a much nicer place, an assumption shared by a wide range of contemporary liberals and conservatives. Maybe America did used to be nicer in some ways—more children who grew up in the 1950s will remember that their mothers were usually at home—but we are HERE now. Forces that have been unleashed in the last forty years—one thinks of technology, popular culture, liberal skepticism, even "liberated" women—may be restricted, but they can't be put back in the bottle. What's more, the past probably was not as nice as we think. Just a brief review of frontier letters, photographs of city slums in the nineteenth century, letters from women living during the Depression, or conversations with women who felt themselves suffocating as housewives in the 1950s, teach us that life in this country has often been rough, though there were not always surveys to register the disorder and suffering.

In fact, I have come to think that the unacknowledged safety and comfort in which a huge proportion of Americans live today actually, perversely, make us avid to search out violent threats. The problem is that when we look for these threats or pathogens, these general causes of America's perceived decline and increasing sickness, we usually find them in somebody else's house. I am not thinking here of James Garbarino and other counselors like him, but of more rough and tumble political fighters. Thus liberals want to ban the guns they themselves don't own, and conservatives want liberals to start going back to church. This political pattern makes liberals and conservatives both inclined to preach and pry in ways that can be sharply insulting—a habit we may have inherited from our Puritanical forebears—and also inclined to recommend restrictions and spiritual reforms for anybody whose politics diverge from their own. What's more, it makes us ignore certain pieces of the puzzle necessary to create, to imagine, an entire, complex picture of this diverse nation. Anti-gun advocates should wonder how it is that the state of New Hampshire allows its citizens to carry guns in public relatively unrestricted, and yet has one of the lowest gun-homicide rates in the nation. And pro-gun advocates should take into account the fact that recent, steady declines in the nation's crime rate have been attributed by many law enforcement officials to proactive police strategies that take advantage of strict gun-control laws in urban areas.

We must make generalizations to figure out who and where we are as Americans. Yet then we must test our generalizations. It is no doubt true that the psychological portraits of troubled, violent young American men resemble one another. Yet the "influences" that characterize inner-city gun violence—influences usually related to illegal drug enterprises, severe economic disadvantages, and poor education—must be distinguished from the "influences" that drive upper-middle-class white adolescents to walk into their school, shoot a mismatched flock of acquaintances their own age, and then kill themselves. Specific kinds of attention and of reforms—many of them educational and economic—are needed to address the first broad problem. Other kinds of attention and reforms are required by the second. Some of these will overlap, but not all of them will.

The series of articles about the Littleton, Colorado, killings published in *Newsweek* concluded with a column by Jonathan Alter, who pointed out the fact that the deaths of white, middle-class students had shocked the public in ways that the more common gunshot deaths of African-American students never managed.

> For years now, an average of roughly forty teenagers a week have been murdered in this country, nearly 90 percent killed by guns. That's the equivalent of 150 Littleton massacres a year. But they happen mostly one by one, off school grounds—no national news potential there—and slightly more than half of the teen killers and victims have been black. [16]

James Garbarino noted the same phenomenon: that the deaths of white teenagers always aroused much more horror, nationally, than the more common deaths of black teenagers, a fact that for years allowed residents of smaller towns to feel safe from the "epidemic" of youth violence. And of course Dr. Weaver, an African-American physician, noticed it as well. When facing a predominantly white audience, he always made sure to begin his slide shows with pictures of dead young white men, not dead young black men.

After the shootings at Littleton, President Clinton and members of Congress rushed to signal their concern. The president hosted a conference on juvenile violence. The Senate approved a few new gun-control measures. The House passed a "Juvenile Offenders Act" to provide states and local governments with more money for prisons, prosecutors, and drug rehabilitation programs, and it voted to increase penalties against minors for illegal possession or use of firearms. Modest gun-control legislation died in the House.

Far from these public displays and efforts, what was going on was going on. The women with whom I'd spoken in Camden, individuals who knew about "juvenile offenders" first-hand, were doing their work. These women generally did not trust the promise that guns in the hands of individuals would act to protect communities, establish order, or guarantee anybody's safety or rights. They appreciated an old-fashioned need for rules and authority, but they also felt the need for skating rinks, movie theaters, jobs, and better schools. And they knew all about living near the edge of a dangerous frontier, and about the sorrows of women whose sons have gone off to explore that frontier. Recall Brenda Roundtree: "My arms are still wanting to put my arms around him."

## Notes

1. See Bureau of Justice Statistics Reports, "Homicide Trends in the U.S.: Trends by Race," http://www.ojp.usdoj.gov/bjs/homicide/race. "Homicide Trends in the U.S: Age, Gender, and Race Trends," http://www.ojp.usdoj.gov/bjs/homicide/ageracesex. "Homicide Trends in the U.S.: Weapons Used," http://www.ojp.usdoj.gov/bjs/homicide/weapons. The graphs in the report on "Age, Gender, and Race" show that in 1995, homicide victimization rates for populations of people aged 18–24 were tallied in this way: black male homicide victims aged 18–24 per 100,000 population: 148.8 (down from 176.2 in 1994). White male homicide victims of the same age per 100,000 population: 17.3. Black female homicide victims of the same age per 100,000 population: 17.1. White female homicide victims of the same age per 100,000 population: 4.2. According to the publication, "Homicide Trends by Race," most homicides are intraracial: 86 percent of white victims were killed by whites; 94 percent of black victims were killed by blacks.

2. Deborah Prothrow-Stith, with Michaele Weissman, *Deadly Consequences* (New York: HarperPerennial, 1993), pp. 6, 18.

3. Ibid., pp. 65–66.

4. Ibid., p. 69.

5. Bill Shralow, "Camden Tightens School Security," *Camden Courier-Post,* February 16, 1996.

6. Sasha Abramsky, "When They Get Out," *Atlantic Monthly* (June 1999), pp. 30–36. Abramsky cites a study by Bruce Western, of Princeton, and Katherine Beckett, of Indiana University, entitled, "How Unregulated Is the U.S. Labor Market? The Penal System as a Labor Market Institution."

7. "Losing the Vote," available from http://www.sentencingproject.org/news/news.html. 1999.

8. Michael Massing, "Crime and Drugs: The New Myths," *New York Review of Books*, vol. XLIII, no. 2 (February 1, 1996), p. 18.

9. Michael Cooper, "Homicides Decline Below 1964 Level in New York City," *New York Times*, December 24, 1998, p. A-1.

10. Ibid., p. 17.

11. Clifford Kraus, "New York Sees Steepest Decline in Violent Crime Rate Since '72," *New York Times,* December 31, 1995, p. 1, 32.

12. See various articles in *Newsweek* (May 10, 1999), pp. 31–58.

13. Barbara Kantrowitz and Pat Wingert, "How Well Do You Know Your Kid?" *Newsweek* (May 10, 1999), p. 38.

14. James Garbarino, *Lost Boys: Why Our Sons Turn Violent and How We Can Save Them* (New York: Free Press, 1999), throughout.

15. Ibid., p. 176.

16. Jonathan Alter, "On the Cusp of a Crusade," *Newsweek* (May 10, 1999), p. 59.

# 8

---

# Conclusion

## Partisans and Their Peoples

Less than a week before Christmas, on December 19, 1998, the House of Representatives voted to impeach President William Jefferson Clinton. Of the 228 members who voted to impeach the president for perjuring himself in misrepresenting his adulterous affair before a grand jury, only five were Democrats. Of the 206 members who voted not to impeach, only five were Republicans. As reporters noted again and again, *this* was *really* partisan politics. Many analysts interpreted the drive to impeach Bill Clinton as the culmination of an intense political struggle between conservatives and liberals that had begun six years earlier with his election and shaped the politics of the 1990s (which were themselves engendered in the 1960s . . . or, some would argue, in the 1780s). Since this discussion has been occupied with aspects of that struggle, we take time here to look back on "The Clinton Era" and the stories people told when they were following, and thereby creating, its history . . . spanking new American history.

The impeachment hearings, proceedings, and subsequent analyses of those proceedings were marked by countless references to the American people. Everybody claimed to be acting on behalf of the American people. Bob Barr, Republican from Georgia, said: "I think there are two Americas, and there is a real America out there. . . . And it is that America that I have great faith in, because it's that America that understands what perjury is." Conservatives of the same political persuasion as Barr inveighed "moral relativism" and exhorted their colleagues to uphold the "rule of law" and thereby set a moral

197

example for America's children. Inside this discourse, Clinton was identified as both a cause and a sign of creeping "moral relativism" in the nation. Draft dodger, occasional ally of homosexuals, blacks, and women, and husband to a liberal female lawyer, he stood as a representative "child of the sixties," that decade when American values were turned upside down by protesters and a host of revisionist historians. According to a *Wall Street Journal* editorial, the prosecutor Ken Starr was trying to nail not just Clinton, "but the generation that produced him," that is, the sixties generation.[1] Bob Inglis, Republican of South Carolina, expressed the same idea to the Judiciary Committee: "One view is that there is absolute truth. The other view is that everything is relative. And really what we're seeing here in President Clinton, I believe, is the culmination of that. He is the perfect embodiment of everything being relative."[2]

To resist this conservative Republican chorus, liberal Democrats never attempted to defend the sexual exploits of Clinton. Instead, they attacked the Republicans, accusing them of hypocrisy and of being so "crazed" by their hatred of Clinton that they no longer attended to the will of the people they'd been elected to represent. Liberals argued that the pro-impeachment troops were being led by white males and right-wing Christian groups. Betty Friedan called leaders of the drive to impeach "a bunch of dirty old white men," and Maureen Dowd described watching the House Republicans deliver the impeachment papers as "a sight at once grotesque and hilarious: a bunch of out-of-touch old white guys trying to fathom truth in sex." The fact that Clinton could himself be characterized as a "dirty old white guy" escaped mention. Representative Charles Rangel of New York noted that the Republican contingent of the House Judiciary Committee was made up of nearly all white men (joined by a single white woman), while the Democratic side included five blacks, three women, and an openly gay man. "It's a political lynch mob," declared Rangel. "They think that America should look like they look—white."[3]

Staring into clusters of microphones, conservatives reported that they could see real America and the American people. The liberals said they could too. The portraits didn't coincide. This is how our democracy works.

Throughout this book, we have paid attention to the polarized public rhetoric —specifically rhetoric contributing to the national discourse on guns, gun risks, gun control, gun rights—produced by conservative and liberal political advocates. We have also attended to individual stories told by American women in the 1990s and explored what happens when personal stories intersect with public debates, and vice versa. The course of this discussion, as it has zig-zagged from articles to Internet sites to historical documents to personal interviews and anecdotes, has been intended to track down The American People and even to discover America . . . and it has been pursued with confidence that the prey will elude capture.

Yet we hunt for it. We hunt for "us." It is impossible to make history without generalizations, and impossible to make identity without thinking of one's history. *The people. The American people. Our children. Americans.*

After the impeachment votes had been cast and counted, reporters spread out across the country to interview people: men eating sandwiches, women shopping for Christmas gifts, guys in bars. The guys in the bars turned out to be more focused on the Buffalo Bills and New York Jets, but everybody had opinions. Pollsters were mobilized. By Monday, *USA Today* could report that President Clinton's job approval rating had "hit a personal high during the weekend in spite of his impeachment. . . ." [4] For avowed conservatives the results were disorienting. A *New York Times* reporter interviewed voters amazed by these polls. Many of them spoke of their efforts to teach their children right from wrong and the need to see that Clinton, who had lied under oath, received swift and appropriate punishment. And they said they couldn't fathom the nation anymore. "It's like I don't even understand what country I'm living in," said one dazed Republican. [5]

To my mind, this man has made a significant discovery, for every genuine search for America should commence with bewilderment and keep coming back to it. Partisan political contests illuminate contrasting strands in American discourse, but to see the entire picture we must allow for, even hunt for, entanglements, contradictions, unresolved dilemmas. This book has examined combative discourses about guns, "gun rights," gun "self-defense" "independence" and "self-reliance" as they've been broadcast and interpreted through the 1990s, and it has sought for entanglements by focusing on contemporary women, whose misfit relationship to many long-lasting American stereotypes helps illuminate those stereotypes. What's more, the discussion has presented the voices of women whose experiences defy easy categorization, and whose different perspectives and reports ought to unsettle anyone whose America includes only two kinds of people, two teams of people: the formulaic good guys and the bad guys, one's designated allies and enemies.

We the people . . . who are these people? Stefani Woodhams is one of the people. She grips the barrel of a shotgun controlled by her husband—"I had a madman on my hands"—while beagles bark outdoors, and the children overhead keep as silent as doorknobs. A few years later she can be found shooting at a target with a new husband. Carole Hockmeyer scrambles down a hallway in Newbury, New Hampshire, falls once, gets up, finds herself locked in the town hall restroom, where she tears out a screen in a little window. She is literally shot full of holes. Shirley Grenoble walks step after step through the woods trailed by the two brothers who, thinking she sounds like a turkey, spray her with heavy shot. Not long after, she returns to the woods to hunt. She hopes her granddaughter will follow. Joanne Carroll sleeps over a new LadySmith 9 millimeter pistol, but more importantly, she keeps an eye on passing cars and on the time, continually tracking her own movements to avoid those places where her estranged husband expects her to be. To be safe, she must live outside habit. Tamara Mechem is missing two children. Brenda Roundtree is missing a son. Ruth Merson sits quietly in a dry valley where gunshot reports echo off automobiles and flagpoles; she hates the wartime shock of any explosion but spends time comfortably here. Sherry shoots target in the field with other militia members and then returns to a basement where a computer hums like a little heater. She lights up a cigarette. Kathryn Blackshear sends her son to his father to fetch her a gun but later wraps the thing and stuffs it in the trash. A girl called Cana grabs a metal pipe. She carries a gun for a while before realizing that it doesn't work well as a shield. She attends college.

Each individual woman named in this list is embedded in the nation, and at the same time more complicated and larger than a nation. She can be and has been placed, *located* as a member of this or that group, not only because the culture has judged the value of her gender, race, or class, but also because she has identified herself in league with allies over the years, and she has often interpreted her own experiences in accord with the ideologies of her friends. Yet her experiences, as they are lived, in the moment they are lived, cannot be duplicated. When she tells stories, she corrals her past and, at the same time, illuminates the edges of vast territories that can't be told. She is one of The People, certainly. And yet that old public phrase is just a buzz in the rooms where she lives.

What good does it do to assert these commonplace mysteries, when even a brief imaginative flight over Washington, DC, shows that political power does not reside in citizens, but in political action committees, corporations, and conduits, in moneyed, opportunistic partisan politics? It may do very little good.

## Recent Histories

In 1992, Bill Clinton was elected. He supported gun-control legislation but in many other areas was described as "vacillating." Six years later, Tanya Metaksa of the NRA would write the history of the early battles between Clinton and the good guys—her good guys—in this way:

> After the Brady Act and the Clinton Crime Bill became law and President Clinton proved that he would do his best to live up to our worst predic-

tions, gun owners who didn't believe our warnings woke up. They got involved at the grassroots, and we all began to work together. The result was the 1994 elections.

You remember 1994. It was payback time. United in our cause, we sent an unmistakably clear pro-Second Amendment, pro-freedom message to the American voters and new pro-Second Amendment Congressmen to Washington. Our overwhelming success in the 1994 elections stymied Clinton's efforts to steamroller his anti-gun agenda legislatively.[6]

From the vantage point of the new millennium, it is surprisingly difficult to recall the public mood of 1994, the widespread jubilation of so many American conservatives and the despair of so many American liberals. In the midterm election heralded by Newt Gingrich's conservative "Contract with America," Republicans won a majority of seats in both houses of Congress for the first time in decades, and Gingrich became Speaker of the House. Post-election reports in 1994 often focused on the leverage of the male pro-gun, pro-NRA vote in support of the conservative Republican candidates who unseated Democratic incumbents. Clinton credited the Democrats' losses to the NRA: "The NRA is the reason the Republicans control the House."

But two years later, in 1996, the vista had changed. Reshaped and resurrected, Clinton was reelected, and his electoral success described as a "victory for studied modesty" by *Time*. What's more, this time around the popular news magazines had virtually nothing to say about the NRA. Somehow it was no longer a big part of the election story. The NRA earned just one sentence in *Newsweek*'s post-election issue, a sentence that was immediately followed by mention of the newly elected House representative, Carolyn McCarthy. Both *Time* and *Newsweek* featured brief reports of McCarthy, a Long Island political novice whose husband was killed and son seriously injured by a rogue gunman, Colin Ferguson, on a Long Island Rail Road commuter train. McCarthy switched into the Democratic party to win a seat in the House, vanquishing a conservative freshman delegate with her one-issue campaign: gun control.

McCarthy's personal history attracted attention in part because it coordinated with the message mainstream journalists used to cap the 1996 campaign and make a story of it (stories require conclusions). That story trumpeted the collapse of the hard-line conservative revolution that was supposed to have been initiated by the midterm election of 1994. The conservative Congress that struck fear into Handgun Control Inc. two years earlier had not managed to repeal the 1994 assault weapons ban in its first term. And though a band of states' rights advocates were challenging the Brady Bill in the Supreme Court, they hadn't yet succeeded in 1996 (though by June of 1997 their efforts would bear fruit and the Supreme Court would declare the provision of the Brady Law requiring a Chief Law Enforcement Officer [CLEO] to conduct background checks on prospective handgun purchasers to be unconstitutional based on the Tenth Amendment).

Still, in November of 1996 it appeared that the conservative political advance had been stopped, and a shift in mood nationwide seemed to have dampened the appeal of the NRA's message and weakened its clout. In October of that year, just weeks before the election, National Public Radio reported that the NRA was *not* likely to wield again the power it had two years earlier for a number of reasons, including the membership's lack of enthusiasm for presidential candidate Bob Dole, a powerful counterattack by labor unions, and a hemorrhaging of the NRA itself. According to one source, within the last year the NRA had laid off staff workers, arranged to rent out a portion of its new headquarters building, and lost a fifth of its membership "in part because of bad publicity surrounding the Oklahoma City bombing and an NRA fund-raising letter that called federal law enforcement agents 'jack-booted thugs.'"[7] That was the letter that prompted former president George Bush to resign his membership in the NRA.

Skimming through media analyses of this kind, trying to figure out the newest state of the nation, people came away with the impression that all sorts of Angry White Males had lost magnetism and influence since 1994, damaged in part by the self-righteously lawless performances of white men associated with right-wing militias. What's more, reporters had decided that female voters played a decisive role in chastening and silencing reactionary male ideologues. The gender gap dividing the electorate became news. According to an analysis in the *Nation* titled "Voting Blocs, Building Blocks":

> "Pink collar" female workers, the new swing voters, are worried about the issues that affect them where they live—wages, family leave, education, the environment, medical care—far more than about abstract left-right labels based on out-of-date ideological conflicts. Clinton owned these issues, and his attempts to deal with them in small steps fit the public mood. The Republican Congress, apparently guided more by ideological abstractions than by *real experience* [author's emphasis] failed to take the concerns of these voters into account, thereby bringing the "Gingrich revolution" to a screeching halt.[8]

Liberals in 1996 were eager to congratulate America women, who appeared to have been key in electing Clinton and therefore to have replaced the Angry White Male as a decisive political force. The 1996 voting stats showed male voters had split evenly between the Democrat, Clinton (44 percent) and the Republican presidential candidate, Dole (44 percent), but female voters preferred Clinton by a substantial margin (Clinton—54 percent, Dole—38 percent).

This story of America's transformation into a country guided by women of "real experience" was partly fiction, however. In reality, the surging "pink collar" vote that reportedly won the presidency for Clinton in 1996 had been just as strong in 1994: in 1994, during the so-called Gingrich revolution, the same percentage of women (54 percent) voted Democratic. Therefore, Clinton must have secured reelection in 1996 not by winning the women's vote, but by holding it, and then positioning himself more skillfully relative to the dreams, interests, and even resentments of white American men (it was not necessary for him to win over African-American men because he had over 80 percent of the African-American vote secured). Ironically, therefore, his success may well have demonstrated not the failure, but the culmination of the 1994 Republican revolution, for in order to win a second term, the candidate accommodated himself to parts of the conservative agenda, most notably welfare reform.[9] (Since we are tracking the American people, let it be noted that 1996 saw the lowest electoral turnout in a presidential campaign since 1924. More than half of the citizens eligible to vote in the United States did not walk into any polling place. It is sobering to think how many people *don't count* in our political contests and to consider the weight, in experience and presence, of this vast host of no-accounts.)

People who have kept track of American political debates for the last few decades will instinctively understand how the nation's gun politics are related to welfare politics, and how it is that the angry pro-gun vote could either metamorphose into or be deflated, because satisfied, by a successful vote for welfare reform. Declarations having to do with American independence and self-reliance bridge the related discourses, and unstated racial discriminations play a part as well, in my opinion, because African-Americans and Hispanics, as groups, are perceived as dependent on welfare. Rebecca John, cofounder of SWARM in Colorado, said to me: "We're more and more dependent on our government for our food, our clothes, our income. It's not healthy for us, as individuals, or for the society as a whole. The way I see it, we're responsible to bathe ourselves, we're responsible to feed ourselves, and we are responsible for our self-defense." This logic equates self-reliant gun ownership with self-supporting work, and, thereby, with "independence" and even, more oddly, "freedom." In a similar way, Sherry, member of the Chemung County Militia, identified the gun as a necessary, even iconic, tool for an independent citizen. She favored actions that cut away some part of the national and international New World Order net that she believed has been cast wide to control, entrap, and ultimately denature

204 • WOMEN AND GUNS

individual Americans. She perceived the nation to be suffering from an over-dose of one sort of "independence"—liberal individualism—and a deficiency of another sort—conservative individualism. In such a mood, idealized images of spare frontier life become especially attractive, for they promise individual sovereignty, control over one's own property, and guns barring the door against invasion: physical self-defense. Old-fashioned frontier virtues defined in this way legislate for Second Amendment rights, against gun control, against welfare entitlements, and, often, against federal environmental legislation.

Those who speak in favor of conservative individualism and self-reliance very often resort to gendered imagery. They identify the United States as elementally masculine—assertive, stoic, competitive—and resist public demands for more "compassionate," that is "feminized," public policy.[10] In doing so, these speakers draw on a tradition that reaches back to the founding of the United States. Gordon Wood, scholar of the American revolution, has shown that the fantasy of creating an ideal nation by uniting independent men under a good government relied on masculine rhetoric to give it force. American writers in the eighteenth century repeatedly contrasted the strengths of their national character—frugality, industry, simplicity, "scorn of ease," "love of valor"—with the corruptions of the feminized European character. According to one such author, Americans were a "hardy virtuous set of men . . . strangers to that luxury which effeminates the mind and body."[11]

In our political era, questions about (1) what it is that constitutes American manhood; (2) what American manhood has to do with guns; and (3) whether American manhood as a presence and an idea should be celebrated or restrained, all contribute to public debates about issues as diverse as welfare and gun control. Our politics are gendered in ways (sometimes clear, sometimes confusing) that the gun debates we have studied illuminate. In March 2000, the *New York Times* ran a front-page article announcing that the upcoming presidential race might be largely determined by whether or not the Republican George W. Bush, who described himself as a "compassionate conservative," could attract the women's vote. The article noted that women had voted "heavily Democratic in two of the last three presidential elections" and that:

> One of the first tests may come on the issue of gun violence and gun control, which pollsters say is a far more powerful issue among women than among men. In a CBS News poll conducted Sunday through Tuesday, 56 percent of the men said laws governing the sale of handguns should be made more strict; 73 percent of the women did. . . .
> Democrats see Mr. Bush's record on guns—especially his signing of a law allowing Texans to carry concealed guns—as a real vulnerability.[12]

The article went on to note that Governor Bush had signed Texas legislation that effectively banned "public health" class action and personal lawsuits against gun manufacturers.

I am skeptical about the prediction that Bush's "record on guns" will prove to be a "real vulnerability" in the presidential race. Public fascination with the gun-control debates flares and dies periodically in the United States, and women across the nation do not impress me as a tight, predictable bloc of voters, or as one-issue voters. The shooting of six-year-old Kayla Rolland by her six-year-old classmate in March 2000 reignited interest in gun politics once again, and Clinton, whose record as an ally of gun-control organizations has been unwavering, helped fan the fires in the early months of 2000 by publicly attacking pro-gun congressmen and the NRA for their intransigent opposition to modest gun-control measures. But Clinton's motives for pressing this wedge issue, this designated women's issue, were surely, in part, political, and people recognize that. Clinton was intent on helping his vice-president, Al Gore, win the presidency in November. He was interested in publicity, in spin. The death of Rolland, followed by a loud barrage of public insults traded between Wayne LaPierre of the NRA and Clinton, all accompanied by the announcement that Smith & Wesson had capitulated to pressure from the pro-gun control lawsuits (see below), did attract media attention. *Newsweek* featured Rolland on its March 13 cover and featured a story, " Inside the Gun Wars," on March 27.

Whether the reverberations from this tragedy and other recent gun tragedies will last until November 2000 and influence the outcome of the presidential election has yet to be seen. Many citizens have become anti-gun activists in the wake of these events, and they have organized to press for the passage of new state and federal gun-control laws. The Million Mom March, a public anti-gun demonstration held in Washington, DC, on April 14, 2000, attracted approximately 750,000 participants (according to the organizers) and showcased impassioned women speakers, many of them mothers of children who had died of gun wounds. Rolland's mother, Veronica McQueen, spoke to the gathering, as did family members of students who had been killed in the Columbine High School shootings. Sarah Brady and Representative Carolyn McCarthy, among others, addressed the demonstrators, and Hillary and Bill Clinton addressed organizers at the White House. The woman who spearheaded the event, Donna Dees-Thomases, explained that she was inspired to begin organizing this Mother's Day demonstration after she watched an August 1999 television news report that described a shooting in a Jewish community center in Los Angeles.[13] Her Million Mom March website was decorated with flowers and showed vocal pro-gun advocates—Tom DeLay, House Majority whip (R-Texas) and, on a later date, Wayne La Pierre,

NRA president—seated in a little time-out chair as punishment. Additionally, the web-site offered a Mom's Apple Pie award to its favorite gun-control advocates (Bill Clinton in July of 2000). After the march was over, the revised web page invited women to become members of the Million Mom March Foundation so that they could continue to organize and advocate for gun control.[14] In short, this public event and the new advocacy organization that sprang from it were very clearly gendered, styled to attract and to represent women as women, as moms, in ways that have become familiar in contemporary American politics and that remain powerful.

These moms generally did not approve of the NRA. According to the *New York Times,* speakers "assailed the National Rifle Association and its power over Congress."[15] One Ithaca, New York, resident returning from the march commented: "I was truly inspired, and when I heard a rabbi say in his speech how the blood of the slaughter of our children is on the heads of the NRA, I came away feeling like I wanted to continue to try to do something back home."[16] Apparently the line between the good guys and the bad guys was very clearly drawn at this political event, and the agents that enable "gun violence" to flourish were sharply identified.

I would like to record my admiration for the women who took part in this demonstration and my support for many of their arguments, while, at the same time, registering some doubt about the discourse and methods that necessarily energize this kind of a political exercise. Though the Million Mom March was remarkable in the way it generated grassroots political involvement, its rhetoric was familiar, adapted from position statements broadcast by established gun-control advocacy organizations. And the same style of political combat, pitting good guys against bad guys, was in evidence, the same contentious, unanswerable, deafening, and sometimes misleading rhetorical machinery employed. If one judged the attitudes of American women based on this event, one would expect that Al Gore, the Democratic candidate for president and a gun-control advocate, would attract more of the women's vote in November, and George W. Bush, who does not favor additional gun control and who, as governor of Texas, signed his state's right-to-carry bill, would make a poor showing. Excited by this prospect, one Democratic pollster present at the march was quoted in the *New York Times* as saying: "Bush ought to be terrified. Look out there—that is the face of the soccer mom." But a *New York Times*/CBS News poll noted in the same article found that "women are almost evenly divided in their views of how the two presidential candidates handle the gun issue. . . . Thirty-five percent of the women said they agreed more with Mr. Gore, while 30 percent said they agreed more with Mr. Bush. Among mothers, 33 percent said they agree more with Mr. Bush, 24 percent with Mr. Gore."[17] It looks like we will have to wait until the very last minute to see how the gun debates, which are often expected to separate the girls from the boys, play out in the upcoming election.

Public speech, private thought. The territory that exists between these modes of action is significant, and I think we must venture here, into the territory that intersects public and private, in order to explore how national identity and individual identity are shaped and how they interact with one another. Assumptions about gender, questions about gender, are an important part of this shaping process. Plenty of Americans would like to see the country become more "compassionate," "feminized," not only for their own sake, but for the sake of their children, who must grow up inhaling American popular culture. But plenty of others dread this promised liberal reform and transformation. It doesn't feel right. They don't like it when actions and symbols that used to be considered normal or good—hunting, cigarette smoking, the Confederate flag, to name a disconnected few—are redefined as sick or unacceptable, while actions and symbols that used to be considered sick or unacceptable are redefined as normal. They dread waking up to find they don't understand what country they're living in anymore. They don't want to wake up as aliens.

But they must, we all must, occasionally, in order to rediscover the nation and ourselves, because the nation is being daily recreated. And this process is not new, not unique to the electrified United States of America in the second half of the twentieth century. The United States has always been protean, and since its inception our most influential thinkers have been continually troubled by inconsistencies between their idealized characterization of The People and, well, crowds of actual local people. Our Constitution was written by a group of exclusively male would-be leaders intent on constructing the government of a nation freshly born of an armed conflict. The document they hammered together was framed according to their understanding of a people that consisted of male citizens, potentially armed. It is amazing that this document, this democratic framework, has been stretched to fit the nation as it exists today. We seem to be a people with such a short memory, with so little grasp of and so little interest in our own history, and yet some traditions, some documents and declarations, have proven to be exceptionally resilient, and the Constitution is first among these. In my opinion, this could happen not so much because the Founding Fathers got all the answers right, but because they focused on significant, enduring *questions* and framed a government to accommodate dissent and change. How should an individual be fitted to a government, and how should a government be fitted to accommodate individuals? What is a people? How can government be kept rooted in the people? It is these long-lived questions, much more than the changing answers, that constitute our most precious democratic legacy.

## The Founding Fathers and Their People

Article I, Section 8 of the United States Constitution, introduced by the pragmatist Alexander Hamilton and eventually ratified by the states, granted Congress the right to "provide for organizing, arming and disciplining the Militia, and for governing such Part of them as may be employed in the Service of the United States." Simply put, this meant that the U.S. Congress would have the power to muster its own standing army. But a number of influential patriots distrusted standing armies, which they pictured as mercenary, parasitic hordes dispatched against the people by a despotic monarch. So in 1789 James Madison proposed a set of twelve amendments—the Bill of Rights—to reinforce the powers of the people against centralized authority. Pared down to ten amendments, the Bill of Rights was adopted in 1791. Its second amendment assured the states that their citizens would retain their weapons and so maintain the power to revolt against a federal government should it turn tyrant.

It states: *"A Well regulated militia, being necessary to the security of a free State, the right of the people to keep and bear Arms shall not be infringed."*

This single sentence was composed more than two hundred years ago by men who lived in a different world—before repeating rifles, before the infected, intestinal rending of the Civil War and the liberation of the nation's slaves, before the enfranchisement of women, before anesthesia, antibiotics, electrical outlets, photographic film, automobiles . . . add to the list all technological advances in medicine, communications, transportation, and weaponry developed in the last two hundred years. And when these men wrote referring to the "people"—*"the right of the people to keep and bear Arms shall not be infringed"*—they did not mean to include servants, slaves, vagabonds, or females. No skirts interrupted the hedge of trousered legs standing in queue for exercises on the drilling field.

The fact that the Constitution was composed in a such different time, and that it named entities that have altered drastically since that time—the states, the government, the people—challenges, but never completely defeats, those who use the document as a guide for contemporary government. Wonderfully, it turns out that this last entity, the people, has from the first been difficult to pin down. The Founding Fathers themselves quickly discovered that America's general population failed to live up to their expectations when it came to virtue. The most articulate revolutionaries, who identified with one another as genteel men, found that their newly enfranchised fellow citizens sometimes neglected to respect or even elect them, and voted instead for noisy upstarts who promised favors and local improvements. "Effrontery and arrogance, even in our virtuous and enlightened days, are giving rank and Importance to men whom Wisdom would have left in obscurity," mourned John Jay, revolutionary and political theorist. By the 1790s, political thinkers had already learned that "the people were not an order organically tied together by their unity of interest but rather an agglomeration of hostile individuals coming together for their mutual benefit to construct a society," according to Gordon Wood.[18] The people were already a ragtail mystery.

And there were other mysteries. The Constitution did not explain how a "well regulated" militia would be created from such a disparate collection of male gun owners. It would require a people practiced in devotion to the common good, but already the people were showing themselves to be headstrong, diverse, and unreliable. The regiments of American patriots mustered against England most nearly approximated such a universal militia, and the authors of the 1789 Bill of Rights were doubtlessly recalling their own experiences as armed and principled rebels when they penned the Second Amendment. But they were also borrowing from similar bills in a number of the states' constitutions, bills that defended the people's right to bear arms and located the abiding source of security in an armed, trained (male) populace, rather than in a standing army.[19] These bills were themselves modeled after a portion of the English Bill of Rights, which had been introduced by Parliament a century earlier in response to the aggressions of the Catholic King James II and his standing army. In all these cases, it was understood that a citizens' militia was meant to unite against tyranny. This honorable goal gave the volunteer militia, as defined, its authority; without such an honorable goal, any restive collection of armed American rebels would be nothing more than pack of traitorous rabble. The propertied Founding Fathers had little use for traitorous rabble. George Washington's forceful suppression of the Whiskey Rebellion of 1794, a citizens' armed protest against a federal excise tax on homemade whiskey, indicated as much. After crushing the Pennsylvania rebellion with a force of 15,000 armed militiamen mustered by the federal government, Washington addressed Congress and spoke against "self-created societies" that prompted small groups of citizens to resist the authority of the federal government.

The authors of the Constitution had been scrupulous in designing a governmental machine that relied on the people for its power and could be altered by the people when they chose. This made it very difficult to imagine when and how such a government could ever be judged despotic—it was much easier to judge an individual king to be despotic—so that a collection of U.S. citizens might justifiably arise, challenge the central government or the United States' standing army through force of arms and, after the dust had cleared, be judged as virtuous, patriotic militiamen . . . not "irregular" riffraff excited by "specious pretexts."

Somewhere between the vision of a mustered regiment marching in step outdoors and the vision of a single Kentucky rifle slung from a nail indoors, the Second Amendment presents us with deep obscurity. This gap between the public, outdoor mustering of arms and the private, indoor keeping of arms creates a fertile ground for conflicting interpretations of the amendment's central meaning. Did the authors of the Constitution intend for the government to regulate the number and kinds of weapons a citizen could keep in his own home, or would they have defined that intrusion as an infringement of the citizen's rights? It seems clear that James Madison and his illustrious colleagues had little fear of guns as poisonous, infectious, or immoral objects, as pathogens. These men did not think of firearms in the way gun-control advocates do now. Their perspective was more plainly masculine and militant. At the same time, it is also clear that the Founding Fathers lived in a young nation where unwritten gun-control laws were at work. Madison and Jefferson equated *freedom* with *regulation*, just as George Washington equated "true liberty" with duty. A well *regulated* militia, being necessary to the security of a *free* state. . . . What's more, they did not grant a universal right to "self-defense." Reviewing eighteenth-century debates about the Bill of Rights, the legal scholar David Williams found that "the references to a popular right of resistance are countless; in contrast, the references to a popular right to arms for self-defense are quite rare."[20] It is clear that Thomas Jefferson, a sterling representative of the people as defined then, would have expected to defend himself and his own extensive property with firearms. But he would not have been ready to grant his slaves, male and (more tellingly) female, the right to bear arms for their own self-defense . . . against him, for instance.

In the late nineteenth and twentieth centuries, the Supreme Court has interpreted the Second Amendment with some consistency by concluding that the American right to keep and bear arms is inextricably linked to a stated purpose—the establishment of a militia to defend the freedom of the state—and this right is empty when divorced from that purpose. A landmark case, *United States v. Miller,* was decided in 1939, after a citizen challenged the National Firearms Act of 1934 prohibiting possession of sawed-off shotguns. In their 1939 ruling, members of the Court judged that the purpose of the Second Amendment was "to assure the continuation and render possible the effectiveness of (militia) forces." The Court said it found no evidence to show that "possession of use of a [sawed-off shotgun] has some reasonable relationship to the preservation or efficiency of a well-regulated militia." But at the same time the justices acknowledged that in the eighteenth century, when the Constitution and the Bill of Rights were written, the militia included "all males physically capable of acting in concert for the common defense" and agreed that "when called for service, these men were expected to appear bearing arms supplied by themselves." Interpreted in this way, the Second Amendment not only accepts, but condones, the existence of a substantial arsenal of privately owned weapons. But the brief amendment does not specify which styles of weapons meet the criteria as firearms appropriate to be used for the common defense (only nonrepeating guns, flintlocks, and pistols would have been available at the time), nor does it make clear whether citizens who would be unlikely to act for the common defense, that is, reprobates and British sympathizers and their ilk, could be stripped of their weapons. At last, it does not make clear whether the public purpose described in the amendment could be used to regulate private ownership of firearms.[21]

Viewed from these many angles, the Second Amendment shows itself to be a problematic document for the eighteenth century and a perplexing document for the late twentieth century. Some critics, notably feminist critics, have argued that it ought to be scrapped. One such author, Wendy Brown, writing in the *Yale Law Journal,* contended the Founding Fathers' "republican intellectual tradition includes a militarism, elitism and machismo that is past due for thoughtful critique and reworking."[22] Even the scholar David Williams, who generally defends the republican tradition, concluded: "The absence of a universal militia is now severe and chronic, and self-deception about its existence has become impossible. . . . As a result, for judges trying to interpret the Second Amendment, republicanism suggests that the Amendment, as worded, is meaningless."[23] Alert to feminist criticism, he acknowledged that the Founding Fathers' eloquence was powered by age-old masculine enthusiasms:

> Republicans' use of metaphors of masculinity to describe militia members, and the centrality of guns, danger, physicality and male-bonding themes in recollections of militia service suggest that, for many, the militia may have offered rich emotional rewards for the same reasons that hunting trips and team sports do.[24]

Yet the Second Amendment remains in the Constitution, and it appears to have been written by men who valued the people's right to keep their own firearms. The legal scholar Sanford Levinson, a self-described "card-carrying member of the ACLU," has studied the Second Amendment and concluded that the Founding Fathers did mean to insure that law-abiding individual citizens would have the right to own and keep firearms untroubled by the state, for they recognized the people as an arm of government. He says: "Arguments on behalf of a 'strong' Second Amendment are stronger than many of us might wish were the case." He moves on to consider the core reason for liberal opposition to the Second Amendment, based on a calculation and measurement of gun deaths in the United States: "It appears almost crazy to protect as a constitutional right something that so clearly results in extraordinary social costs." But Levinson wonders if those who would happily discard the Second Amendment have looked hard enough at contemporary examples of people effectively resisting—or failing to resist—a massively armed state. He cites the situations in Northern Ireland and Palestinian territories occupied by Israel, "where the sophisticated weaponry of Great Britain and Israel have proved almost totally beside the point . . ." and mentions Tiananmen Square. His conclusion: "A state facing a totally disarmed population is in a far better position, for good or ill, to suppress popular demonstrations and uprisings than one that must calculate the possibilities of its soldiers and officials being injured or killed."[25]

This ongoing analysis of the very brief Second Amendment—and of the much longer Constitution to the United States—illuminates how history *works*. Not only do the words and actions of our forebears continue to influence us in significant ways, but our own changing lives alter our perceptions of our forebears, so that even dead men and women may be given new voices through historical studies, through efforts to rediscover individuals who had been neglected and forgotten, or to reassess individuals who previously had been revered without question as national heroes. In this way we begin to hear what our predecessors have to say to us. Again, when we try to understand the meanings of these familiar, resounding texts, we must take into account not only what they signified to the original authors and their audiences, but how their meanings have changed over time as they have been newly interpreted, again and again, in an effort to make them fit a growing, protean nation of people. Our attempts to grapple with these inherited texts, to guard and to adapt them, make history.

We the People of the United States speak the same language as Thomas Jefferson . . . with some difficulty. Our modern cities would shock him, as a blood-spattered eighteenth-century surgeon's theater would shock us, but time-travel visitors from both centuries would recognize elemental American traits in the people they encountered. We are occupied with many of the same political questions: How can order be maintained in a democratic republic when such a wide range of people have been invited to share in the power of the state? Is it possible to educate citizens in virtue so that order can be maintained by agreement, by cooperation, and not by coercion? How can the majority of the people be prevented from dealing unjustly with a misfit minority? Which is the more trustworthy body, a collection of distant federal representatives who may be better able to judge national issues impartially, or a collection of local, states' representatives who understand the territory?

This is all our heritage—a markedly masculine, thoughtful, democratic heritage. It is always necessary to sort out and refine it, for The Enfranchised People continues to expand to include those who were "Not-People" just yesterday. Which of the Founding Fathers' gifts will we keep, discard, or alter? We debate to decide that question.

## Not Just Machismo

The women I met who picked up shotguns or pistols partly to assert their status as inheritors and preservers of an American legacy certainly appreciated the fact that guns gave them a plain source of power. At the same time, macho fascination with raw power did not fully explain their interest in guns. Because they were women, I watched them more carefully than I would have watched gun-owning men, and so I was better able to appreciate that their pride, their feisty acts of resistance, their distrust of a faraway and potentially despotic federal government, and their determination to keep and maintain their own firearms were rooted in national traditions. I was struck by how many proved eager to undergo discipline in one form or another, following rules of conduct or training that had been codified by their fellows, people with whom they felt some connection. Thus, some satisfaction was derived from getting hold of an explosive weapon and then inventing or accepting rules to control oneself. This process effectively allowed a small group of compatriots to invent an alternative government for itself. In some cases, they codified, published, and distributed sets of game rules (I think of the Practical Shooters) for everyone to follow. Members wished to retain, practice, and assert the adult prerogative of self-government—government of these people, for these people, by these people—on a local scale. Taken to extremes, these experiments in self-government can lead to bloody business, as the 1990s proved. But kept within bounds, they remind us how government is, in fact, formed: out of nothing.

I remember Shirley Grenoble on a heavily wooded autumn hill placing the heel of one boot against the toe of the other boot slowly, slowly—imagine a cat dressed in twenty pounds of insulated clothing—and then repeating the movement with her opposite foot. She was demonstrating how unnaturally patient one must be to "still hunt." And there was Michael Maroni: "Is the line clear, the line is clear. Clear to the right, clear to the left. This is five rounds, hip level, one shot." And Robert Hohberg: "Diligencia, Vis, Celeritas." Standing alongside her husband, Ruth Merson asserted that this motto was no joke. The practical pistol shooting contestants on the long field in front of her, a few of whom were at that moment riding a small golf cart with their firearms tucked behind them in place of woods and irons, had a "calm" about

them, she said, an "emotional serenity" that they had acquired through responsible practice drills with dangerous weapons. And Ruth Merson was not
naive. She had experienced war and understood the difference between a
killing battle and a game.

The physical attributes of firearms attract people. They really do shoot
real holes in things. The opportunities guns provide for individuals to invent
and practice *discipline* may be as powerful an attraction, however. Writing
this, I hear a collective groan rise from American women and men who perceive most gun owners—hunters, target shooters, self-defense devotees—to
be macho slobs out for a thrill. It is true that the rules and regulations weekend gunners impose on themselves look pretty flimsy to any outsider who
watches a series of competitors blast away at the target "zones" of distinctly
human silhouettes and emerge with their faces quietly alight. But in my opinion liberals who make a sport of denouncing guns and all activities and institutions having to do with guns seem as content, and sequestered, in their
favorite arenas, since the security they (we) take for granted is sustained, in
part, by immense, often functionally invisible, state military and police networks to which they (we) give very little credit.

I cannot shake the impression that there is something gun owners know
about the American landscape and the—masculine?—visceral forces still at
work in the landscape that detractors must acknowledge. It is difficult to
relinquish all one's raw power, especially as government grows more distant
and faithless. Too much acquiescence feels like servitude. Many of the days
people live in the United States are, in fact, days of servitude, for despite our
heroic stories, we function inside a hive of commercial activity and electronic mysteries. The muscular, plain, bloody powers—power to kill to eat,
power to shoot threatening attackers, power to kill British soldiers—did in
fact clear the way for a rich, national lifestyle enjoyed by millions who today
think themselves *free* by right. Those who have inherited riches thanks to the
unapologetic, imperialistic, bloody powers of their predecessors must beware denouncing those same predecessors. In this regard, politically conservative women have something to teach. They remind us that the American
urge to resistance and outdoor independence is not just a white man's game,
and they ask one to remember that pioneer foremothers struggled in league
with their husbands to grab and keep what they could.

Contemporary gun debates focusing on the Second Amendment "right to
keep and bear arms" are good places to study this national veneration for
*resistance* and *independence*. Listening to conservatives and liberals discuss
the people's relation to government, we notice how difficult it is for citizens
to confront and define what *is* government in the United States. Is the government inside the Beltway? Or is it inside us, does it derive its authority

from us? Do we still continue to create it, in truth, or has it solidified and expanded beyond our control? When and how can an individual justifiably resist government? Every time I listen to a pro-gun speaker defending his or her constitutional right to own firearms in order to maintain his or her capability to resist the U.S. government should it turn tyrannical, I want to ask: "Have you looked at an F-15 fighter plane? You plan to SHOOT this thing from the porch?" And every time I hear my own friends deride institutions and groups of people committed to the defense of boundaries (national boundaries, neighborhood boundaries, the walls of their own houses), I want to ask similar, but opposite, questions about modern weaponry and Defense with a big D. Are we confident that we would all be able to live, work, and complain so securely if the United States were "cured" of its big and little guns and all boundaries left unprotected?

I am not nonpartisan. Liberal policies make more sense to me than conservative policies, and I am a fervently grateful inheritor of 1960s reforms. I favor most gun-control laws, waiting periods, and check-systems implemented to help prevent the sale of guns to criminals and convicted spouse abusers. I'm in favor of laws that hold a homeowner liable if harm occurs because he or she kept a loaded gun in a place accessible to curious children. (What constitutes "accessible"? What constitutes "children"? Legislation would decide.) Much of the rhetoric broadcast by opponents of gun control strikes me as paranoid and wrong-headed. In a country so well-stocked with old and new firearms, it is difficult for me to figure how people can be afraid that they will wake up some day and find themselves unable to buy enough guns. I can't fathom it. I admit to being bewildered by people who value the Second Amendment to the Constitution with such passion, who consider the Second Amendment key to the Bill of Rights, and who regard guns as iconic, elemental tools for being and staying *American*.

I have tried. Having listened to women who felt this way, I understand that they find liberal prescriptions intrusive and find liberals, generally, to be self-righteous, judgmental, predictably anti-American, and condescending. They don't like it when Sarah Brady or the American Medical Association lobbies to impose new safety restrictions on their households, in part because they don't think of Brady or members of the AMA, all of whom appear so ready with paternalistic advice, to be people who would ever bother to visit their households. Trying to get nearer the source of this perspective, I remember the words of Kim Clark (who herself favored gun-storage liability laws): "I think if we start regulating everybody's rules, what they can and can't do in their house, you start there and the next thing they're saying you can't smoke in your house, you can't drink Pepsi in your house. It can get out of control." And the words of Sherry:

But it does mean that if the government insists on passing laws that make us criminals, if the state of New York passes a law that says if I'm in possession of a semi-automatic weapon that is capable of holding a magazine with more than ten rounds, then I'm a Class D felon, then they, with a legislative swipe, have made me a criminal, made me a felon. Well, the day before they signed it into law, I'm not a felon, I'm a law-abiding citizen. The day after they sign it, I'm a felon and I can go to jail for ten years. Who's right and who's wrong?

In these words, I hear Sherry say that any government that would pass legislation arbitrarily outlawing certain citizens is not a proper American government, because it is no longer acting as an institution that derives its authority from the people, but instead has become government that imposes its authority on the people. Here lies a key to Second Amendment advocacy. I expect Sherry would have little patience with the relativist argument that it's *always* laws that make criminals, that the "law-abiding person" is invariably defined, and thus created, by the state, rather than by the person herself. Thus, Sherry's position derives imaginatively from an individual's own conviction that he or she continues to exist, to think, to work, even when the agents of the government pay her no attention or, more dangerously, misunderstand and miscategorize her. She asserts that she *is herself basically good and lawful and trustworthy* regardless of the government's changeable labels, and that her existence and identity precede and outweigh the state's. And if a gun is an iconic tool for both law enforcement and resistance, she will keep one for herself, in her house, because she is the source of government.

This defense of *one's self* makes great sense to me, for a moment; it seems brave and pragmatic. But then I recall how eagerly many pro-gun advocates welcome the incarceration of people they identify as criminals—"Jail works!" wrote Tanya Metaksa enthusiastically—and I find my appreciation waning. Maybe jail does work; liberals should be prepared to credit certain Republican "get-tough" policies for contributing to the recent decline in crime rates, for instance. But when conservative pro-gun advocates insist on maintaining their own freedoms relative to the state while at the same time calling for "bad guys" to be made subject to the full disciplinary powers of a strong state, they fail in imagination, I think, and in Americanism. They effectively call for two governments, rather than one, and for two peoples, rather than one, and they forget that the formulaic "bad guys" probably see themselves as good, as citizens deserving their own rights. In my opinion conservative advocates who show so much eagerness to defend themselves and incarcerate others fail to acknowledge how often the U.S. government has arbitrarily criminalized or stripped people of their civil rights over the centuries. People who contracted to an interracial marriage could find themselves defined as criminals in the South under Jim Crow. Gay men and women can still find themselves defined as criminals in many states. More recently, young men caught with drugs in amounts that a few years ago would have earned them misdemeanor convictions are now being convicted of felonies. The new laws make them felons, though they may not *feel* like felons. Conservatives who trust that they *know* what a *criminal* is, because they trust that the definition of criminal behavior is fixed and unchanging, absolute rather than relative or constructed, are duty-bound to look back over the haphazard evolution of our laws and our government.

Conservative pro-gun advocates who are shocked when the state turns its cold eye on them—"Hey I'm not the bad guy here!"—and who feel impelled, therefore, to delineate areas of individual civil, constitutional authority with the help of their firearms, must sometimes sense how nearly they must resemble criminals to any functioning state. States do not welcome unauthorized armed insurrection; acts of armed resistance against the police, military forces, or National Guard are classed as illegal, as traitorous . . . as criminal. Perhaps it is because Second Amendment advocates realize this dilemma—they realize instinctively that a mature government does not happily accommodate resistant, armed citizens—that they fight so hard to maintain their legal place on the knife edge.

Guns in the home. I am happy to visit people who have shotguns in their home . . . and usually just tell myself those guns are unloaded. But I am frightened by the idea of my sons visiting a house where handguns, in particular, are kept; I would want to know that all the guns in that house were unloaded and locked apart from their ammunition. I would not keep a gun in my own home for reasons that derive entirely from my own experience and informal statistical reckonings. In our home, my two sons and their friends have entered thousands of times. An intruder has not yet entered. I judge that the likelihood that a gun would accidentally wound a beloved boy or girl in our house is greater than the likelihood that I or my husband would be able instantly to grab a pistol and scare off—or kill—an intruder. This conviction has been strengthened by hearing a few women tell me that they, or their brothers, discovered the guns hidden by their parents in the houses where they grew up and that they picked up those guns out of curiosity and played with them, and their parents never knew it.

At the same time, I would not promise that I will never buy a gun.

## Those Other Roads

Women may not save the nation, but we ought to be able to complicate its politics. Victim of an abusive husband, Joanne Carroll appreciated both the powers of legal networks that must be staffed with enlightened judges and educated cops if they are to provide women with a measure of justice and security (typically liberal) and, also, the plain power of guns as weapons of resistance and self-protection (typically conservative).

Now, having said that I think women can do little more than blessedly muddle our partisan politics, I must also admit to sustaining a dim faith in a generalized, even "compassionate," female character that elects diplomacy before attack. The fact that women globally have been assigned to shield human lives rather than destroy them, and that they've played so little part in weapons manufacturing, arms sales, and combat, impresses me as an advantage of a kind that ought to be enlarged. I am not hopeful that the increasing political and financial influence of women in the West will gradually move the world toward a pacifist utopia, but I am hopeful that greater attention paid to women will draw their experiences and ideas into the light, giving birth to alternative national myths, methods, and definitions of heroism.

For instance, when a person reviews American frontier myths from a traditionally female perspective, it becomes obvious what sort of everyday, heroic work a gun might be expected to accomplish and what sorts of everyday, heroic work it would leave undone. Even 200 years ago, a firearm would be of little use preparing children for school, building houses (you could try to hammer with a revolver, but watch out), curing diphtheria, facilitating correspondence, increasing crop yield, or effectively propping up any human identity. But this kind of work—work to raise a family and maintain a home—is essential to settling any frontier, and when we allow ourselves to be lured by stories featuring resistant, gaudily independent males—unattached guys on horses, unattached guys on the road, costumed guys with guns—we forget an immense portion of our history and, in that way, skew our perception of the present. For instance: maybe the nation isn't becoming "feminized" in the 1990s as analysts contend; maybe it was always largely "feminine," but scholars, politicians, and culture critics have only just begun to recognize it. Women who have experienced true frontier conditions, where the legal, educational, and financial networks that undergird family security are either unformed or shredded, understand that firearms just don't do much of the development work that needs to be done in such a place. Frontiers remain in this country, and a lot of the effort being invested to survive there is being invested by women . . . as usual.

Following passage of the welfare reform act (i.e., The Personal Responsibility and Work Opportunity Reconciliation Act of 1996), a variety of citizens are undoubtedly finding it necessary to work harder for food and shelter to sustain not just themselves, but their children. Since it is women who head 95 percent of welfare families in the United States, it will be largely women who must discover how to manage these challenges: how to find a job in a city or rural county where businesses have fled and old farm towns collapsed, how to pay for daycare while working for relatively low wages, and how to raise their children in the time remaining. Contemporary American politics tends to focus on "the ghetto" as the place where criminals and dependents gather, making it necessary for "responsible" citizens to defend themselves against forces generated by the "ghetto." That focus is skewed, but we don't seem to be able to repair it, in part because the "inner city" has been granted its own mythic role in the American landscape as the "anti-frontier." This is the place where good guns turn bad, where armed men shoot people instead of deer, where the family disintegrates. This is the inner city, not the great outdoors. Like most persistent national stories, this one is partly braced by fact. But even more, it's propped up by convenience, for it compliments those people who identify with the old frontier by contrasting them against the people who inhabit the anti-frontier. One should note, however, that the male gangs of gamblers and miners whom Luzana Wilson knew in the Wild West—"Nearly every man carried in his belt either knife or pistol, and one or the other flashed out on small provocation to do its deadly work"—and the flocks of young male dealers whom Blackshear and Keyes kept chasing off their corner display common characteristics. Our nation has made a cult of renegade machismo that effectively denigrates in our imaginations and, thus, in our logic and our policies, the patient, cooperative work required to raise children well.

Once the "inner city" has been defined as the anti-frontier, it loses distinctness, so that those who have never been at home there find it difficult to credit its everyday physical variety. Instead, outsiders think of the "ghetto" as part of a finished story, so that it becomes a predictable, cinematic place, rather than an actual place inhabited by individuals whose futures have not yet been determined, who happen to be living in real life. Now, it might not seem like much of an effort or an accomplishment to acknowledge the actuality of people who live at a distance from ourselves, yet it is important for voters to appreciate the simple fact that real life, local life, continues in places they have never visited and good sense can be found in people they never hoped to meet.

It was Patricia Murray who steered me toward Rosemary Jackson. When I spoke to Jackson, she was serving her first term as school board president of Camden, New Jersey, having won election to the board after two failed attempts. Over the years, Jackson had worked in the Camden Home for Children, taught preschool, taught children with disabilities, worked with young teen mothers at Alpha House under the New Jersey Department of Corrections, taught troubled youth—mostly girls—in the public school system, initiated a system of Urban Women's Centers throughout New Jersey, and, most recently, became involved in setting up entrepreneurship programs for women "to help welfare mothers get off welfare and set up their own businesses."

As one might expect, Jackson's politics do not fit inside the conventional conservative/liberal grids. Her description of the massive welfare system that had developed in Camden was scathing. Camden City was "nine square miles of pure poverty by design," in her opinion. Echoing conservatives, she recommended accountability and reductions in aid. "I believe that if the government didn't pass so much money down here, they [the welfare administrators] would have to think."

> You take out those welfare systems because they create that dependency, they create it so they can be in control of people's lives. And if they couldn't get money off of dependency, and the only way they could get money was to prove results—people getting jobs, people finishing school—that would be the litmus test. If that didn't occur, why would you keep funding the same institutions?

Accountability, responsibility, discipline, training, jobs: she trusts these forces to rebuild her community. She favored consistent punishments for women and saw no benefit in a criminal justice system that went easy on them:

> The juvenile justice system, the court system, they do not know what to do with women, they never did. What they've been doing is smacking them on the hand, sending them back home. They don't get any kind of treatment, they don't get any kind of discipline either. So here we had two women for homicide. They had their ankle bracelets [electronic monitors] on and they were playing with their babies. I mean, what does it take before they decide that this is really a dangerous person who needs to be incarcerated?

As a result of the lighter court sentences generally dealt to young women: "The young women will take the weight. They will take the weight for a guy. They'll carry the gun for them, drugs for them, anything they want for them because they still believe that a girl can get a lighter sentence, and it's true."

Jackson had met plenty of young women who she thought deserved stricter punishment. And she had met plenty of young women who passed through the courts and the jails and eventually reshaped and reclaimed themselves, with help. She advocated for discipline. She also advocated for treatment.

And she liked girls. She found a wealth of spirited power in them.

> When I go to court, the judges say: "How in the world do you deal with 'em?" And I say: "Well I'm glad they're emotional, because at least I don't have to worry about them taking up a gun and walking in here and blowing your brains out 'cause they couldn't discharge their emotions." Thank God for that, at least they're healthy, mentally healthy. I think they are healthier than males in some respect because they have taken a lot. They do a lot, they take a lot. But I think they do have stamina, will, a spirit, if you can get to it, to do a lot, because they're the ones who have to be responsible not only for themselves, but often for family members, children, even mothers and husbands. I really do feel women are the ones who will do the job.

One of the jobs that women need to do in Camden is to stop the gun deaths. Referring back to 1995, Rosemary Jackson said: "We had sixty murders in this city, and those mothers were calling me: 'What can we do? What can we do?'" She gave a group of Camden mothers some direction, and they moved on to lobby the city council and the mayor. They traveled to Trenton on buses and exerted the pressure that brought state troopers to Camden as a kind of peacekeeping force.

But that peace was shattered by a bullet. In 1995, one of the New Jersey state troopers who had been called in shot and killed a young black Camden resident. The city started to bubble. Jackson recalled: "It was a real volatile situation. I talked to some of the guys who were there when that boy was killed, and they were telling me, 'Miss Rose, we're going to retaliate.' I said: 'The only thing you're going to do is cause the National Guards to come out, some of the military, and that will be a no-win situation.'" Meetings were organized. The parents of the dead boy spoke, asking for calm. Rosemary Jackson directed one of the meetings.

> When the one young man was shot and killed by a trooper, the governor called me up and asked if I would intervene, hold a group to see if the people in Camden still wanted them [the state troopers]. We had that group and I led it just like I do regular support groups, only this was a bigger audience. But I did not want people pointing fingers at the state trooper, or vice versa. So I start every meeting with our ground rules. You speak in your own person. No put-downs of yourself or other people. Don't give advice, unless someone asks you for advice. Speak from your own personal experience. There are about four or five basic rules. Then we talk, we discuss, have a dialogue. We had over a hundred people come out, and it was very uneventful. All the press was there, thinking this was going to be a knock-down, drag-out fight between the police and the community, be-

cause typically it is, but because I used that format, it really took all that thunder out, because if you only talk from your own personal experience, starting with what you feel and think, who can tell you right or wrong?

Rosemary Jackson's four or five rules for defusing a battle and initiating a dialogue can be reeled off in less than a minute. She developed them through her own experiences with small support groups, and she learned some of her techniques for organizing support groups from workable projects in Third World countries, "like Africa, India, because Camden is really Third World USA." In Costa Rica, she found that women were organized in cooperative groups of ten, and now in New Jersey Jackson has organized entrepreneurial women's groups of a similar size. "We usually have nine or ten women in each group, and once we've trained them how to do it, then each one of them has to go and get a group of ten, so it multiplies."

The groups Jackson described most enthusiastically are committed to training women to start up their own businesses or secure jobs. She mentioned one woman who set up a bridal shop, one who began a cleaning business, two who organized beauty salons. Five went into construction and maintenance, one worked as a dressmaker, a few got into t-shirt sales, others designed centerpieces for weddings and conferences. Rules and mutual responsibilities governed participants in a typical group, and the network helped maintain their courage. The process was not easy.

> In the entrepreneurship program, if you had a time-lapse camera . . . I've seen them come in rough, rowdy—probably had a lot of that in their lives—and in six months, they wanted something better; [they] did not want to go back to what they had been a part of. And in some instances, while they were there, many of them made that choice, and it was rough, because guys [from their old life] knew where they went to school, knew where they would come for classes. . . .

Rosemary Jackson did not have all the answers. She didn't say how Camden City or the State of New Jersey could bring large, thriving corporate employers back to the area where she lived so that residents would have opportunities to move beyond wedding centerpieces, t-shirts, and hair styling. She didn't say how it would be possible to reform the entrenched welfare bureaucracy so long as a number of residents and their children continued to need the services. At the same time, I was struck by the good sense of many of her observations, which were based on years of experience with challenging, often difficult, young women and on research into grassroots development experiments that had succeeded in other parts of the world. Jackson denounced the effects of welfare dependency, but she never just said "no."

She understood that experiments must be attempted, workable programs sustained, and time and money invested if one hopes to train disadvantaged teenagers, young women and men, to discipline themselves as they worked to fulfill reasonable hopes for the future.

Rosemary Jackson described to me her personal experience with a household gun:

> I was like twenty-five, twenty-six years old at that time, and my boyfriend and I had a fight, an argument; he was drunk. You could not have told me he would do that, to point a gun and shoot it. I ran, jumped fences, hopped over cars, and ran, and my nephew who was running with me was telling me: "Run Rose, 'cause he's just smacked out." I know on one occasion I took the gun and put it in his face; there weren't bullets in it, but he made me mad, and I grabbed that gun. That was the first thing I thought. And then when we had a fight, the first thing I thought of was: "Get the gun." So I didn't have an enjoyable time having that gun around. I was terrified of that gun, because every time I thought: "If I went to do it when I was mad, imagine what he would do when HE was mad."

## Smoke and Fire

As the nation moved past the grotesque impeachment holiday season of 1998 and into the final year of the millennium, the media reported on the American people's growing impatience with divisive, partisan politics in the capital. The people just want closure, they said. They want it to be over. Hearing the message, members of the Senate let it be known that they would try to conduct their impeachment deliberations expeditiously. Members of the Senate would be more statesmanlike. Tom Daschle, Democrat, and Trent Lott, Republican, made a show of bipartisan cooperation and congratulated themselves and their colleagues vigorously whenever they agreed on any plan.

Reports that America was becoming more conciliatory, that the ideologues were losing ground, had been delivered before in the decade, as noted above. In fact, newspaper stories reporting on the losses sustained by ideologues had been broadcast just a few months earlier in November of 1998, when the Republicans, who had funded advertisements focused on the Clinton scandal and expected to increase their majorities thanks to Clinton's humiliation, lost five seats in the House. Following this disappointment, Newt Gingrich, hero of the "conservative revolution" of 1994, resigned his post as Speaker. That seemed a neat and significant conclusion to a four-year story.

But then came the impeachment vote, a partisan display that showed the antagonisms, agendas, insults, and culture wars fomented throughout 1992, 1994, and 1996 were very much alive. It was payback time. William Jefferson

Clinton was impeached. He was nailed. But the sport of payback, as usual, cost both sides. Shots ricocheted. House members were briefly stunned by the surprise resignation of Robert L. Livingston, newly elected Republican Speaker, the man chosen to replace Gingrich. It turned out that Livingston's own adulterous affairs had been exposed as a result of a bribe offered by soft-porn publisher, Larry Flynt.

Partisan politics are with us. We will never be rid of them because they focus opinions and give people enemies, and enemies orient us. What's more, the issues that drive partisan politics are serious; they usually engage people's fears and hopes for both a national and personal future and guide their interpretations of both a national and personal past.

There were some signs that these gun debates were cooling in reaction to a more temperate public mood. In the summer of 1998, Charlton Heston was elected to become the new president of the NRA. In his acceptance speech, Heston, an actor best remembered for his on-screen depiction of Moses, announced his interest in ". . . restoring the image the NRA has enjoyed for, what, 120 some years. I think we will find ourselves back in the mainstream of American public life." The Associated Press paraphrased Heston saying that under his leadership the NRA would "worry less about changing policy than about doing a better job communicating the message that the NRA's members are regular, all-American folk."[26] The Associated Press article attributed Heston's concern about image to a recent 18 percent decline in NRA membership from its peak in 1995.

But only a few weeks after the election of Heston, Tanya Metaksa broadcast one of her usual calls to arms, reminding the NRA membership that 1994 had been "payback time" (as quoted above) and encouraging members to unite against the foe, Bill Clinton, and his political cohorts. She invoked the revolutionary spirit of 1775:

> We must come together again, and we must do it today, not tomorrow, not next month, not next year. The fight won't become any easier if we let Bill Clinton, Al Gore, and their anti-gun lobbyists and powerful media friends have their way for a few more weeks, months, or years. The fight won't become any easier when, step by step, "ugly" semi-autos are banned, "junk" handguns are outlawed, "arsenal licenses" are required to collect guns, or *all guns and their owners are registered in a federal computer.* (author's emphasis)
>
> You remember 1775. That was the year Patrick Henry gave us his famous "Give Me Liberty or Give Me Death" speech. Henry's words speak to us today: "They tell us we are . . . unable to cope with so formidable an adversary. But when will we be stronger? Will it be next week, or next year? Will it be when we are totally disarmed?"

In that same glorious speech, Henry said: "I know of no way of judging of the future but by the past." In the past when we gun owners have come together to fight for freedom, we have won the day. The fight continues and so must we.[27]

Metaksa's partisan battle cry—"it was payback time"—and Heston's vow to lead his people along a course of moderation appear to have been working at cross purposes, or even to have been competing for the soul of the NRA. The subsequent demotion of Metaksa suggested that the more (apparently) moderate Heston had won. But the fight wasn't over. The practiced antagonists, the NRA and Handgun Control Inc., were still going at it.

In November of 1998, the National Instant-Check System (NICS) was implemented by the FBI as a follow-up to the Brady Bill. The NICS truly introduced a "federal computer" into the gun-control picture, for now all licensed gun dealers were required to contact the NICS—or an equivalent state check system—before completing any transaction; the instant-check systems would quickly identify individuals with criminal records that made it illegal for them to purchase guns.

Handgun Control Inc. was happy that the instant-check system was up and running but unhappy that the five-day waiting period for gun purchases was now eliminated in many states:

> Because the FBI does not have access to many local records, including vital categories like domestic-violence restraining orders and mental health, some prohibited purchasers will be getting guns. And because the purchase is instant, people who are looking to commit crimes of passion or impulse suicides now have no barrier to almost-instantaneous violence.[28]

And it was disgusted with the NRA for carping against the NICS:

> What is particularly troublesome, however, is the National Rifle Association's newfound opposition to the system it insisted on creating. On Tuesday, the NRA filed a lawsuit against the Justice Department, whose instant-check system will retain the records of gun purchases for some months. Never mind that those records are critical for evaluation of the system—and never mind that new research demonstrates that a very high percentage of legally bought guns are getting into the criminal market very quickly after purchase. Despite the reasonable concern for thoroughness and public safety that underlies the temporary retention of Brady records, the NRA is more concerned about placating hard-line gunowners who object to any records at all of their transactions.[29]

Indeed, the NRA had filed suit in U.S. District Court to stop the FBI from retaining NICS records of legal gun sales. According to a posting titled, "*NRA v. Reno:* Round One":

> NRA's position is simple—the law that established NICS clearly directs that all information submitted on a firearm purchaser be destroyed once the system determines that the transfer should not be denied.[30]

In addition, the NRA had opposed a federal plan to charge a fee for every use of the NICS, asserting that the fee was just one more "gun tax."

No one was happy. It was policy not to be happy, though the institution of a national check system to keep guns out of the hands of convicted felons appeared to benefit all parties involved, and both pro-gun and anti-gun organizations could take some credit for the implementation of this system. In short, the gun debates were still frozen and still hot. It did not seem like the argument had evolved or progressed in essentials since 1993. It was and is always payback time. Watching not only gun politics, but *all* politics with a cold eye, one begins to wonder if the antagonistic parties engaged in any long-running partisan contest aren't tacitly complicit, for designated enemies clearly serve to keep passions running high and contributions flowing.

It's trench warfare. Nobody seems to move. But the battles continue, and new weapons are introduced. Some of them prove surprisingly effective. In 1998, lawsuits became the weapons of choice for anti-gun advocates, many of them initiated by cities and aimed against gun manufacturers and dealers. The City of Chicago and Cook County filed their multimillion dollar "public nuisance" lawsuit against the gun industry in late 1998. The City of New Orleans also filed suit against gun manufacturers, but based its argument on the fact that manufacturers had failed to include sufficient safety devices with their "unsafe product." By August 1999, according to Handgun Control Inc., similar lawsuits had been filed by twenty-seven cities and counties located in eleven different states. Then President Clinton announced that the federal government would consider suing the gun manufacturers for the gun violence costs sustained in federally subsidized housing projects.

These legal campaigns were all being informed and guided by recent successful lawsuits against big tobacco companies, and they relied on liberal political logic that interpreted gun control as a public health issue. Individual citizens were also suing. In a successful class-action lawsuit, *Hamilton v. Accu-Tek,* the families of seven New York shooting victims accused Smith & Wesson, Beretta USA, Sturm, Ruger, Accu-Tek and more than thirty other defendants of "negligent marketing." The lawyer in "Hamilton" argued that dealers could reduce the flow of guns to criminals by instituting inventory controls and distribution restrictions more like those employed by "makers of other hazardous products, like scuba gear and certain chemicals and paints."[31]

These lawsuits did garner results. In March 2000, the Smith & Wesson Company capitulated to the pressure and agreed to: (1) build safety locking devices into guns and sell all guns with trigger locks; (2) design their firearms so that they would be difficult for small children to fire; (3) introduce new "smart gun" technology within three years so that a gun could only be fired by its owner; (4) establish restrictions on purchasers, so that an individual could buy multiple guns, but take only one home and retrieve the remainder after a fourteen-day waiting period; (5) establish restrictions on sellers, to prevent Smith & Wesson firearms from being sold at gun shows that did not require background checks for all purchases; and (6) cut off supplies of Smith & Wesson guns to any dealers who attempted to sell to juveniles or criminals or to market modified versions of banned "assault" weapons. In return for its commitments, Smith & Wesson received a promise from the chief government negotiator, Housing Secretary Andrew Cuomo, that he would convince the cities to drop their suits against Smith & Wesson. Just a few weeks later, newspapers reported that the move had profited the company. Not only had Cuomo succeeded in removing Smith & Wesson from the lists of gun manufacturers being sued in most cases, a number of cities had also announced that they would buy Smith & Wesson guns for their law enforcement agents to show their appreciation.

I applaud this development. And I wonder about its full significance. Politically, as a signpost to the future, the success of these lawsuits is very important. Gun manufacturers—American businessmen—have been frightened by the litigation, and this will alter the political landscape by shifting the debate away from territory where the troublesome Second Amendment has any relevance at all. This was a first step, an unexpected shift in the trench wars. But how important was the compromise as policy? What was accomplished? A single gun manufacturer agreed to provide locks with its guns (no one can insure that those locks will be used once the gun gets home) and to restrict sales and marketing in modest ways (if you buy a lot of guns, you have to wait two weeks to pick them up) and to cease providing guns to dealers who illegally supply criminals (but who will identify unqualified dealers? Smith & Wesson can't send out its own police, so local law enforcement must investigate and identify negligent dealers . . . this means effective law enforcement is still a prerequisite to effective gun control). What's more, this compromise obviously only restricts sales of new guns, and the United States remains very well supplied with slightly used guns. We could create plenty of noise, and havoc, with those slightly used guns for many years.

That such a relatively small compromise could provoke such jubilation on the part of gun-control advocates and the media tells us something about the frozen state of the gun wars over the last many years. As a person who generally favors the imposition of new gun-control measures, I am pleased by the Smith & Wesson compromises. Yet I am not compelled by the logic of this new method. I am not convinced that cities or individuals ought to be able to sue gun manufacturers for the "public health" threat posed by their products, or that guns equate neatly with cigarettes. Cigarette manufacturers knowingly withheld evidence that cigarettes were addictive and/or carcinogenic. But consumers know guns are potentially lethal. People (if they are sane) buy firearms understanding that they shoot deadly projectiles—that's their purpose. If these functioning firearms are being illegally peddled to individuals with criminal records, then police ought to investigate and prosecute the culpable dealers. I do not think manufacturers should be held responsible for improper/illegal use of their product or for failing to abide by regulations that were not codified at the time of sale. I do not speak here as an expert but as a nondescript citizen and magazine reader. The broad logic doesn't make sense to me, and I wonder about the precedents that will be established by this litigation.

Mere citizens, nonexperts, who try to form independent opinions about this campaign of lawsuits against gun manufacturers must take into account the philosophical questions raised in the first chapter of this book. Do guns kill people or do people kill people? Is the gun an active or passive object? Should a dangerous product be defined, legally, as a kind of pathogen, as contagious? If so, what does that tell us about the evolving perception of individuals in a community? Are individuals helpless against the spread of guns in the same way they are helpless to withstand a contagious virus, the flu, or the common cold? Are people who own guns "sick" and people who sell guns even sicker? The evolving national perception (and legal definition) of agency, of individual, collective, and corporate responsibility and liability will shape our laws and thereby shape the life of the country in this new century.

Sometimes the pro–Second Amendment vs. pro-gun-control debates make me think of a big gear that has detached from the machine it was meant to serve and has gone spinning and bouncing down the hill, its momentum strengthened by counterweights. Where does this big gear fit in context? Does it function properly anymore? Do the people guiding it forward with sticks ever pause to examine and question their own intent sport?

Since the mid-1990s, the crime rate in the United States has been decreasing steadily. Statistics show the crime rate declined again in the first half of 1998, dropping 5 percent and continuing a six-year trend. Yet the most powerful pro–Second Amendment/pro-gun-control advocacy organizations have shown relatively little interest in analyzing or even acknowledging this development. An Internet posting by Handgun Control Inc./The Center to Prevent Handgun Violence, still online in 2000, stated: "As the rate of American gun violence dramatically increased over the last fifteen years, American children paid the price. . . ,"[32] this despite the fact that Bureau of Justice Statistics studies show gun homicide rates have been decreasing in the second half of the 1990s.

When pro-gun and anti-gun advocacy organizations do address the steady drop in the national crime rates and gun homicide rates, they usually credit their own policies—either the implementation of widespread background checks and waiting periods or the proliferation of right-to-carry laws—as instruments of reform. In fact, the policies that appear to have worked most effectively to reduce crime have been fashioned from a mix of items on the liberal and conservative agendas. Gun-control laws (liberal) helped police move proactively to get young, armed men off the streets in high-crime urban areas.[33] Tougher, more focused mobilization of police forces and stricter sentencing laws (conservative) also helped. Notably, the city of Boston instituted programs that effectively reduced juvenile homicide by sending out "curfew patrols" of probation officers to track the actions of young offenders, facilitating cooperation between city and federal law enforcement agencies and black churches, instituting an "Operation Cease Fire" "to keep drugs and weapons off the streets," and enforcing strict policies that slapped federal warrants on intractable offenders. By the summer of 1997, Boston could boast that it had gone two years without a single juvenile gun homicide. "No other American city with a population over half a million can match this record," reported *Time*.[34]

"Operation Cease Fire" has been lauded by the Clinton administration's Justice Department in part because it mixes tough enforcement and sentencing with community involvement and proactive intervention, these latter marks of "compassion." (Conservatives advocate policies that are almost entirely punitive, e.g., Project Triggerlock and Project Exile.) But even less compassionate cities have enjoyed a decrease in crime. By the end of the 1990s, New York City under Republican mayor Rudolph Giuliani had experienced one of the most dramatic reductions in crime in the nation. Giuliani's police commissioner, Howard Safir, credited the drop to tougher police methods that replaced the (typically liberal) "community policing" strategies of the early 1990s, before Giuliani's inauguration. "I'm not going to be bullied by community activists who say, 'We want feel-good cops,'" Safir announced in an interview.[35]

This is gendered discourse. Under Safir's pronouncement lies the assumption that no police department could provide both (feminine, "compassion-ate") community policing services and (masculine) tough cop enforcement. The commissioner—who holds a job once manned by Teddy Roosevelt—assumes that the two breeds, or sexes, of cops are mutually exclusive. Un-happily, Safir's police force has run into some trouble recently. A few of his plainclothes officers have proved to be overly zealous in accosting, and maiming or shooting, unarmed black men.

As it turns out, the police department of the city where I live has been split by this same issue and is reported to be in turmoil. The traditional cops resent the community cops for their cushy schedules and friendly strolling, while the community cops claim that their efforts to learn about the neighborhoods and in this way help to defuse potential violence in those neighborhoods are misunderstood and despised. It's not difficult to read gender issues into the contest. The recent appearance in downtown Ithaca of bicycle-riding policemen dressed in navy-blue shorts is reassuring to me but possibly not to people who prefer more definitively masculine cops in big patrol cars. Yet I wouldn't want *all* police on bicycles. It wouldn't work. I like living in a place where some are pedaling and others are cruising.[36]

In cases like this, partisan, gendered, politicized discourses serve, once again, to camouflage central issues and to polarize discussion in a way that makes it very difficult to discover which public policies are actually working, which are functioning *in conjunction with other policies*. Ideally, men and women engaged in spinning the gun-control debates back and forth across the country ought to be required to lift that great gear together and try to fit it back into context, to acknowledge and discover together which of their many proposals have actually helped reduce deaths. I know this won't happen. Given the way the institutions and the alliances that have grown up in response to these public issues work, it is impossible. But more attempts to make something like this happen might at least redirect the questions we ask of our representatives and advocates and transform the questions that public representatives and advocates ask of themselves.

Because in fact nobody seems to be able to explain very well why the crime rate, particularly the gun homicide rate, has been dropping in the United States. Is wholesale incarceration of young men the central cause? Did improvement in the economy have an effect, and if so, how much of an effect? What about the welfare reform bill? Is it at all possible that imposed economic "self-reliance" can invigorate neighborhoods? A few researchers have argued that legalized abortions reduced the nascent population of troublemakers. Is this true? Did right-to-carry laws or NICS background checks contribute? Where and how do culture and fashion play a part? Is it possible that a number of young men and women in crime-plagued neighborhoods came to recognize that the glamour of the drugs/guns trade was poisonous after seeing so many of their peers die? This last possibility, the possibility of a shift in local fashion, in local culture, interests me the most, but I've seen few magazine or newspaper articles addressing the topic. Most media reports credit top-down police strategies, the incarceration of young drug dealers, and the increasingly healthy job market for the drop in crime. I expect these diagnoses of national trends are essentially accurate, and I continue to wonder about local conditions. Do the people living in those Boston or New York City neighborhoods where crime has declined approve the transformation?

And what about all the young men in prison now? Are they part of the picture, or not? This is not a mere rhetorical question. It's relatively easy to erase large groups of people from the general portrait—and political life—of a nation. It has been done often enough.

Decent public policy cannot be made unless the electorate and its representatives repeatedly attempt to correct their perceptions of the people, trying to fit those perceptions to the real world as it exists moment by moment. We waste too much time fighting over whose constructed depictions of the people are most worthy. Nobody knows, and nobody has ever fully known who the people are, and so everybody is responsible to keep trying to find out, by listening to conflicting stories, by descending into confusion, by trying to imagine those we habitually forget or dismiss or dislike, by forgoing the pleasures of secure partisanship and team spirit, be it liberal or conservative. Of course, this is a frustrating exercise, and no one can sustain it for long. But even a brief attempt is salutary.

A newspaper story from 1998 shows the pictures of seven boys, at least six of them Caucasian, all under the age of seventeen, five of them younger than sixteen. They have boy faces: smooth skin, delicate chins. Three of them wear glasses. They made the news by shooting and killing school classmates. One shot fellow students in an algebra class. Another opened fire on a prayer meeting. Two of the kids lay down in the grass after setting off an alarm and then took aim at students and teachers exiting the building. The article talks about the interest many of these boys showed in violent video and computer games, in rap music and movies about vengeance. It reports on depression among youth in the United States: "more than 1.5 million Americans under age 15 are seriously depressed, the National Institute of Mental Health says." And it reports that the boys had easy access to guns.[37] The next year, magazine and newspaper stories from April, May, and June 1999 described and then analyzed the attack at Columbine High School in Littleton, Colorado. Many of the same cultural factors—violent video games, adolescent loneliness, family dysfunction, guns—were identified as influences that might have predisposed Klebold and Harris to attack and murder their classmates in high school.

Some questions beg to be asked and answered. I am curious to understand better why all these shooters were young males, why girls didn't stage any of these attacks. And I wish I could understand, but I despair of comprehending, how it is possible that two young men, together, could have told themselves this bleak adventure story—they would walk to the school in their long cowboy coats, guns hidden, then take out their firearms, surprise! and walk the halls as triumphant killers—and then could have sustained their belief in the story long enough to fashion the bombs and acquire and adapt the guns and then enact the fantasy to the end, to death, and never wake up out of it in all that time, even when they saw the bullets strike real people.

American stories are powerful. American dreams are often replayed on the ground.

These bleak events have now become national anecdotes. They enter the canon—they will undoubtedly enter American history books—and they mean a great deal, because stories don't have to be widely representative to be potent and significant and to change our behavior and our laws. Storytelling that uses heroic or demonic characters as tokens to help clarify the state of the nation always simplifies real life. It highlights one figure and consequently throws many others in shadow. It ignores misfit details. It shapes the questions we think to ask about our situation. By this means, anecdotes in magazines, in newspapers, in history books, in novels, in letters, in imagination, lead a nation of diverse people calling themselves Americans into the future. And we are traveling there at a great rate now, so that the reports and images available to interpret, and to ingest, are piling up. Which will we respond to? Which will we reenact? Are there any we should try to squash?

This book has been largely constructed from women's stories meant to increase the canon of recorded American personal histories and to illuminate the varied interactions of American women with their own country and its peculiar traditions. I will conclude the book with one last story of a woman: Abigail Adams, wife to the second president of the United States, mother to the sixth. In making this choice, I certainly fail as a groundbreaking historian or explorer, since this white American matriarch is very well known. I also indulge myself in the pleasures of simple patriotism, since she is a national heroine familiar to me since grade school. I include it here because Adams lived through the Revolutionary War that engendered the United States. Her own husband was one of the Founding Fathers, and she had contact with the actual militiamen whose idealized images have proliferated in our own time, especially in pro-gun literature. In short, she was involved with and surrounded by men who would one day be designated American heroes and recreated as icons and logos. As one might expect, she herself was neither a soldier nor a legislator, but certainly her efforts, like the efforts of so many other struggling people in those unpredictable times, were remarkable: they deserve to be remarked upon. Adams's letters offer a picture of a daily life sustained by courage, intelligence, reasonable doubts, duty to family, love, impatience, ambition, and loyalty. Thus I invoke her for the same reasons I invoked the voices of pioneer women in an earlier chapter, because by her example Adams enlarges our pantheon of heroes and our awareness of the women who made, and continue to make, the nation.

Abigail Adams passed through most of the Revolutionary War living on the family farm in Braintree, Massachusetts, where she managed everyday business and raised her four children (she gave birth to six) largely without the help of her husband, who had been called to Philadelphia as the Massachusetts representative to the First Continental Congress. She recorded her experiences in letters to her husband. When the British invaded Boston, forcing residents into the country, she struggled with a stubborn tenant, trying to coax him to share his rooms with the Trotts. She moved the dairy things to make space, but "he positively tells me he will not and all the art of Man shall not stir him, even dares me to put any article out of one room into an other." Many times she heard the sounds of drums and alarms pass over the farm, and once there came news of Redcoats approaching near Braintree, but they had come to steal hay from Grape Island and were put to rout by armed volunteers—including two of John Adams's brothers. Occasionally in her letters she speaks of gunpowder supplies and is glad to hear of "Ten Companies of Rifle Men to be sent from Pennsylvania, Maryland and Virginia, to join the Army before Boston." The rifle was new to her. "They use a peculiar Kind of [weapon called] a Rifle—it has circular . . . Grooves within the Barrell, and carries a Ball, with great Exactness to great distances." She never mentions the possibility that she might defend herself or her children with a gun. The tension she experienced waiting for letters from her husband appear to have distressed her more than concern for her own safety.

Adams repeatedly requested and followed her husband's advice, though there were times she acted on her own initiative without consulting him. Frightened by a devastating outbreak of smallpox among American troops who had ventured north into Quebec, she made an independent decision to take herself and the children to Boston to be inoculated. At that time, men and women were inoculated by being infected with the actual smallpox virus under "controlled" conditions; judging from her own description, this was done by slicing into a vein with a razor and then pressing a contaminated thread into the vein. She described the condition of her children as they began to erupt with the pox. Her youngest son, Charles, resisted the infection for a long time. "I hope they have all pass'd through except Charlly, and what to do with him I know not. I cannot get the small pox to opperate upon him, his Arm both times has been very soar, and he lives freely, that is he eats a small Quantity of meat, and I have given him wine but all will not do." A few weeks later she would write to her husband: "I was talking of sending for you and trying to procure horses for you when little Charles who lay upon the couch coverd over with small Pox, and nobody knew that he heard or regarded any thing which was said, lifted up his head and says Mamma, take my Dollar and get a Horse for Pappa." (One of Benjamin Franklin's children died of a smallpox inoculation.)

John Adams was able to return home occasionally, and in late 1776 after one such visit, his wife found herself to be pregnant. Their baby, a daughter, was born dead the following July. John Adams was in Pennsylvania at the time. Abigail Adams had felt apprehensive the weeks before the birth and described her fears in a letter—"Slow, lingering and troublesome is the present situation"—that moved on to describe wartime deprivations and farm production: "The fruit was injured by the cold East winds and falls of, the Corn looks well, Hay will be plenty, but your Farm wants manure. I shall endeavour to have Sea weed carted every leasure moment. . . ." After the stillbirth, she wrote again to him: "Vapours had taken hold of me. I was as perfectly sensible of its discease as I ever before was of its existance. I was also aware of the danger which awaited me; and which tho my suffering were great thanks be to Heaven I have been supported through, and would silently submit to its dispensations in the loss of a sweet daughter; it appeared to be a very fine Babe, and as it never opened its Eyes in this world it lookd as tho they were only closed for sleep."

Led by General Howe, British forces captured Philadelphia a few weeks after the baby's birth and America's ragtag government was forced to evacuate to York. But good news followed bad, and by the end of the year 1777, John Adams secured a leave of absence from Congress to visit his home. Then Congress commissioned him as representative to France, and by February, 1778, he was sailing to France with his eldest son, John Quincy (future president), ten-years-old. He and John Quincy would spend the next six years (except for three months) in Europe, apart from Abigail Adams, whose letters during this period are often marked by heavy complaint, for twelve months, thirteen months would pass with no word received from her husband. To send a letter across the Atlantic at the time, one had to find friends or acquaintances taking passage on a boat from a harbor that hadn't been closed by the war. The same procedure was employed for the delivery of young men. The Adams's younger son Charles, eleven-years-old, lived in the Netherlands with his father for a while, but grew sick and had to be sent home. Unfortunately, he was shipped out with a rogue captain who docked in Spain weeks later for repairs. Major William Jackson, the man chaperoning Charles, eventually discovered another boat, and the boy touched shore in the United States and was claimed by his mother five months after his journey's starting day.

Abigail Adams herself feared braving the Atlantic without her husband, and after he had served the Republic in Europe nearly ten years, she wanted him home. "There was a time when I had brought my mind to be willing to cross the Seas to be with you, but . . . the train of my Ideas for six months past has run wholy upon your return." Eventually, in summer of 1784, she booked passage with her daughter, Nabby. Everybody was seasick. "The Ship was very tight, and consequently very loathsome, in addition to this our cargo was not of the most odifferous kind consisting of oil, and potash, one of which leaked, and the other fermented, so that we had that in concert with the Sea Smell." They passed through storms. "We could not however sit without being held into our chairs, and every thing that was moveable was in motion, plates Mugs bottles all crashing to pieces." Eventually they arrived in Portsmouth. It took some time before John Adams learned from letters that they had arrived and made his own way to England, but eventually he left his responsibilities at The Hague and reunited with his wife in London.

Letters grow over separations. The reunion of Abigail and John Adams after six years did not produce letters. It was described obliquely by their daughter, Nabby. "At 12, returned to our own apartments; when I entered, I saw upon the table a hat with two books in it; every thing around appeared altered, without my knowing in what particular." Father was come home.[38]

When we go hunting into the past for slogans or images to inspire us, we should try to call to mind the full span of everyday experiences granted to the living and to the dead of this continent. Wisdom is not extinct in this country. Patient and elusive, it waits in the thickets.

### Notes

1. As quoted by Jonathan Alter, "The Era of Bad Feeling," *Newsweek* (December 28, 1998), p. 58. Alter also quotes Leonard Garment, Richard Nixon's former lawyer, who explains why so many conservatives hate Bill Clinton: "Because he represents the sixties."

2. Bob Inglis quoted in Frank Bruni, "A Debate on Something Bigger than Words," *New York Times*, December 20, 1998, The Week in Review, p. 6.

3. Betty Friedan and Charles B. Rangel quoted by Frank Bruni, "A Debate on Something Bigger Than Words" [see note 2]. For Maureen Dowd's quote about "old white guys" see Dowd, "Avid Ovid Readers," *New York Times*, January 10, 1999, The Week in Review, p. 21.

4. The *USA Today*/CNN/Gallup poll showed Clinton's approval ratings were up

to 73 percent, 10 percent higher than just before the impeachment vote. Judy Keen and Richard Benedetto, "Clinton Poll Ratings Surge," *USA Today*, December 21, 1998, p. A-1.

5. Sam Howe Verhovek, "Outnumbered but Steadfast Against Clinton," *New York Times*, December 23, 1998, p. A-1.

6. Tanya Metaksa, "United We Stand, Divided We. . . ." July 1998, http://www.nra.org.

7. Report on the National Public Radio, Morning Edition, October 8, 1996, 6:00–8:00 A.M. (Eastern Time). The NRA response and a transcript of the report was broadcast on the Internet: http://www.nra.org.pub.ila/96–10–09_biased_npr_broadcast.

8. Mark Green, "Voting Blocs, Building Blocks," the *Nation* (December 9, 1996), p. 23.

9. The monumental welfare reform law that took effect October 1, 1996, gave state legislatures substantially more power to administer welfare in their own domains, instituted a five-year lifetime limit on benefits for each recipient, required able-bodied recipients to work in order to qualify for food stamps, denied benefits to most legal immigrants who are not citizens, and established a deadline requiring states to switch a quarter of their caseloads into jobs within the next year.

10. A contemporary article by George Will, well-known conservative columnist, helps to illustrate how gendered associations influence conservative/liberal perceptions of the United States and its elemental nature. In January 1999, Will argued that culture, not policy, determines whether a nation will succeed or fail. He went on to assert that America is strong because its culture is grounded in masculine, capitalist virtues, which he opposed to a newly fashionable "feminized conservatism" characterized by "compassion." He quoted an economist and the head of the American Enterprise Institute to make his point:

> In 1990 Herb Stein, drawing on fifty years' experience making and analyzing economic policy, told some visiting—and probably perplexed—Russians that "The basic reason for our prosperity is that 120 million Americans get up in the morning and go to work to do the best they can for themselves and their families and previous millions did the same thing for two centuries." Which is why [Christopher] DeMuth believes that, in spite of the current talk about compassion as the saving social value, and all the recommendations of a feminized conservatism, "the hard, competitive, masculine virtues—assertiveness, willingness to take risk, stoicism, cussed determination to prevail—are receiving much less attention than they should."

Rather oddly, Will's tribute to the American masculine virtues was prefaced by this sentence: "The history of nineteenth-century Britain and America is replete with examples of social movements, often religious, that improved marriage, child rearing, and schooling practices and promoted temperance, all of which contributed to cultural vitality."

Judging from this comment, it would appear that the assertive women who manned so many of the progressive social movements in the last century must have been inspired by, and helped to inspire, American masculine virtues.

See George F. Will, "The Primacy of Culture," *Newsweek* (January 18, 1999), p. 64.

11. Gordon S. Wood, *The Creation of the American Republic, 1776–1787* (Chapel Hill: University of North Carolina Press, 1969), p. 76.

12. Robin Toner, "Presidential Race Could Turn on Bush's Appeal to Women," *New York Times*, March 26, 2000, p. 1.

13. Robin Toner, "Marches Across U.S. Demand Strict Laws," *New York Times*, May 15, 2000, p. A-14.

14. See http://www.millionmommarch.com; downloaded April 2000, July 2000.

15. Toner, "Marches Across the U.S. Demand Strict Laws," p. A-14.

16. "Tompkins County and Southern Tier Citizens Travel to Support March," *Ithaca Journal*, May 15, 2000, p. A-1.

17. Toner, "Marches Across the U.S. Demand Strict Laws," p. A-14.

18. Wood, *The Creation of the American Republic;* see p. 477 for John Jay quote, p. 607 for Wood's assessment.

19. For a fuller description of eighteenth-century republican literature and states' rights constitutions, see Robert E. Shalhope, "The Ideological Origins of the Second Amendment," in *Gun Control and the Constitution: Sources and Explorations on the Second Amendment*, ed. Robert J. Cottrol (New York: Garland Publishing, 1994), pp. 257–72. This collection also includes copies of the articles by Sanford Levinson and David Williams cited in this chapter.

20. David C. Williams, "Civic Republicanism and the Citizen Militia: The Terrifying Second Amendment," *Yale Law Journal* 101, no. 3 (1991): 551–615, esp. p. 587.

21. In *United States v. Cruikshank* (1876), *Miller v. Texas* (1884), and *Presser v. Illinois* (1886) the Court held that the Second Amendment limited the actions of the federal government, but was not intended to limit actions of the state governments, which were thus free to regulate firearms as they saw fit. In the 1976 *United States v. Warin* decision, the Court rejected the argument that the defendant's participation in the state militia of Ohio conferred on him the right to own a submachine gun. The Court declared there was no evidence showing that a machine gun in the hands of an individual would facilitate the preservation of a well-regulated militia.

22. Wendy Brown, "Guns, Cowboys, Philadelphia Mayors and Civic Republicanism: On Sanford Levinson's 'The Embarrassing Second Amendment,' " *Yale Law Journal* 99, no. 3 (1989): 661, 663.

23. Williams, "Civic Republicanism and the Citizen Militia," p. 596 [see note 20].

24. Ibid., p. 607.

25. Sanford Levinson, "The Embarrassing Second Amendment," *Yale Law Journal* 99, no. 3 (1989): 637–59. For further discussion of the Second Amendment and a critique of Levinson, see Robert J. Spitzer, *The Politics of Gun Control* (Chatham, NJ: Chatham House Publishers, 1995), chap. 2.

26. David Kinney, "Heston Climbs Mount of Second Amendment," [The Associated Press], *Ithaca Journal*, June 9, 1998, p. B-1.

27. Metaksa, "United We Stand, Divided We. . ." [see note 6].

28. Handgun Control Inc., news release, December 5, 1998, "Statement of Sarah Brady re: President's Address and the Instant-Check System," http://www.handguncontrol.inc.

29. Ibid.

30. NRA, "*NRA v. Reno*—Round One," *Grassroots* 5, no. 50, http://www.nra.org, or groots@nra.org (no longer online in 2000).

31. The *New York Times* reported that this cascade of new suits against gun dealers and manufacturers would be supported by a new federal law-enforcement study that had discovered guns passed from dealers into the hands of criminals much more quickly and directly than had been supposed. Lawyers in the Hamilton suit used BATF fig-

ures to argue that nearly 40 percent of the handguns used in crimes nationally had been purchased from licensed dealers in the preceding three years. Quotations are from Fox Butterfield, "New Data Point Blame at Gun Makers," *New York Times*, November 28, 1998, p. A-9.

32. "Issue Brief: The School Shootings . . . and Beyond: Kids and Guns in America," Internet posting by Handgun Control Inc./Center to Prevent Handgun Violence, http://www.handguncontrol.org/chldgns; downloaded February 2000.

33. Michael J. Sniffen, "Crime Rates Decline 5% in First Half of '98," Associated Press Report, *Ithaca Journal*, December 14, 1998, p. A-1. The Associated Press wrote that "academic experts, law enforcement and elected officials have attributed the now six-and-a-half-year decline [in crime] to the aging of the baby boom generation beyond its crime-prone years and police efforts to get guns away from teens, especially in big cities."

34. Sam Allis, "How to Start a Cease-Fire: Learning from Boston," in *Time Magazine* (July 21, 1997), pp. 28–29. For further information on successful violence prevention programs, see the web sites for the Coalition for Juvenile Justice, http://www.nassembly.org/html.mem_cjj, 1211 Connecticut Avenue, NW, Washington, DC 20036. See also information on Boston's Operation CeaseFire, http://www.reeusda.gov/pavnet/new/YF-ceasefire, Operation Cease Fire, Office of Strategic Planning and Resource Development, Boston Police Department, 154 Berkeley Street, Boston, MA 02116.

35. Michael Cooper, "Homicides Decline Below 1964 Level in New York City," *New York Times*, December 24, 1998, p. A-1.

36. Our county's crime rate is, in fact, quite low, nearly 70 percent lower than for either New York State as a whole or for the upstate region. See Anne Gearan, Associated Press, "U.S. Violent Crime Drops to 25-year-low," and sidebar, "Violent Crime in Tompkins," *Ithaca Journal*, December 28, 1998, p. A-1.

37. Timothy Egan, "From Adolescent Angst to Shooting Up Schools," *New York Times*, June 14, 1998, p. A-1.

38. Quotes taken from L. H. Butterfield et al., eds., *The Book of Abigail and John: Selected Letters of the Adams Family, 1762–1784* (Cambridge: Harvard University Press, 1975), throughout.

# Index

Accu-Tek, *Hamilton v. Accu-Tek*, 226–27
Adams, Abigail, 232–35
Adams, Carol, 57
Adams, John, 233–35
Adams, Samuel, 26
*Adventures of Colonel Daniel Boon, The* (by John Filson), 32–33
*Adventures of Huckleberry Finn, The*, (by Mark Twain), 34
Adventure tales, American, 13, 32–35
Advocacy organizations, 3–4, 12–13, 17, 21, 26, 83, 85–89, 91, 95, 142, 205–206, 224–225, 228–229; *see also* Center to Prevent Handgun Violence; Handgun Control Inc.; National Rifle Association (NRA); Violence Policy Center
African-American, 180, 191
    males and criminal justice system, 178–79
    males as gunshot victims, 6, 161–62, 164–69, 172, 173–77, 180–181, 185, 187, 193, 221
    reports of gunshot trauma, 6, 161–62, 164–69, 172, 173–77, 180–81, 185, 187, 193, 221; *see also* Stories, first-person stories of gunshot trauma
Agrarian societies, 60, 63
Algonquin, 63–64
Alter, Jonathan, 6, 193
Animal rights, 48, 57, 60
Anticrime Bill, the; *see* Violent Crime Control and Law Enforcement Act of 1994
Antigovernment, 143, 144
Anti-gun conference, 21–25
Anti-hunters, anti-hunting, 48, 53, 56–59, 71
Armageddon, 132, 151–52

Arming Women Against Rape and Endangerment (AWARE), 110–11, 114, 137
Artemis, 61, 63
Assembly line production, 36
Ayoob, Massad, 101–3, 138

Background checks, 14, 123, 202, 215, 225–26, 227, 229, 230
    at gun shows, 15, 82
    *see also* National Instant Check System (NICS)
Baltzly, Mary Francis (Aunt Fannie), 40–41
Barr, Bob, 148, 197
Bates, Lyn, 110, 137
BATF; *see* Bureau of Alcohol, Tobacco, and Firearms
Battered women; *see* Domestic violence
Batterers; *see* Domestic violence
Becoming an Outdoors-Woman (BOW) program, 17–21, 52, 63
Bennett, Denise, 118–19
Bethel, Martha A., 144
Bill of Rights, the, 131, 148, 208–10
    English Bill of Rights, 209
Blackshear, Kathryn, 172, 180, 183–85, 200
Boone, Daniel, 32–33, 44
Boone, Rebecca Bryan, 33
Boston, Massachusetts, 229
Brady Bill, the, 14, 82, 123, 200, 201, 225
Brady, Sarah, 8, 9, 10, 13, 87, 205, 215
Branch Davidian; *see* Waco, Texas
Breechloaders, 35–36
Brown, Wendy, 211
Browne, Angela, 108–9
Buffalo Bill's Wild West Show, 37–38
Bureau of Alcohol, Tobacco, and Firearms (BATF), 143, 146

Bureau of Justice Statistics, 94, 161, 229
Bush, George H., 202
Bush, George W., 15, 81, 82, 92, 204–6

Camden, New Jersey, 21, 162–64,
    167–77, 180, 183, 185, 187, 192, 194,
    219–22
Cana, 187–90, 200
Capwell, Allen, 155
Case, Gene, 84
Castano Group, 11
Catlin, George, 37
Center for Disease Control, 11, 83, 162
Center to Prevent Handgun Violence, 13,
    80, 123–24
Centerville, New Jersey, 171
Chelton Terrace, 167, 169–72, 183–84
Chemung County Militia, 146, 148,
    154–55, 203; see also Militias
Chenoweth, Helen, 148
Chicago, lawsuit against gun industry, 11,
    226
Christian, Christ, 151–53, 156, 184, 198
Cigarettes; see Tobacco, public health threat
    similar to guns
Civil War, the, 35–36, 44
Civilization, women as "civilizers," 35
Clark, Kim, 118–19. 215
Class divisions, 65, 67–68, 158
Clinton, Hillary, 25
Clinton, William Jefferson, 5, 7, 11, 14, 82,
    149, 152, 197–98, 200–3, 205,
    223–24, 229
Coalition to Stop Gun Violence, 21
Colorado Sovereignty Act, 123; see also
    Antigovernment
Colorado, State of, 5, 85, 122–24; see
    also Columbine High School,
    shootings at
Colt, Samuel, 35–36
Columbine High School, shootings at, 5, 15,
    26, 81–82, 89, 134, 191,
    193–94, 205, 231–32
Concealed-carry
  legislation, 4, 5, 15, 27, 81–85, 88–90, 92,
    95, 111, 127, 163, 206, 229, 230
  permit, 4, 5, 15, 27, 81–85, 88–90, 92, 95,
    111, 127, 163, 206, 229, 230
Congress, U.S., 14–15, 81–82, 89, 91, 94,
    123, 143, 148, 157, 194, 201, 202,
    205, 208–9, 223, 233; see also
    Government; Federal government
Conservation, 54–56, 58–59
Conservationists, 54–56, 58–59

Conservative, 11–12, 27, 76, 86, 100,
    133, 144, 157, 163, 165–66, 179, 192,
    193, 197–99, 201–4, 214,
    216–17, 223, 229, 236 n. 10
  attitudes toward guns, 10, 12
  perceptions of threats to women, 106–7
  perceptions of traditional American
    heroes, 13–14
  opposed to intrusive government, 7, 12,
    25–26, 86, 123; see also
    Government
Constitution, U.S., 5, 8, 10, 13, 32, 131,
    148, 150, 155, 158, 207–13
Constitutional, 5, 8, 10, 13, 32, 131, 148,
    150, 155, 158, 207–13
Controlled chaos, 152
Cooper, Jeff, 134
Cooper, Marc, 145
Courage, 44, 110
Crime rate, 5, 179, 216, 229–30
Criminal, 8, 10, 12, 15, 27, 83, 85, 87, 90,
    100–2, 106, 122, 127, 149–52, 158,
    161, 163, 191, 215, 216–17, 225, 227
Crockett, Davie, 33
Cuomo, Andrew, 227
Cuomo, Mario, 91

Dacey, James, 154–55
Daschle, Tom, 223
Davies, Sandy, 118, 120–21
Deadly force, 117
Debates, 203; see Gun debates
Deer hunting, 61, 66, 69–70, 93
Dees-Thomases, Donna, 205
Defensive Gun Use (DGU), 87–88, 95
Delay, Tom, 205
Department of Environmental Conservation
    (DEC), 18, 19
Deshaney v. Winnebago, 86
Diallo, Amadou, 180
Diana; see Artemis
Dillon, Darlene, 19–20
Dole, Robert, 202–3
Domestic, novels, 39
Domestic violence, 100, 102–16, 185, 225
Doom, 5, 134, 152
Dowd, Maureen, 198
Drug sales, 124, 127, 165, 166–67, 170,
    172–73, 178–81, 184, 186, 193, 194,
    216
Drugs, illegal, 124, 127, 165, 166–67, 170,
    172–73, 178–81, 184, 186, 193, 194,
    216
Due process, victim's rights to, 86

Eco-feminist, 59, 61
Ecology, ecosystem, 58
Elections, 1994 Congressional, 14–15, 81, 91, 201, 203, 223, 224; *see also* Congress
Environmental, 14, 54, 57–58, 61, 144–45, 204
Environmentalists, 14, 54, 57–58, 61, 144–45, 204
Epidemic, of violence, 5, 10, 191–92, 194; *see also* Pathogens, guns as; Public health and guns; Toxic, contemporary culture as
Ethic of submission, 39
Evers, Medgar, 165

Family, and hunting, 48–52, 54
Farms, and hunting, 47, 49–52, 54, 68, 93
  decline in farming, 51
  ecologically destructive, 60–61
  *see also* Agrarian societies; Rural life
Farrakhan, Louis, 182
Faulkner, William, 33, 34
Federal Bureau of Investigation (FBI), 87, 95, 109
Federal government, 131, 142–43, 149–50, 157, 208, 209; *see also* Congress, U.S.; Government
Feminine, 13, 16, 35, 56, 59, 76, 81, 121, 154, 204, 207, 218, 236 n. 10
Feminist, 14, 16, 38, 56, 57, 60, 61, 63, 100, 102–7, 109, 121, 158, 170, 187, 211
Ferguson, Colin, 201
Fiedler, Leslie, 32
Filson, John, 32
Finn, Huckleberry, 34
Firearms, manufacturing and types, 35–36, 43; *see also* Guns
Florida, 151–52
Founding Fathers, 132, 157–58, 207–13, 232
Friedan, Betty, 198
Frontier, 156, 163, 164, 183, 192, 194, 204, 218–19
Frontiersmen, 13–14, 27, 32–35, 42, 55, 94, 144, 157
Frontierswomen (or pioneer women), 27, 39–43, 55, 163, 218–19, 233

Gabaree, Gordy, 65, 67, 68
Games
  with guns, 131–32, 136–41, 150
  paintball, 138
  video target games, 134, 231

Games *(continued)*
  *see also* Practical Shooters Association; Practical shooting competitions; War, and gun games
Garbarino, James, 191–94
Gatling gun, 36
Gender, 4, 13, 27, 31, 59, 65, 158, 200, 204, 206–7, 229–30, 236 n. 10
Gianaris, Camille, 21–22
Gibson, William, 134–35
Gingrich, Newt, 5, 15, 81, 148, 201–3, 223
Giuliani, Rudolph, 180, 229
*Go Down Moses*, 34
Gopnik, Adam, 145
Gore, Albert, Jr., 82, 205, 206
Government, 6, 7, 86, 151, 157, 204, 210, 211, 213, 214–16
  critiques of intrusive government, 12, 25–28, 119, 123, 142–43, 146–48, 151–52
  *see also* Congress, U.S.; Elections, 1994 Congressional; Gun-control legislation; State legislation
Gray, Ellen, 144–45
Grazia-Hupp, Suzanna, 81, 87
Grenoble, Shirley, 69–75, 199, 213
Grossman, David, 134
Gun-control legislation, 14, 15, 28, 81, 82, 89, 92, 101, 123, 125, 127, 133, 177, 180, 194, 198, 200, 201, 204–6, 210, 228; *see also* Concealed-carry legislation; Safe storage of guns; Safe storage legislation; State legislation
Gun debates, 10–13, 25–27, 76, 81–83, 128, 228, 230
  women in gun debates, 81, 83, 86–87, 92–93, 103–6
  *see also* Brady, Sarah; McCarthy, Carolyn; Metaksa, Tanya; Stories, women's personal stories in the gun debates
Gun safety locks, 15, 117–18, 124, 227
Gun violence, 10, 21, 26, 81, 165, 181–82, 187, 188, 193, 204, 206, 228; *see also* Stories, first-person stories of gunshot trauma
Guns
  active or passive, 9–11, 26, 228
  deterrents to crime, 25, 87–89, 95, 115
  health hazard, 10–11, 16,17, 89–91, 95, 102
  nature of, 9–11, 31

Guns *(continued)*
  ownership by women, 80, 121; *see also*
    Self-defense
  and Native American women, 64
  as tools, 10, 47, 53, 90, 94, 101
  *see also* Handguns; Homes, guns in
*Guns: Who Should Have Them?*
    (ed. David Kopel), 104–5
Gunfighter nation, 13
Gunsite Ranch, 134

Hamilton, Alexander, 208
*Hamilton v. Accu-Tek*, 226
Hammer, Marion, 16
Handgun Control Inc., 10, 13, 14, 89, 117,
    123, 201, 225–26, 229
  ratings of states, representatives, 14, 84,
    91
Handgun permit course; see Pistol permit
    course, 99–101
Handguns, 4, 7–8, 10, 11, 13, 16, 17, 21, 23,
    27, 54, 68, 71, 75, 76, 80–81,
    83–84, 88–89, 93–95, 100–2, 103,
    105, 116–21, 123, 126, 129, 161, 172,
    181, 204, 217
  *see also* Concealed-carry legislation;
    Guns; Handgun Control Inc.;
    Practical Shooters Association;
    Practical shooting competitions
Harlem, New York, 187, 190
Harris, Eric, 15, 134, 232; *see also*
    Columbine High School,
    shootings at
Health; *see E*pidemic, of violence; *see also*
    Guns, health hazard; Public health and
    guns
Hemingway, Ernest, 33, 34, 35
Henigan, Dennis, 11
Heroes, American, 14, 26, 31–32, 35, 37,
    38, 44, 157, 212, 218, 232
Heroism, 14, 26, 31–32, 35, 37, 38, 44, 157,
    212, 218, 232
Heston, Charlton, 223–24
Hidden Children, 140
Hispanic-American, 162, 178, 203
History, American, 157–58, 165, 199, 218,
    232
  reevaluation of, 14
  shaping of, 13, 63, 197, 212
Hockmeyer, Carole, 22–25, 26, 199
Hohberg, Robert, 139–40, 213
Holden, Jennifer, 118–20
Homes, guns in, 16, 17, 89–91, 93,
    109–10, 114, 117–21, 217

Homes, guns in *(continued)*
  hunting and, 54
Homicides, gun, 95, 108, 161–62,
    170–71, 180, 229–30
Hotchkiss, Benjamin, 43
Hotchkiss gun, 36
House Judiciary Committee, 82, 89, 142,
    198
Hunters, 101, 144
  as heroes, 33–34, 55
  and nature, 58–60, 72
  Native American, 63–65
  women, 17–18, 47–77 (chap. 3)
Hunter-gatherers, 60, 63
Hunting, 47–77 (chap. 3)
  decline in, 18, 20, 33

Implantable transponder, 152–53
Independence, as a national trait, 5, 13, 32,
    143–44, 199, 203–4
Indians; *see* Native American
Industry, American, and guns, 35–36
Inner city, 162, 219; *see also* Urban
Instant Check System; *see* National Instant
    Check System (NICS)
Internet, 11, 27, 58, 81, 85, 87, 123, 143,
    144, 150, 229
Invasion, 143

Jackson, Rosemary, 219–23
Jay, John, 209
Jefferson, Thomas, 26, 210, 212
Joanne Carroll, 111–16, 200, 217–18
John, Rebecca, 85–87, 90, 101, 124, 203
Johnson, Karen, 48–49, 54
Jones, Ann, 86, 103–4, 108, 109
*Journal of the American Medical Associa-*
    *tion (JAMA)*, 89, 97
Journals, of women, 39–43
Judiciary Committee, House; *see* House
    Judiciary Committee
Justice system, 117, 127, 152, 175–76,
    178–79, 218
  women and, 86, 112–16, 218, 220

Kates, Don B., 90
Kellermann, Dr. Arthur L., 89–91,
    104–6
Kennedy, John, 165
Kennedy, Robert, 165
Keyes, Deborah, 172–73, 183–86
King, Martin Luther, 163, 165
Kinkel, Kip, 26, 191
Kitt, Edith Stratton, 41

Klebold, Dylan, 15, 134–35, 232; *see also* Columbine High School, shootings at
Kleck, Gary, 87–88, 91, 95, 122
Koop, C. Everett, 89
Kopel, David, 104, 122, 142, 144
Koresh, David; *see* Waco, Texas

Lamplugh, Harry, 143
LaPierre, Wayne, 82, 89, 143, 205
LaSalata, April, 109–10
Lawsuits, 11, 82, 124, 205, 225, 226–28
Legislation, 147, 151, 156; *see also* Concealed-carry legislation; Gun-control legislation; State legislation; Safe storage of guns; Safe storage legislation
Lethal Force Institute (LFI), 8, 101–2, 138
Levinson, Sanford, 211
Liberal, 11, 12, 13–14, 27, 58, 76, 91, 92, 100, 142, 145, 157, 165, 192, 193, 197–98, 201, 202, 207, 212, 215, 216, 218, 229
  attitudes toward guns, 10, 12
  perceptions of threats to women, 100, 102, 107, 110
Literature, American, 32–35, 39
Littleton, Colorado; *see* Columbine High School, shootings at
Livingston, Robert L., 224
Locks; *see* Gun safety locks
Long, William J., 56
Loper, Jerry, 146, 154–55
*Lost Boys: Why Our Sons Turn Violent and How We Can Save Them* (by James Garbarino), 191
Lott, John, Jr., 88–89, 94–95
Lott, Trent, 15, 223
Louima, Abner, 180
Lyon, Shirley, 7–10, 17, 101

MacNutt, Karen, 11–12
Madison, James, 208, 210
Magazines, high-capacity, 15, 151
Manhood; *see* Men
Mark of the beast, 152–53
Maroni, Michael, 117–18, 213
Masculine, 13–15, 31, 35, 38, 54, 56, 59, 75–76, 81, 135, 144, 157, 204, 210, 214, 230, 236 n. 10
Massing, Michael, 178–79
McCarthy, Carolyn, 201, 205
McPherson, James J., 35–36
McQueen, Veronica, 205

McVeigh, Timothy, 15, 141–42, 145, 150; *see also* Murrah, Alfred P. Federal Building, bombing of
Mechem, Tamara, 123–27, 200
Memoirs, of women, 39–43
Men
  American, 204, 207–9, 218
  African-American, 161–62, 203
  white males, 14–15, 91, 135, 198, 202–3
  *see also* African-American, males and criminal justice system, males as gunshot victims, reports of gunshot trauma; Masculine
Merson, Ruth, 139–40, 200, 213–14
Metaksa, Tanya, 11, 16, 26, 58, 83–84, 87, 104, 143, 200–1, 216, 224–25
*More Guns, Less Crime* (by John Lott, Jr.), 88
Mother Earth, Mother Nature, 59, 72
Michigan, 141–42, 145, 149, 154
Michigan Militia, 141, 149, 154, 159 n. 6
Militia of Montana (M.O.M.), 145, 149, 150, 159 n. 6
Militias, 15, 28, 123, 132, 141–42, 144–50, 154–56, 202, 208–12, 232, 159 n. 6
Million Mom March, 205–6
Montana, 144–45, 149, 150
*Ms. Magazine*, 16, 103–4
Mucci, J. Michael, 154
Mule, 167
Murrah, Alfred P. Federal Building, bombing of, 5, 15, 141–44, 148–50, 154–55, 201
Murray, Patricia, 21, 164–71, 177–78, 186–87, 219
Mustard, David B., 88
Muzzleloaders, 19, 35–36
Myths, frontier, 13, 32–33, 37, 40, 42, 47, 218–19

National Crime Victimization Survey, 87
National Instant Check System (NICS), 225–26, 230; *see also* Background checks
National Institute of Justice, 88
National Opinion Research Center (NORC), study of gun ownership, 80
National Rifle Association (NRA), 7, 11, 12, 14, 15, 17, 20, 58, 81–85, 87, 88, 91, 94, 103–4, 106–7, 114, 122, 126, 143, 201–2, 205–6, 224–26

National Rifle Association (NRA)
  *(continued)*
  annual meeting 1998, 26–27, 84,
    200–1, 224
  ratings of states, representatives, 14, 15,
    84, 91, 94
  role of women in, 16, 83–84
National Shooting Sports Foundation
  (NSSF), 17, 63
Native American, 14, 37, 63–65
  introduction to hunting guns, 64
  resistance, 36
  women's roles, 63–65
Nazi, 140, 145
*New England Journal of Medicine,* 89, 90,
    97, 104
New York City, 19, 21, 117, 172, 179–80,
    187, 229
New York State, 7, 8, 18, 21, 48, 49,
    51–52, 65, 67, 68, 133, 135, 146–47,
    151, 154, 187, 191
*New York Times,* the, 179, 190, 199, 204, 206
New World Order, 156, 203; *see also* One
    World Government
News reports, 14, 15, 201, 205, 223, 231
  public reactions to, 6, 16, 81–82,
    141–42, 232
*Newsweek,* 6, 141–42, 154, 191, 193, 205
*Next Time She'll Be Dead* (by Ann Jones),
    86, 108
Nicholl, Diane, 87, 89, 90, 127–28
North American Free Trade Agreement
  (NAFTA), 148
Nostalgia, 35, 38, 44, 59, 127, 163, 171,
    177, 191–92

Oakley, Annie, 37–38, 44
O'Hair, Madalyn Murray, 165
Oklahoma City, Oklahoma; *see* Murrah,
  Alfred P. Federal Building, bombing
  of; *see also* McVeigh, Timothy;
  Militias
Olson, Norman, 154, 155; *see also* Militias;
  Michigan Militia
One World Government, 123, 151; *see also*
  New World Order
Operation Cease Fire, 229
Orwell, George, 152, 153

Paintball, 138
Paramilitary, 135, 142; *see also* Militias
Partisan politics, 10, 12–13, 25–26, 89, 197,
    199, 200, 217, 223, 226, 230; *see also*
    Advocacy organizations

Pasco, Pat, 122–23, 128
Pathfinder Fish and Game Club,
    135–36
Pathogens, 192
  guns as, 10, 11, 181, 210, 228
  *see also* Epidemic, guns as; Guns, health
    hazard; Public health and guns;
    Toxic
Patriarchy, patriarchal, 57, 60, 183
People for the Ethical Treatment of Animals
  (PETA), 57
Peterson, Tammy, 17
Phillips-Taylor, Byrl, 81–82, 86, 103, 123
Pioneers; *see* Frontiersmen;
  Frontierswomen
Pistol permit course, 99–101, 111,
    116–22
Pistols; *see* Handguns
Pittman-Robertson Act, 56, 58
Plains Indians, 64–65
Planck, Doreen, 133
*Point Blank* (by Gary Kleck), 87
Police, 8, 11, 23–24, 54, 79, 84–86, 101,
    104, 109, 111–16, 117, 120, 124–25,
    127, 154–55, 174–75, 179–80,
    188–89, 193, 214, 221, 229–30
*Politics of Gun Control, The* (by Robert
  Spitzer), 25–26
Practical pistol shooting; *see* Practical
  Shooters Association; Practical
  shooting competitions
Practical Shooters Association, 133, 135,
    137, 139, 155
Practical shooting competitions, 8, 28, 131,
    133, 135–41
Project Triggerlock, Project Exile, 229
Property rights, 144–45
Prothrow-Stith, Deborah, 161–62
Public health and guns, 11, 88, 89–91, 104,
    181, 205, 226, 227–28; *see also* Center
    for Disease Control; Epidemic, guns
    as; Guns, health hazard; Pathogens,
    guns as
Public nuisance, guns as a, 11, 226

Racial profiling, 180
Ramboz, Sharon-Jo, 81, 86
Rangel, Charles, 198
Real world, "real life," as concepts, 9, 34,
    39, 43, 65, 67, 101–2, 110, 126,
    128–29, 197–98, 202–3, 219, 231
Refuse To Be a Victim program, 16, 83,
    104, 106, 107
Reno, Janet, 83, 180

Repeaters, 36, 211
Revelations, 151
Revolutionary War era, 35, 39, 131, 157, 204, 207–13, 224–25, 232–35
Richards, Ann, 15, 91–94
Right-to-carry laws; *see* Concealed-carry legislation
Right to keep and bear arms; *see* Second Amendment
Rolland, Kayla, 82, 205
Romantic, myths and heroes, 34, 36, 47, 131
Roosevelt, Theodore, 54–56, 230
Roundtree, Brenda, 170, 173–78, 183, 200
Roundtree, Gregg, 173–78, 183
Ruby Ridge, Idaho, 142, 150; *see also* Weaver, Randy
Rupe, Joan, 7–8, 17, 155
Rural life, 48, 49–50, 67, 68, 148, 156, 173
and guns, 119, 133
and hunting, 47–52, 65, 67, 76
Ryker, Jake, 26
Ryker, Robert, 26

Safe storage of guns, 93, 114, 117–18, 119, 122–25, 127; *see also* Gun safety locks
Safe storage legislation, 93, 114, 117–18, 119, 122–25, 127; *see also* Gun safety locks
Safety, women's, 102, 106, 107, 110; *see also* Self-defense; Concealed-carry legislation
Safety for Women and Responsible Motherhood (SWARM), 84–87, 89, 92, 106, 127, 203
Safir, Howard, 229–30
Saunders, Esther, 49–51, 54
School shootings, 5, 15, 26, 44, 81–82, 134, 191, 193, 194, 205, 231–32
Seamans, Barbara, 138
Second Amendment, 10, 13, 26, 28, 102, 106, 121, 123, 142, 143, 148, 150, 204, 208–12, 214–17, 227, 228–29
Self-defense, 8, 16, 27–28, 38, 76, 79–130 (chaps. 4 and 5), 103, 105, 107, 110, 114–20, 128, 129–30 (esp. n. 17), 163–64, 189, 199, 203, 204, 210, 216
Self-reliance, 5, 13, 32, 37, 94, 153, 156, 199, 203–4, 230
Sentencing Project, The, 178
Sentimental novels, 39, 43

Sherry, 146–54, 200, 203, 216
Sixties, the, 13–14, 21, 25, 29 n. 15, 56, 163, 164, 165, 177, 191, 192, 197–98, 215
Slotkin, Richard, 13, 33
Smith & Wesson, 82, 117, 133, 135, 138, 205, 226–27
poll of women's gun ownership, 16, 80
Smith, Horace, 35
Smith, Tom, 80
Spencer Repeater, 36
Spitzer, Robert, 25–26
Stange, Mary Zeiss, 59–63, 104–6
Starr, Ken, 198
State legislation, 15, 82–85, 122–23, 125–26; *see also* Concealed-carry legislation; Legislation
Statistical studies, 80, 87–91, 92, 94–95, 108, 228–29, 231
homicide victimization rates by sex and race, 161–62
Arthur Kellermann's studies, 89–91, 104–6
Gary Kleck's studies, 87–88, 95
John Lott, Jr.'s studies, 88–89, 94–95
showing that guns deter crimes, 25, 87–89, 94–95
showing that guns are a hazard, not useful for self-protection, 16, 17, 25, 89–90, 103
Stauffeneker, Carol, 7
Stoecker, Martha, 41
Stories, 232
first-person stories of gunshot trauma, 21–25, 72–75, 123–26, 166, 167–69, 172, 173–77, 180–81, 185, 187, 193
frontier adventure, 13, 27, 31–45 (chap. 2)
frontierswomen's, 40–43
nineteenth-century women's, 38–39
women's personal stories in gun debates, 86–87, 123, 125–26, 128, 201, 205–6
Stout, Becky 52–54
Stowe, Harriet Beecher, 39
*Straight From the Heart* (by Ann Richards), 92

Targets, 134
paper, 99–101, 116, 122
practical shooting targets, 133, 136–38
interactive target video games, 134
Technology, 35, 44, 58
Texas, 15, 91–94, 106, 142, 204–6

Thomas, Christine, 17
Tobacco, public health threat similar to guns, 10, 11, 226
Tompkins, Jane, 39
Toxic, contemporary culture as, 191; *see also* Epidemic, guns as; Guns, health hazard; Pathogens, guns as; Public health, and guns
Trochmann, Randy, 145
Turkey hunting, 69, 72–75
Turner, Frederick Jackson, 44, 54
Twain, Mark, 38, 39, 56

*Uncle Tom's Cabin* (by Harriet Beecher Stowe), 39
Uniform Crime Reports, 87
United Nations, 151
*United States v. Emerson*, 106
*United States v. Miller*, 210
United States Practical Shooters Association (USPSA); *see* Practical Shooters Association
Urban, 192, 193, 218–19, 229
disadvantaged neighborhoods and guns, 161–195 (chap. 7)

Veverka, Joy, 65–69, 75
Victims of gunshot wounds, reports, 22–25, 72–74, 124–26, 164–66
Victorian, 164
American literature, 39
Video games; *see* Games
Violence, 132–33, 135, 142, 166, 230; *see also* Gun violence
Violence Policy Center, 96, 103
Violent Crime Control and Law Enforcement Act of 1994, 14, 15, 81, 83, 200

Waco, Texas, 142–43, 149–50
War, and gun games, 132, 134, 138–40, 150

Warner, Charles Dudley, 56
Warner, Susan, 39
*Warrior Dreams: Violence and Manhood in Post-Vietnam America* (by William Gibson), 134
Washington, DC, 21, 144, 164–66, 169, 170, 205
Washington, George, 157, 209–10
Weaver, Martin, 162–63, 170, 172, 180–82, 186, 194
Weaver, Randy, 142, 150; *see also* Ruby Ridge, Idaho
Webster, Sue, 23–24
Welfare, 86, 203, 204, 218–20, 222, 230
Wesson, Daniel Baird, 35
Wexler, Ann, 79–80, 107–8
*When Battered Women Kill*, 108–9
Whiskey Rebellion, 157, 209
Whitman, Christine, 180
*Wide, Wide World, The* (by Susan Warner), 39
Wild West Show; *see* Buffalo Bill's Wild West Show
Wilderness, 18, 20, 32–35, 37, 47, 53, 54, 58, 66, 153, 183, 190
Wildlife management, 52, 56, 57
Williams, Claytie, 92
Williams, David, 210, 211
Williams, Joy, 57
Wilmer, Mary Ann, 164–66, 186
Wilson, Luzana, 42–43, 190, 219
Winchester Repeater, 36
Wise Use, 144
*Woman the Hunter* (by Mary Zeiss Stange), 59, 61, 63, 104
*Women & Guns*, 11–12, 110, 137
Women's Shooting Sports Foundation (WSSF), 17
Wood, Gordon, 204, 209
Woodhams, Stefani, 7–9, 90, 199